Gustav Friedrich Waagen, Franz Kugler

Handbook of Painting

The German, Flemish, and Dutch schools

Gustav Friedrich Waagen, Franz Kugler

Handbook of Painting
The German, Flemish, and Dutch schools

ISBN/EAN: 9783337735050

Printed in Europe, USA, Canada, Australia, Japan

Cover: Foto ©Thomas Meinert / pixelio.de

More available books at **www.hansebooks.com**

HANDBOOK OF PAINTING.

THE

GERMAN, FLEMISH, AND DUTCH SCHOOLS.

BASED ON THE HANDBOOK OF KUGLER.

ENLARGED AND FOR THE MOST PART RE-WRITTEN.

By DR. WAAGEN,
DIRECTOR OF THE ROYAL GALLERY OF PICTURES, BERLIN.

WITH ILLUSTRATIONS.

IN TWO PARTS.—Part I.

LONDON:
JOHN MURRAY, ALBEMARLE STREET.
1860.

The right of Translation is reserved.

LONDON: PRINTED BY W. CLOWES AND SONS, STAMFORD STREET,
AND CHARING CROSS.

PREFACE.

ALTHOUGH the translation of Kugler's excellent Handbook of German, Flemish, and Dutch Painting, not only gave a faithful version of its contents, but also contributed much additional information—the result of great judgment and erudition—yet the researches which have since taken place regarding these schools have brought so much new and important matter to light as greatly to alter the conditions under which the work was originally written. Mr. Murray accordingly, always anxious to keep his Handbooks in every respect on a par with the scientific standard of the age, has, not without reason, considered it necessary to prepare a new edition; the more so, as the Handbook by Kugler devoted to the Italian Schools has, with the assistance of Sir Charles Eastlake, been, in the present third edition, made to include all essential knowledge hitherto obtained of the history of Italian art. Having, therefore, consented to undertake the remodelling of the Handbook of German, Flemish, and Dutch art, I have laboured at it the more gladly from the consciousness that the experience of a number of years devoted to the study of these very schools in their various periods, as seen in the principal public and private galleries of Europe, had enabled me to collect materials peculiarly fitted for the task. In the performance of it I have not only left but a small portion of the original text standing, but have considerably extended the historical details. Much, also, as I concur, in essential points and in the estimate of the principal masters, with the late lamented author—who in 1858, then in the full activity of his labours, was suddenly snatched away—I equally differ from him in some particulars which my own researches have elucidated. Under these circumstances it appeared the most advisable plan completely to recast certain portions. Generally speaking, what survives of the first edition refers chiefly to the earlier periods, inclusive of Albert Durer and Holbein. In the admirable account of Albert Durer, namely, I have had occasion to make but few additions. Yet even in this early portion, especially in the department of miniatures, my fresh matter is of considerable amount. But in the later periods—such, for instance, as the notices of Rubens and Rembrandt—while the text has been greatly enlarged, I may say that only a small portion of the original work has been preserved. In comparison with the degree of labour bestowed by the late Dr. Kugler upon the masters of the 15th and 16th centuries a large number of eminent painters of a later time may be said to have been far too scantily noticed. Thus, while several pages were devoted to Albrecht Altdorfer, such a painter as Cuyp was dismissed with a few words, and not one of his works referred to; another great landscape painter, Philip de Koninck, being omitted altogether. Considering the extensive knowledge of art attained by Dr. Kugler, which, besides the entire department of painting, included those of sculpture and architecture, it is easily credible that he should not have had time to devote to that close study of the later Dutch painters which they deserve. My endeavour has been, by means of a closer analysis of the chief masters of the Dutch school, and by reference to their most notable works, to supply this deficiency. In the selection of examples, not only of these works but of the productions of all other periods, I have been guided by the conditions of their accessibility; since I am especially interested that every reader of this Handbook should have it in his power, by personal inspection of the pictures quoted, to verify the justice of my opinions. In this respect I have strictly borne in mind the position of the English public, referring them for examples either to the National Gallery or to the collection at Hampton Court; and, next to these, to the galleries most accessible to the Englishman abroad, such as the Louvre, and the Museums of Antwerp, Brussels, the Hague, and Amsterdam. My references also extend to the Galleries of Dresden, Munich, Vienna, Berlin, Cassel, Frankfort, and Florence. Private collections are only sparingly alluded to, partly from their inaccessibility, and partly from their liability to be dispersed; it being my object to ensure to this Handbook as lengthened a period of usefulness as may be possible. At the same time I have brought forward those galleries which are either distinguished for the importance of their contents or for the kindness with which they are opened to the public. Such, for either or both of these reasons, are the royal collections in Buckingham Palace and Windsor Castle, those of Lord Ellesmere, Lord Ashburton, Messrs. Baring, Holford, and Munro, and the collection of the Duke d'Aremberg at Brussels. Where I have, on a very few occasions, alluded to other private collections in England or on the Continent, it has been to point out either a picture of extraordinary merit or the specimen of some extremely rare master; as, for instance, Van der Meer of Delft. In order further to facilitate the inspection of pictures in large galleries I have added the numbers from the latest catalogues, only, in most instances, omitting this practice with the Vienna Gallery, as the mode of numeration there is too intricate to be always given.

Although this Handbook is devoted to the art of painting, yet I felt it incumbent on me to add short notices of those painters who either engraved, etched, or designed for woodcuts from their own compositions. In such cases as Martin Schongauer, whose pictures are extremely rare, his great power of invention and whole style of art can be only gathered from his engravings and etchings. Others, such as Herrmann Swanevelt, who lacked feeling for colour, are seen to far better advantage in their etchings than in their paintings. Another again, like Simon de Vlieger, who painted almost exclusively marine subjects, can scarcely be known in his other compositions, namely, in his landscapes, but by means of his etchings. One reason also for noticing these various forms of the art of engraving lies in the multiplicity of their examples, and in the facility with which they may be seen, which is the first condition of knowledge in the formative arts. At the same time, considering the great rarity of many engravings, and the difference between one impression and another, I feel it right to add that, for the study of the "Peintres Graveurs" in all these different styles, especially in that of etching, no place in the world offers such advantages as the collection of engravings in the British Museum. It must be understood that my remarks on this class of art chiefly refer to power of invention and picturesqueness of effect. To have entered more deeply into technical merits, or to have given a closer description of particular plates, was beyond the scope of this Handbook, though in both cases I have referred the reader to Bartsch's well-known work, 'Le Peintre Graveur,' and to Rudolph Weigel's additions to it. As regards that important form of art, the drawings of the masters, the immense number of them, as well as the difficulty of access to most, have compelled me to limit myself to a very few notices. If the reader also should be struck by the omission of a large number of painters, I may remark that the omission has been intentional, and not from inadvertence. The object of a Handbook is to give a short account, both as respects historical facts and æsthetic merit, of the more important examples of the schools under consideration at their various periods, and to indicate the sources of knowledge to those who are desirous of making further researches. All such painters, namely, who have neither stood in any relation to a notable master, nor have raised themselves above mediocrity, nor, further, exercised any influence on any known painter, I have therefore omitted, as tending to complicate the subject and as unconnected with the object of a Handbook. Painters of this class belong more properly to dictionaries of artists. On the other hand, I have noticed painters even of less individual importance when connected with a master of the first rank, such as Rubens or Rembrandt, in order to exhibit as completely as possible the extent of influence exercised by these great men. Nor with such as Rubens and Rembrandt have I attempted to describe all their works,—a task which belongs rather to the sphere of biography, as in Passavant's 'Life of Raphael.' In some instances, also, there must exist some diversity of opinion as to which painter or which examples of a painter should be given.

As regards, for example, a master so well known for his admirable etchings as Waterloo, I think it right to observe here that I have purposely omitted all mention of him, and for this reason—that neither I, nor so experienced a connoisseur as Mr. E. Hartzen, have ever seen an authentic picture by him, so that I feel it doubtful whether he may be said to have ever painted at all. Here, however, I venture to bring forward a plea in favour of this work above all other works known to me upon these schools in their whole extent—namely, that, with the exception of a very few, and those openly avowed, I have myself seen every picture which I quote, and on which I found my opinions. Notwithstanding this, if the reader should find that, in comparison with Kugler's 'Handbook of Italian Art,' as remodelled by Sir Charles Eastlake, this work is very meagre in notices of notable painters or important works of the earlier periods, and also in the later periods far more uncertain as regards such historical facts as the birth and death of masters, he must in both instances attribute the difference to the far less favourable conditions attending the compilation of a History of Painting in Germany and in the Netherlands. I feel it therefore expedient, under these circumstances, to give some account of what these conditions are.

The two chief sources from which every history of art is drawn are, first, the existing monuments of art; and secondly, all written notices both of these monuments and their authors. Various circumstances have, however, conspired to leave but sparing relics of painters' works of the larger class before the year 1420. From that date also to the year 1550, a time including the whole school of Van Eyck, and the German masters from Martin Schongauer and Michael Wohlgemuth to Albert Durer and Hans Holbein, but little is left for our guidance in comparison with the large amount of works originally produced. Even the comparative rudeness of the climate, with its trying alternations in spring and autumn, had in many instances a destructive effect upon pictures. But the Reformation may be considered as the arch destroyer of the works of that early time, especially where it took effect under the auspices of the Swiss Reformers,[1] who left no pictures at all in the churches; as in the Netherlands[2] and in Switzerland. Nor was less injury done in the Catholic portions of Germany and the Netherlands by the preference felt for the later forms of art: a preference which in the time of Rubens had a kind of excuse, but which was equally active at the periods of the most positive decline; viz. in the latter half of the 17th and in the 18th century, when the earlier pictures were driven from the churches.[3] A further reason for the barrenness of the land, as respects the earlier pictures, may be found, in the Netherlands, in the long-continued wars with the Spaniards in the 16th century, and in those with France in the 17th and 18th centuries; and in Germany by the Thirty Years' War, when pictures were either destroyed, or stolen and carried away to other lands. Many pictures owe their destruction also to the general low estimation of them which prevailed in the 18th century. The knowledge also of those masters whose pictures have survived all these prejudicial elements is much obscured by the circumstance that they very seldom signed their names, or only left a monogram on their works, the meaning of which is in many cases lost. Nor

[1] On the other hand, in those parts, for instance in Breslau and in Saxony, where the Reformation was in conformity with the dogmas of Luther, not only many altars of Roman Catholic origin were retained in the churches, but numerous pictures, chiefly by Lucas Cranach and his school, were added to the sacred edifices. Thus it would be unjust to charge the Reformation altogether with the destruction of pictures.

[2] This was especially attributable in the Netherlands to the Iconoclasts, who began their ravages in the August of 1566.

[3] Striking proofs of this are seen in Brussels especially, where the Iconoclasts never came, and in St. Stephen's, Vienna, and the Cathedral of Freisingen, where the Reformation never took effect: the first place has retained but very few pictures of the earlier time; the two others are totally stripped of them.

is there more encouragement to be found in the written notices of the history of painting in Germany and the Netherlands. The earliest accounts, and scanty, are derived from a few Italian books,[1] and especially from the works of *Vasari*. As this writer's biographies were published, however, as early as 1550, and refer back to painters of the 13th century, we may assume that *Carel van Mander's* work, which appeared in 1604,[2] and which goes no further than to Hubert van Eyck, therefore only to the beginning of the 15th century, was the *first* to give a nearer description of the Netherlandish and German painters. Imperfect, therefore, and incorrect as his work is in many respects, it nevertheless remains the chief source of information regarding the masters of these schools up to nearly the end of the 16th century, and takes a far higher place than that of the earliest author who wrote in Germany upon the history of painting—I mean Joachim Sandrart, whose 'German Academy' first appeared in 1675. As regards the Netherlandish, and even the greater part of the German painters up to the end of the 16th century, this work is little more than an inaccurate translation, and often even a very meagre abstract from Carel van Mander. The notices of those masters only who were cotemporary with Sandrart are original, and most of them valuable. A work by *Cornelis de Bie*,[3] published 1661–62, contains much that is available upon the subject of the Netherlandish painters. Two other authors—*Arnold Houbraken*[4] and *Campo Weyermann*[5]—who wrote upon the

[1] In the work by Facius, 'De Viris Illustribus,' written in 1455 and 1456, are found the earliest notices of Jan van Eyck and Rogier van der Weyden the elder. And in the journal of a traveller written in the early part of the 16th century, first published by Morelli, ' Notizie d' Opere di Disegno,' Bassano, 1800, are also accounts of the same masters, and of others of the Van Eyck school.

[2] 'Het Schilderboek, &c., door Carel van Mander, Haarlem, 1604, bei Paschier van Wesbusch.' 1 vol. 4to. The Lives of the Netherlandish and German painters, however, only occupy one portion; viz. from p. 196 to p. 300. My quotations, however, are taken from the 2nd edition, also 4to., which came out in Amsterdam in 1618.

[3] ' Het Gulden Cabinet van de edel vry Schilderkonst.' 1661-1662. Antwerpen. 1 vol. 4to.

[4] 'Grote Schouburgh der Nederlantsche Kunstschilders en Schilderessen.' 1718. Amsterdam. 3 vols. 8vo.

[5] 'Levens Beschryvingen der Nederlandische Kunstschilders en Schilder-

second great period of Netherlandish art in the 17th century, are very defective. In such notices as they have not borrowed from Van Mander or De Bie, they are as scanty as they are incorrect, though all the more abundant in idle gossip and false anecdotes, which often shamefully traduce the memory of a painter. *Johann van Gool*,[1] who continued Houbraken's work, is also little to be relied on for the history of the earlier painters, but gives us at all events many a valuable notice regarding those who lived in his time. *Descamps'* 'Biographies of Painters'[2] are scarcely more than an abstract from the above books, which, owing to his only partial knowledge of the Dutch language, he has not always rightly interpreted. The faults we have alluded to are therefore all transcribed into his work. By his habit, however, in cases of painters the date of whose birth was unknown to him, of placing, by way of approximation, the birth year of some cotemporary painter on the margin, he has greatly increased these inaccuracies; for most later writers, who have made use of Descamps for their authority on these subjects, have taken these dates on the margin for the actual date of the painter's birth. This especially occurs in *Fiorillo's*[3] work, as far as concerns the painters of the 17th and 18th centuries, though he offers far better information of the earlier schools; and in the Dictionaries of Painters by *Füssli*,[4] *Bryan*,[5] *Pilkington*,[6] and *Nagler*.[7] The same blame attaches to *Immerzeel*,[8] though

essen.' 'S Gravenhaage, 1729. 4 vols. in 4to. We need not wonder that this writer should have carried on Houbraken's slanderous tales to a still greater extent—knowing that he finished his days in prison as a 'Pasquillant' by profession.

[1] 'De nieuwe Schouburgh der Nederlandische Kunstschilders en Schilderessen.' 'S Gravenhaage, 1750. 2 vols. in 8vo.
[2] 'La Vie des Peintres Flamands, Allemands, et Hollandais.' Paris, 1753. 4 vols. in 8vo.
[3] 'Geschichte der Zeichnenden Künste in Deutschland und den Vereinigten Niederlanden.' Hanover, 1815-1820. 4 vols. 8vo.
[4] 'Allgemeines Künsterlexicon.' Zürich, 1810-1820. 3 vols. folio.
[5] 'Dictionary of Painters and Engravers.' 2 vols. 4to. London, 1816.
[6] 'Dictionary of Painters.' 4to. London, 1810.
[7] 'Neues Allgemeines Künstler-Lexicon.' München, 1835-1852. 22 vols. 8vo.
[8] 'De Levens en werken der Hollandische en vlaamsche Kunstschilders, Beeldhouwers, Graveurs en Boumeisters.' Amsterdam, 1842. 3 vols. 8vo.

he has treated the disgraceful calumnies of Campo Weyermann with becoming contempt, and has added also many a valuable notice. *Rathgeber's*[1] work is also a very careful compilation.

As regards Germany, it was in the first decennium of the present century that, stimulated by the writings of Ludwig Tieck and Frederick Schlegel, a lively sense of the importance of the monuments of art belonging to the middle ages was first awakened. With the desire, therefore, to obtain the utmost possible information regarding them, the scantiness of the objects themselves as regards painting, and of all historical records of them, soon became apparent. Efforts were therefore made to find pictures of the earlier periods before the year 1550, and to form collections of them. But though these endeavours were in some measure successful—as in the instance of the Boisserée Collection, now passed into the Munich Gallery; in that of Mr. Edward Solly, now forming part of the Berlin Museum; in the collection of the Chevalier van Ertborn, bequeathed by him to the Antwerp Museum; and in that of Mr. Abel, of Stuttgard, recently purchased by the Wirtemberg Government—yet these collections still offer, comparatively speaking, but sparing examples of the period between 1380 and 1550. This deficiency was still more observable in specimens of the antecedent period, chiefly consisting of important wall-paintings, generally discovered in ecclesiastical buildings under a coating of whitewash. In the desire, partly to obtain a more connected view of the pictorial art of these early times, partly to complete that of a later epoch, the investigators of these subjects took refuge in the miniatures of the richly-decorated manuscripts, extending from the 8th to the 16th century, in which the character of the writing, or the knowledge of the individuals for whom they were executed, furnished evidence, more or less trustworthy, of their date. The merit of having first traced this course belongs to *D'Agincourt*, in his well-known work.[2] Next to him, I may venture to say

---

[1] 'Annalen der Niederländischen Malerie.' Gotha, 1842. Folio.
[2] 'Histoire de l'Art par les Monumens.' 3 vols. folio. Paris.

that I have pursued the same road, with still greater research, having given, both in my works on the Treasures of Art in Paris, and in England, as well as in an article in the German 'Kunstblatt' of 1850, a close description of a number of manuscripts with miniatures. After me *Kugler* may be said to have entered the same lists. In order also to increase as far as possible the amount of historical facts, notices of painters or of pictures were eagerly sought for in poets or historians, and in civic or conventual chronicles. Even the tedious labour of examining guild and church books, old accounts, and other archives was gone into; an important result of which is seen in *Merlo's* work upon the painters of the city of Cologne.[1] The same interest being excited in Belgium, after the year 1820, for the native school of painters, of which the brothers Van Eyck were the heads, similar researches took place: among the earliest annotators were *Louis de Bast, Delepierre,* and *Van Lockeren;* among the more recent, *Wauters, Schayes, de Stoop, Goetgebuer,* the *Abbé Carton,* and *Edward van Even.*[2] Some foreign labourers in this field may be also mentioned here. Thus the work by *Gaye,*[3] a Danish writer, though chiefly important for Italian art, includes many a valuable notice of the schools here treated. The labours of *Count Léon de Laborde* also—the fruits of patient examination of the various archives of the old dukedom of Burgundy[4]—have added a large number of notable contributions to this class of literature.

Next in order arose the desire to draw up works of more or less compass on the history of art, based on the accurate

---

[1] 'Nachrichten von dem Leben und den Werken Kölnischer Künstler.' Köln, 1850. 2 vols. 8vo.

[2] The results of the researches of these gentlemen have chiefly appeared in the 'Messager des Sciences et des Arts de Belgique,' Gand; and in the Annual Reports of the Belgian Academy of Science and Art at Brussels. The names of many other meritorious investigators in the same path, as well as the results of their labours, will be found in the introduction to the Catalogue of the Antwerp Museum of the year 1857—a masterly notice both as respects historical records and the lives of painters, and one which I have copiously referred to.

[3] 'Carteggio d' Artisti.' Firenze, 1839-1840. 3 vols. 8vo.

[4] 'Les Ducs de Bourgogne.' Paris, 1849. 8vo. This work will comprise six volumes, only two of which have yet appeared.

knowledge of early pictures, and of such scattered notices as should possess that scientific character hitherto quite absent from writings of this class. I was the first who came forward, as early as the year 1822, with a work upon the brothers Van Eyck,[1] in which I endeavoured, according to the standard of knowledge then existing, to demonstrate the high significance of these great masters, not only for the art of painting in the Netherlands, but for that of the rest of Europe. This effort on my part was followed up, somewhat later, and with the happiest results, by *Schnaase*,[2] *Passavant*,[3] *Kugler*,[4] *Hotho*,[5] and *Jacob Burckhardt*.[6] The same desire, arising in Belgium, found the support of the Government, who furnished assistance to *M. Alfred Michiels*, a French writer, in his compilation of the History of Netherlandish Art.[7] This gives, upon the whole, a careful abstract of all hitherto instituted researches, and takes us as far as the end of the 16th century. An Essay upon the Brothers Van Eyck and their School, by *M. Heris*,[8] which obtained a prize in the Royal Belgian Academy, is principally based on the labours of the above-mentioned German investigators. Finally, a work, profiting by all

---

[1] 'Über Hubert und Jan van Eyck.' Breslau, 1822. 1 vol. 8vo. Additions and corrections of this also occur in various lengthy articles contributed by me to the Kunstblatt, and to the German Kunstblatt.

[2] 'Niederländische Briefe.' Stuttgart, 1854. This is replete with intelligent opinions, which extend even to pictures of a later time.

[3] First published at the end of his 'Kunstreise durch England,' Frankfurt, 1833, 1 vol. 8vo; and later in various long and instructive articles in the Kunstblatt and in the German Kunstblatt; more recently in his 'Christliche Kunst in Spanien.' Leipsig, 1853. 1 vol. 8vo.

[4] Given to the world not only in his Handbooks, but in a collection of his smaller essays on art. Stuttgart, 1854. 3 vols. 8vo.

[5] 'Die Malerschule Huberts van Eyck.' Berlin, 1855. 2 vols. 8vo. In this work, which treats these schools from the year 1250 and onward, he has availed himself of the historical circumstances of the time, both secular and ecclesiastic, in deciding the course taken by the art of painting. When completed, this work will be the most important hitherto produced on this subject, combining, as it does, the personal knowledge of almost all the pictures, excepting those in Spain, with the discriminating use of all materials collected.

[6] The results of Mr. Burckhardt's researches are seen in his 2nd edition of Kugler's 'Handbook of Painting,' Berlin, 1844, 2 vols. 8vo.; and here and there in his 'Cicerone,' 1 vol. 8vo.

[7] 'Histoire de la Peinture Flamande et Hollandaise.' Bruxelles, 1845 and 1846. 3 vols. 8vo.

[8] 'Histoire de l'École Flamande.' Bruxelles, 1856. 1 vol. 4to.

these existing materials, and assisted also by the personal inspection of most of the pictures, was published in 1857, by the combined labour of *Mr. G. B. Cavalcaselle*, the Italian critic on art, and *Mr. J. A. Crowe*. This is a history, properly speaking, of the early Netherlandish Schools, and which, little as I am disposed to concur in all the opinions expressed, gives a very complete description of them. As regards the critical character of the work, it suffers from the circumstance that the reader is sometimes left in doubt whether the opinions of the authors have been derived from their own examination of the pictures, or from the reports of another.[1]

In Belgium also it soon began to be felt on what insufficient foundations rested all the knowledge of the second great epoch of Netherlandish painting in the 17th century. Accordingly researches began to be instituted in the same earnest spirit, which have borne the happiest fruit for the present, and promise far more for the future. To the students of this period of history belong more especially *MM. de Laet, Van Lerius, Gerard,* and *De Burbure*.[2] To these may be added *M. Edmond Fetis*, the compiler of a series of biographies of single painters, which appeared in the already-mentioned annual Records of the Belgian Academy. In Holland, I regret to say, the desire to prosecute similar researches regarding the great masters of their historically neglected schools has been but little aroused. At the same time, the public has to be thankful for a few small writings of this class; the most important being that by *Dr. P. Scheltema*,[3] the keeper of the archives at Amsterdam, whose notices upon Rembrandt have thrown quite a new light upon the life and character of this great master. Next in order *M. T. van Westrheene's* 'Jan Steen' deserves

---

[1] 'The Early Flemish Painters.' London, Bohn, Murray, 1857. 1 vol. 8vo.

[2] The researches of these and other gentlemen have been partly published in pamphlets, partly in the 'Messager des Sciences Historiques de Belgique.' The results have been also made use of in the Catalogue of the Antwerp Museum, which gives information regarding the pamphlets.

[3] This essay, which was first published in Amsterdam in 1853 in Dutch, was translated in 1859 into French by Mr. W. Burger, and was published, accompanied by notes, in the 'Revue Universelle des Arts,' and also separately in Brussels.

honourable mention.[1] Several valuable contributions also have been published in periodicals. In the way of opinions and descriptions of pictures of this time *Smith's Catalogue*[2] furnishes us with rich materials and copious examples of a certain number of masters, most of them the first in their department of art. The critical opinions expressed in this last work shows the writer to be a thorough connoisseur; and if some mistakes have crept in, they may be well overlooked, in consideration of the abundant and admirable information he gives us. Two writings also, by *Mr. C. J. Nieuwenhuys*,[3] give very valuable notices upon an equally limited number of pictures. A critical report of numerous pictures by a large number of masters forms the principal features in my works upon the Art Treasures in Paris[4] and Great Britain.[5] The same may be said of various works from the hand of the late *Mrs. Jameson*.[6] Finally, the present age has found a recent and zealous labourer in *Mr. W. Burger*, a French gentleman, who, by the close study of pictures and the signatures and inscriptions upon them, by his artistic judgment, and by the additions to and corrections of historical data, has, in his various works,[7] much contributed to lay the foundations for a history of this great school, which may claim the meed of scientific value.

While I have thus rendered an account both of the earlier and present conditions of the history of painting in Germany and the Netherlands, I have also indicated

[1] Jan Steen, 'Etude sur l'Art en Hollande.' La Haye, 1856. 1 vol. 8vo.
[2] 'A Catalogue raisonné of the Works of the most eminent Dutch, Flemish, and French Painters.' 1829-1842. 9 vols. 8vo.
[3] 'A Review of the Lives and Works of some of the most eminent Painters.' London, 1834. 1 vol. 8vo. And 'Description des Tableaux de S. M. le Roi des Pays Bas.' Bruxelles, 1843. 1 vol. 8vo.
[4] 'Kunstwerke und Künstler in Paris.' Berlin, 1839. 1 vol. 8vo.
[5] 'Treasures of Art in Great Britain.' London, 1854. 3 vols. 8vo. And 'Galleries and Cabinets of Art in Great Britain — Supplement.' London, 1857. 1 vol. 8vo.
[6] 'A Handbook to the Public Galleries of Art in and near London.' London, 1842. 1 vol. 8vo. 'A Companion to the most celebrated Private Galleries of Art in London.' London, 1844.
[7] 'Trésors d'Art exposés à Manchester, 1857.' Paris, 1857. 1 vol. 8vo. 'Musées de la Hollande, Amsterdam, et la Haye.' Paris, 1858. 1 vol. 8vo. 'Galerie d'Aremberg, Bruxelles, 1859.' Paris, Bruxelles, et Leipsic. 1 vol. 8vo.

the sources I have exhausted in the remodelling of this Handbook, and which, at the same time, furnish a standard for any who may desire to pursue similar researches. Other sources, which only relate to isolated facts, will be acknowledged in their due place. Various reasons determined me not to continue the history of painting in these countries as far as living painters; for mature and impartial judgments are only passed on epochs of art, or on separate painters, when each may be said to belong to the past. It is only then that prejudices for or against, and from which cotemporaries can never be free, cease to exist, and also that indulgence which is due to a living painter. There is no doubt, also, that the lovers of the old masters, for whom this Handbook is especially destined, take frequently less interest in the art of the present day. The knowledge of it, however, is so diffused among the educated classes, that any general allusion here would have been superfluous, while a closer examination of the subject would have considerably increased the size and cost of this work.

G. F. WAAGEN.

Berlin.

CONTENTS.

	Page
Preface	iii
List of Illustrations	xix

BOOK I.
A.D. 800–1250.

Chapter I.—Early Christian-Byzantine Epoch. 800–1150	1–15
" II.—The Byzantine-Romanesque Epoch. 1150–1250	15–26

BOOK II.
THE TEUTONIC STYLE.—FIRST EPOCH, 1250–1420.

Introduction	27
Chapter I.—The Period when Painting was principally restricted to the Illumination of Outlines. 1250–1350	28–34
" II.—Development of Painting in its more independent character. 1350–1420	34–49

BOOK III.
THE TEUTONIC STYLE.—SECOND EPOCH, 1420–1530.
Complete Development of the Teutonic Feeling for Art in the Spirit of the Middle Ages.

Chapter I.—The Brothers Van Eyck	50–74
" II.—School of the Brothers Van Eyck till near the close of the 15th century	74–108
" III.—The Van Eyck School, up to the period of its termination. 1490–1530	109–119
" IV.—The German School, in its transition from the Style of the preceding period to the Realistic Tendency. 1420–1460	120–125
" V.—The German Schools which adopted the Realistic Tendency of the Van Eycks. 1460–1500	125–140
" VI.—The German Schools from 1500 to 1550	141–215

BOOK IV.

THE TEUTONIC STYLE.—THIRD EPOCH, 1530–1600.

Deterioration of the Teutonic Style of Art, as regards Historical Painting, arising from the imitation of the Italians. Further development of other classes of Painting—Genre, Landscapes, &c.

	Page
Chapter I.—Painting in the Netherlands	216–248
„ II.—Painting in Germany	248–256

BOOK V.

THE TEUTONIC STYLE.—FOURTH EPOCH, 1600–1690.

Second Development of the Teutonic Feeling for Art.

Chapter I.—Introduction. Rubens	257–273
„ II.—The Cotemporaries and Scholars of Rubens	273–326
„ III.—The Dutch School. The Influence of the Italian Naturalisti, and of Rubens' Style of Art	327–336
„ IV.—Rembrandt Van Ryn	336–348
„ V.—Scholars and Followers of Rembrandt	348–362
„ VI.—The Painters of Genre	362–479
„ VII.—The Painters of Plants, Fruits, and Still Life	480–487
„ VIII.—The German Painters of this Period	488–498

BOOK VI.

THE DECLINE OF ART. 1700–1810.

Introduction	499–500
Chapter I.—The Flemish School	500–503
„ II.—The Dutch School	503–516
„ III.—The German School	516–533

INDEX	534–548

ILLUSTRATIONS.

The Joys and Sorrows of the Virgin; a picture by Hans Memling: in the Gallery at Munich (see p. 105) .. .. *Frontispiece.*

Pictures on an altar-chest at Dijon. No. 1 .. .. *To face page* 39

,, No. 2 .. .. ,, 39

,, No. 3 .. .. ,, 39

,, No. 4 .. .. ,, 39

The Triumph of the Church: in the National Museum, Madrid .. ,, 55

The Altarpiece of The Adoration of the Lamb; painted by John and Hubert van Eyck for the Church of St. Bavon at Ghent .. .. ,, 58

The Adoration of the Lamb .. .. ,, 60

The Holy Warriors } in the Berlin Gallery .. .. ,, 60
The Holy Pilgrims

Outer shutters of the great Van Eyck picture at Berlin.. .. .. .. ,, 62

The Last Judgment; by Rogier van der Weyden the Elder .. .. ,, 88

Outer shutters of Last Judgment; by Rogier van der Weyden the Elder ,, 88

Adoration of the Kings; by Rogier van der Weyden the Elder: in the Gallery at Munich. (The standing King is a portrait of Charles the Bold of Burgundy) .. .. ,, 89

Large Altarpiece, by Hans Memling, of the Last Judgment: at Dantzig ,, 97

The Reliquary of St. Ursula; by Hans Memling: in the Chapel of St. John's Hospital at Bruges .. .. ,, 103

Death of St. Ursula; one of the pictures by Memling on the Reliquary of St. Ursula at Bruges .. .. ,, 105

The Misers; a picture by Quentin Massys: at Windsor Castle .. .. ,, 116

A Card Party; by Lucas van Leyden: at Wilton House . .. .. ,, 118

"The Dance of the Magdalen;" from an engraving by Lucas van Leyden in the British Museum .. .. ,, 118

Temptation of St. Anthony; from an engraving by Lucas van Leyden in the British Museum .. .. ,, 118

Altarpiece, by Stephan Lothener, in Cologne Cathedral, in five parts ,, 121

The Annunciation; from an engraving by Martin Schongauer in the British Museum .. .. ,, 131

Christ appearing to the Magdalen; from an engraving by Martin Schongauer in the British Museum .. .. ,, 131

ILLUSTRATIONS.

St. Anthony tormented by Demons; an engraving by Martin Schongauer, which Michael Angelo is said to have copied: from the British Museum *To face page*	131
Albert Durer; painted by himself: in the collection of Artists' Portraits at Florence .. ,,	147
Adoration of the Trinity; painted by Albert Durer: now in the Belvedere at Vienna .. ,,	154
The Knight, Death, and the Devil; an engraving by Albert Durer ,,	157
Melancholy; engraving by Albert Durer .. ,,	157
Border from the Prayerbook of Maximilian; drawn by Albert Durer: in the Royal Library, Munich .. ,,	159
Border from the Prayerbook of Maximilian; drawn by Albert Durer: in the Royal Library, Munich .. ,,	159
From Albert Durer's woodcut of the "Car of Maximilian," in the British Museum .. ,,	161
From Albert Durer's woodcut of the "Car of Maximilian," in the British Museum .. ,,	161
The Apostles Mark and Paul; by Albert Durer: in the Gallery at Munich .. ,,	163
Altarpiece in the Church at Weimar, containing portraits of Luther, Melanctrhon, and the Painter himself; by Lucas Cranach .. ,,	180
The Burgomaster Meyer's votive picture; painted by Hans Holbein, and now in the Gallery at Dresden .. ,,	192
The Triumph of Riches; from a design by Holbein: in the collection of Sir Chas. Eastlake, P.R.A. .. ,,	199
The Triumph of Poverty; from a design by Holbein: in the same collection .. ,,	199
The Descent from the Cross; by Rubens: in the Cathedral at Antwerp ,,	266
Battle of the Amazons; by Rubens: in the Gallery at Munich .. ,,	266
Rubens' small picture of The Fall of the Damned: in the Gallery at Munich .. ,,	267
Castor and Pollux carrying off the Daughters of Leucippus; by Rubens: in the Gallery at Munich .. ,,	269
Apotheosis of Henri Quatre, and Assumption of the Regency by Marie de Medicis; from the series of pictures by Rubens in the Luxembourg, illustrating the history of Marie de Medicis .. ,,	269
Portraits of Rubens, his Brother, Hugo Grotius, and Justus Lipsius; from the picture by Rubens in the Pitti Palace at Florence .. ,,	271
Rubens' portrait of his two Sons .. ,,	271
Holy Family with Angels; by Van Dyck: formerly in the Houghton Collection, now at St. Petersburg .. ,,	283
King Charles I.; by Van Dyck: from the original picture at Windsor ,,	288
The Pembroke Family; by Van Dyck: in Wilton House .. ,,	288
Peter denying Christ; painted by David Teniers in 1646: now in the Louvre .. ,,	305

ILLUSTRATIONS.

TAVERN SCENE; painted by Teniers: now in the Munich Gallery *To face page*	306
THE ANATOMIST NICHOLAS TULP AND HIS PUPILS; painted by Rembrandt in 1632: in the Museum of the Hague .. „	341
DUKE ADOLPHUS OF GUELDRES THREATENING HIS FATHER; by Rembrandt: in the Berlin Museum .. „	344
" CONSEIL PATERNEL;" a picture by Gerard Terburg: in the Amsterdam Museum .. „	364
REPRESENTATION OF HUMAN LIFE; by Jan Steen: in the Museum of the Hague .. „	372
SURGEON REMOVING THE PLASTER; painted by Adrian Brouwer: in the Gallery at Munich .. „	386
THE ITINERANT FIDDLER; by Adrian van Ostade: in the Hague Museum ,,	389
THE JEWISH CEMETERY; by Ruysdael: in the Dresden Gallery .. „	441
SEAPIECE; by Backhuysen: in the Munich Gallery .. „	469

HANDBOOK

OF THE

HISTORY OF PAINTING

IN

GERMANY AND THE LOW COUNTRIES.

BOOK I.

A.D. 800 TO 1250.

CHAPTER I.

EARLY CHRISTIAN-BYZANTINE EPOCH.

800—1150.

NEITHER in Germany nor in the Netherlands are there indications to be found of any practice of the art of painting previous to the introduction of Christianity. Charlemagne, who endeavoured to infuse something of the culture of the ancient world into his widely-extended dominions, caused the cathedral erected by him at Aix-la-Chapelle to be adorned with mosaics, and his palace with wall pictures. The mosaics of the dome represented that subject so frequently given in this form of art—Christ enthroned, with angels hovering above, and the four-and-twenty elders extending their crowns to him. The paintings in the palace showed forth events in the life of Charlemagne himself—among them that of his campaign in Spain, with sieges of towns and feats of arms by Frankish warriors; also the seven liberal Sciences. His palace at Upper Ingelheim, on the Rhine, was also richly decorated in the same way. The chapel contained scenes from the Old and New Testament, doubtless arranged in strict traditional sequence; while the banqueting-hall exhibited on one wall the deeds of the great Pagan rulers, such as Ninus, Cyrus, Phalaris, Romulus, Hannibal, and Alexander, and on the opposite side those of the Emperors Constantine the Great and Theodosius—the victory of Charles Martel over the Frieslanders, the seizure of Aquitaine by Pepin, Charlemagne's own conquest of the Saxons, and finally, himself enthroned as conqueror. Although no trace remains of all these paintings, yet contemporary miniatures belonging to manuscripts, and executed by order of this great monarch, enable us to form some idea of the style of art in which they were rendered. According to these, the paintings of religious subjects were chiefly based upon the types of early Christian art. Such subjects, however, in the manuscripts exhibit an awkwardness and stiffness of motive, a feebleness of drawing, and a gaudiness of colour indicative only of the feeling of a still semi-barbarous nation. We may, therefore, conclude that the secular scenes, for which the painter had no models at all, and in which the story frequently entails great vivacity of action, must have had a very unrefined appearance. The treatment, with broad lights and shadows laid upon the same unvarying middle tone, which occurs also in the miniatures, was unquestionably derived from that we observe in antique painting. In some parts of these paintings, as in the peculiar type of many a head—in the mean and meagre character of the draperies—in the gold hatchings of the dresses—in the green tone of the shadows, and in the repeated use of vermilion and unbroken blue—the influence of Byzantine art may have taken effect, as we know it did in the miniatures. The manuscripts with miniatures to which we allude are the following:—

An Evangeliarium, in the Imperial Library at Paris. This contains the four Evangelists—Christ represented under a youthful form, giving the benediction according to the rite of the Byzantine Church; and the Fountain of Life, within an octagon building surrounded by stags, by peacocks, and other birds. The heads are here of an elongated oval, the eyes large and widely opened—the temples over the eyes strongly arched, the noses very narrow, but with wide nostrils.[1] This manuscript, according to a Latin poem it contains, was indited by one Gottschalk, who, as often the case in the art of the cloister, was probably the painter also. At all events it is an ascertained fact that painting was, with few exceptions, practised only by monks till towards the beginning of the twelfth century —all intellectual culture, down to that time, being engrossed by the religious orders.

An Evangeliarium (Supplement, Latin, No. 686), also in the Imperial Library at Paris, and far richer in contents than the preceding; originally from the church of St. Medardus, at Soissons. The pictures, including the subjects already described, and also the Church of Christ represented as a building, exhibit a far more skilful artist. Two of the Evangelists are of very animated action.[2]

An Evangelistarium, in the civic Library of Trèves. The four youthfully conceived Evangelists here give evidence of a still more advanced artist. The motives have throughout something grand and free, and justly express the character of Divine inspiration; the features of St. Matthew may be even termed noble. But the ornamentation of the borders of the canon, and of the initials in the manuscripts of this time, show a far more developed stage of art than the human figures. Two elements of art are especially distinguishable here—the one antique in character and of great purity, as appears frequently in the acroteria, genii, and animals; and the other of Irish tendency, displaying itself in the no less beautiful than original taste of the scrolls of the divisions and spaces, and in various dragon and serpent shapes, here first announcing the fantastic element which prevailed in the Middle Ages, and executed with astonishing mastery and correctness. This peculiar form of art, which continued to be developed in the Irish convents from the sixth century downward, was disseminated through the various countries of Europe by numerous Irish missionaries; in France and Suabia by

[1] See further description in my 'Kunstwerke und Künstler in Paris,' p. 234.
[2] See 'Kunstwerke und Künstler in Paris,' p. 237.

St. Columbanus; in Switzerland by his scholar St. Gallus (founder of the convent of St. Galle); in Franconia by St. Kilian; in Belgium by St. Lievin; and in Friesland by St. Willebrord.[1] Both these elements, antique and Irish, are here combined with the application of the most costly colours, especially purple; gold and silver are also abundantly used, and thus a system of ornamentation worked out which unites the utmost splendour of effect with a very original and attractive form of taste, and great technical mastery. The same architectural feeling is observable here which afterwards found so grand a development in the architecture of the Germanic race.

Subsequently, when France and Germany, under the grandchildren of Charlemagne, lapsed into separate states, we soon perceive a distinct character in the art of each. I propose, therefore, only so far to consider the form of art practised in France, as it occasionally is found to influence that of Germany. In this French school Byzantine feeling may be said to vanish, though traces of the types of early Christian art, such as had taken root in Italy and France, are still recognisable. Meanwhile, in the course of the ninth century, a barbaric element becomes more and more perceptible. This is seen in the character of the heads, with noses of monstrous thickness and length—in the brick-red tones of the flesh, and in a coarser style of treatment. As regards the ornamentation of initials and borders, however, upon the above-described system, art retained a far higher character. The chief specimens of this time are the Bibles of Charles the Bald in the Louvre, and in the Royal Library at Munich, formerly in the convent of St. Emmeran at Regensburg, and the Bible of the Emperor Charles the Fat, in the church of St. Calixtus at Rome.[2] Another series of miniatures belonging to manuscripts written in France discover an Anglo-Saxon tendency; these, however, as

---

[1] See my Supplement to Kugler's 'Handbook of the History of Painting,' in the 'Kunstblatt' of 1850, p. 53.

[2] There erroneously given out for the Bible of Charlemagne. See last-mentioned Essay in 'Kunstblatt,' 1850, p. 92; also 'Kunstwerke und Künstler in Paris,' p. 258.

exercising no influence on the art of Germany, I have no occasion to consider.

The one class of art which has been preserved in Germany consists chiefly of very rude and slight pen-drawings, in which reminiscences of antique feeling are traceable only in the motives of the drapery. Of this kind are the miniatures in the manuscript, dated 814, and belonging to the Bavarian convent of Wessobrunn, now in the Library at Munich. This manuscript is also celebrated as containing the Wessobrunn Prayer, one of the earliest examples of the German language. It is decorated with sixteen small pictures, illustrative of the Finding of the true Cross by the Empress Helena.

Translation of the Four Evangelists into German verse, undertaken in the ninth century by Ottfried, a monk belonging to the convent of Weissenburg, in Alsatia; now in the Imperial Library at Vienna. Two pictures here, the Crucifixion and Palm Sunday, probably both by the same monk, occupy each a whole page. Christ is represented upon the Cross under a youthful form, and is upright and still alive. The expression of sorrow in the Virgin and St. John is well rendered by lively gestures. Above, in two circles, are the half-length figures of the Sun and Moon, looking at Christ, and about to cover their faces with their drapery. A third picture, representing the Last Supper, is the work of a later and far ruder hand, to whom also the insertion of the eight Apostles in Palm-Sunday is attributable.

In point of art, however, the above-mentioned works are far surpassed by a picture of Christ as Salvator Mundi, p. 369 of a manuscript in the library of the convent of St. Galle (No. 877), which contains the Grammar of Donatus and other writings of similar import. The motive of the figure is free and noble, the proportions slender, the arms astonishingly well drawn, and the antique style of the drapery well understood. This picture, dating from the ninth century, proves how early the school of art belonging to this convent had attained a very respectable development.

The second class of miniature pictures preserved in Germany consists of subjects very carefully executed in body colours. In the conception of these, antique types are clearly discerned, but also, especially in the tenth century, the strong influence of Byzantine art. The chief specimen of this kind, belonging to the ninth century, is a Psalter, No. 23 of the Library at St. Galle. Among the scenes from the Old and New Testament, contained in the richly-decorated Litany, the figure of Christ, conceived in a youthful type, and that of David playing on the psalter, are most remarkable. As regards initial decorations, this is the richest and most splendid memorial of German art I know, and may be justly placed in the same category as the Bibles of Charles the Bald.

Far richer, however, in point of number of pictures, is a stately Evangeliarium, in the Library of the Cathedral of Trèves, which in its initials, in the attributes of the Evangelists, and in the use of several of the colours, betrays the especial influence of the Irish school of miniatures. At the same time, in other decorations, the style of the above-described French school is discernible, while in the motives of the figures, and partially in the tone of colouring, Byzantine feeling may be seen. One Thomas, who styles himself the writer, was probably the author of some of the pictures, which are evidently the work of different hands. There is reason to believe that this codex was executed in the convent of St. Galle.

The prosperity which Germany enjoyed from 919 to 1066 under the Saxon and the first two Frankish emperors has left its impress in the only surviving form of art—the miniatures attached to manuscripts. Among the artists of this time several bishops take a prominent position. The antique types of art are adhered to with no inconsiderable technical skill in body-colours, while side by side with them may already be remarked signs of original composition. Frequently also, and especially at the period of the marriage of the Greek Princess Theophanu with the Emperor Otho II. in 972, a strong savour of Byzantine influence is apparent. As characteristic of the German painting of this and the succeeding period may be pointed out the frequent use of the colour green, evidently as much a favourite with the Germans as that of azure with the French. MSS. with miniatures of this period exist in considerable numbers, of which I need only give a few examples. A codex, No. 338, of the Library of St. Galle, containing an Antiphonarium, a Sacramentarium, and other ritual works, and which is very important in the history of Swiss art, is incomplete at the beginning and at the end. A Crucifixion and a Descent of the Holy Ghost show a monk of the name of Gottschalk, mentioned in the text, and probably the author of the pictures, to be an excellent artist for his time. The motives are speaking and dignified, the drawing comparatively good. In the broad, antique mode of treatment which still prevails may be seen here and there half tones introduced.[1]

An Evangelistarium entirely written by the hand of St. Ulrich, Bishop of Augsburg, in the Royal Library at Munich, constitutes one of the chief specimens of the Suabian school. The pictures of the four Evangelists, also probably the work of the bishop himself, and that of the Archangel Michael and the Dragon, which is very successful, are, with the exception of the tone of the flesh, free from all Byzantine influence, showing the antique modes of conception proper to early Christian art, combined with much skill of execution. Only in the crude and strong colours, and in the ill-understood motives of the drapery, is a new element, and one indicative of the period, apparent. Another Evangeliarium by the same holy hand, from the easy access which every English reader may obtain to it, it is as well to mention: it is preserved in the British Museum (Harleian MSS. No. 2970), and is of similar character of art, only that the colours are kept more light.[2]

As a specimen of Bavarian art may be quoted an Evangeliarium with the pictures of the four Evangelists, ori-

---

[1] 'Kunstblatt' of 1850, p. 92.
[2] 'Kunstblatt' of 1850, p. 98; also 'Treasures of Art in Great Britain, vol. i. p. 196.

ginally from the Monastery of Tegernsee, 1017–1048, now in the Library at Munich (No. 31). They exhibit strict drawing, a simple cast of drapery, and a clean mode of execution.

At the head of the numerous MSS. representing the Franconian school may be named an Evangelistarium, written about the year 1000, and now in the Munich Library (iv. 2, b). The pictures are interesting, both in point of subjects and of artistic skill. One of the four artists here distinguishable, by whom the Nativity was executed, shows a decided Byzantine influence. Another hand, to which the enigmatical representation, p. 5, is attributable, is a complete specimen of that mode of art observable in the MSS. written at Bamberg, and chiefly decorated with miniatures by order of the Emperor Henry II., who reigned from 1002 to 1024. Some of these are still preserved in the Library at Bamberg, some in the Library at Munich. They are distinguished most decidedly from the works of the Carlovingian period by their peculiarity of style and treatment. On the one hand, they are far less pleasing, but on the other they are in a technical point of view far more important. In spite of the want of certainty, and the clumsy rudeness of execution, the Carlovingian works always show a feeling for form, and always preserve the general proportions of the human frame, and the large lines of the drapery. In the Bamberg MSS. we find no trace of these merits; the figures are most unhappily distorted and crippled, the outlines are whimsical and capricious, the forms of the heads full and exaggerated. Nevertheless the lines are throughout drawn with more certainty and precision. The system of colouring also differs. The juiciness of the impasto disappears, and in its place we find the dry manner of laying on the colour which henceforth belongs particularly to miniature painting; with this are united the finest and neatest execution and the most careful finishing, forming a strong contrast, and for the works in question for once an advantageous one, with the uncertain pencilling of the Carlovingian period. Still more surprising than this elegance of execution is the peculiar, and if I may use the expression, the phantasmagoric play of colour, which appears especially in the grounds of these illuminations. Stripes of delicate colour intermingle in beautiful harmony behind the figures, and produce a very peculiar and pleasing effect to the eye. Besides these technical defects and advantages, we must finally mention that ingenious ideas are often embodied in symbolical forms, suited to the infantine state of art, and that, in spite of the imperfect drawing, there is considerable expression in the gestures and position of the figures.

A description of the illuminations in one of these MSS. in the Munich Library, B, No. 2, which contains a collection of the Gospels, will better explain these observations. After the canons with which for the most part MSS. of this kind begin, and of which the columns are as usual enclosed in pillars and arches, the general contents of the book are indicated by a peculiar allegorical representation: Christ within a rainbow, closed elliptically, stands in the centre in front of a tree, of which he holds a branch with his left hand; in his right is a globe, the symbol of sovereignty. The tree is adorned with mushroom-shaped groups of leaves and small red fruits, and represents without doubt the Tree of Knowledge, from the branches of which, according to old tradition, the Cross was formed; this accounts for its introduction here. In the four rounded corners of the rainbow are—on the right of Christ, Sol, a red head with rays; on his left, Luna, blue, with the crescent; above, Uranus, an old head of a bluish-grey colour; and below a brown figure of a woman for Tellus, with the upper part of her body nude, and holding the stem of the tree. In the outer corners are the four symbols of the evangelists, borne by siren-like figures of a greenish hue. These last signify, as the text explains, the four rivers of Paradise, from which the rivers of the earth receive their supplies, and which at the same time, according to the old system of symbols, betoken the four evangelists. The rainbow, with the four rounded corners, is enclosed in stripes of gold—the ground within it is olive-green, with a bluish-green edge—the outside is lilac, in the upper part melting into rose-colour, in the lower into green. Before each Gospel is also, as is common at this time, the figure of the evangelist, seated at a desk. Each of these figures is enclosed between two columns, which support a horizontal scroll with an explanatory inscription; over it is a flat arch, always containing the symbol appropriated to each evangelist, and also a figure which has reference to the sacrifice of Christ. Here also we meet with ingenious allusions : for example, at the side of the lion of St. Mark, Christ is represented rising from the grave with the Cross; in the lower part of the picture the evangelist himself raises his hands and head in an attitude of astonishment, which the following inscription explains:—

" Ecce leo fortis transit discrimina mortis:
Fortia facta stupet Marcus qui nuntia defert."

St. Luke, on the contrary, over whom is represented a dying Lamb, looks down and drops the scroll he has just been writing. In other MSS. we find perhaps a greater abundance of historical subjects, that is, of events from sacred history, in which, as the meaning has to be conveyed by the figures themselves, the defective drawing strikes the eye far more forcibly than in mere allegorical designs.

Another work, with far more numerous pictures, some of them very interesting in import, is the MS. of a missal in the same library, presented by the Emperor Henry, on occasion of his coronation in 1002, to the Chapter at Bamberg.

The following MSS. are particularly important as illustrative of painting in Saxony :—

An Evangeliarium, in the treasury of the church at Quedlinburg, probably presented by the Emperor Henry I. It may be supposed that the paintings executed in the palace of this sovereign at Merseburg, representing his victory over the Hungarians, were much in the style of the miniatures in this MS.

An Evangeliarium, in the Imperial Library, Paris (Supplement Latin, No. 667), probably written for the Emperor Otho II. (reigned 974-983), and of considerable artistic value as specimens of the above-mentioned form of treatment, though showing a strong Byzantine influence.[1]

An Evangeliarium, also written for Otho II., formerly in the convent of Echternach, now in the Ducal Library at Gotha. Some of the pictures here contained afford an example, more than any others known to me in a German work, of the above-described and little-attractive style of French art appertaining to the ninth century. With these exceptions, however, this MS., both as respects number and value of pictures, and rich decoration of canons and initials, may be considered one of the first class.[2]

Three Evangeliaria, in the sacristy of the Cathedral at Hildesheim. The miniatures in these MSS. coincide much with those in the missal at Bamberg, but are somewhat ruder in execution, and doubtless the work of St. Bernward, Bishop of Hildesheim (reigned 993-1022), who was well known as a painter.

Westphalian art is represented by two Evangeliaria, in the Cathedral Library at Trèves. One of them (No. 139), scarcely later in date than 950, shows, as compared with the South-German and Rhenish miniature painting of this time, a great inferiority in figures: on the other hand, the initials and ornamentation of the canons are very skilful. The other Evangeliarium is of far higher artistic value ; its miniatures may be adjudged to about the year 1000, while its cover contains a carving in ivory of the tenth century, and enamels of the twelfth century.

As regards the position which miniature painting attained in the Rhine country, an Evangelistarium, executed for Bishop Egbert of Trèves (reigned 978-993), now in the civic Library of that ancient city, gives very favourable testimony. It contains fifty-seven large pictures, among which six different hands may be distinguished. These are, in part, very happily composed, and display in the principal motives and in the good feeling of the drapery a

---

[1] 'Kunstwerke und Künstler in Paris,' p. 266.
[2] Rathgeber's ' Beschreibung des Herzoglichen Museum zu Gotha,' p. 9, &c.

successful adherence to antique tradition. A small number only of these pictures give decided evidence of the imitation of Byzantine types.

There is proof also in an Evangeliarium of very splendid execution, in the University Library at Prague, that a similar style of painting was also practised in Bohemia. Various departures from the types of tradition—for instance, in the Baptism, where the river Jordan is represented as a naked youth, pouring the water over the head of Christ—show a mode of conception peculiar to Bohemia.[1]

In the neighbouring country of the Netherlands, judging from the scanty specimens of MSS. with miniatures belonging to this time, the style of art was very similar, only not so successful. An Evangeliarium, in the Royal Library of the Hague, which may be attributed to about the year 900, shows, though rude in forms and crude in colouring, a very powerful reflection of Irish art. The portraits at the end of the MS. of Count Dietrich II. of Holland, and his wife Hildegard, with St. Albert, by whom they are recommended to the care of the Saviour, who appears in a mandorla, belong to the latter half of the tenth century, when this MS. was presented by both these personages to the church of the Abbey of Egmond, dedicated to that saint. This representation is only drawn in black outlines with the pen, and, though rude in character, is interesting as showing the first movement of an original mode of art, in contradistinction to that imitation of the antique types which was then becoming more and more mechanical in practice.

An Evangeliarium, from the church of St. Jacques at Liège, now in the Library of the old Dukes of Burgundy (No. 18,383) at Brussels, belonging to the tenth century, and executed throughout in body colours of light and harmonious effect, is incomparably richer and more careful in manner.

An Evangelistarium, in the same library (No. 9428), of the beginning of the eleventh century, is again richer still

---

[1] 'Kunstblatt,' 1850, p. 129.

and more important. The pictures agree in style of art and type of heads with that above described belonging to Bishop Egbert of Trèves, only that they are ruder. The cool violet flesh tones and the whole scale of bright and harmonious colouring show a striking affinity to the miniatures at Bamberg executed for the Emperor Henry II., proving the wide spread of this style of art.

After the middle of the eleventh century, and owing probably to the great public disorders under the long reign of the Emperor Henry IV., a suspension of pictorial progress is observable in Germany. Side by side with the style of the previous epoch—the use, namely, of size-colours, of a general light tone more or less indicative of Byzantine influence—are perceived those simple outlines, only filled up with slight illumination, which are independent of Byzantine feeling. At the same time, while this period shows more and more the decline of antique tradition, no development of original modes of conception is found to ensue. Besides the single figures of Christ, the Virgin, and Saints, scenes also from the Scriptures occur, and those symbolical representations which are so characteristic of the spirit of the Middle Ages. By the beginning of the twelfth century, however, instances of moderate progress are traceable, which continues until the end of that century. I give a few examples:—

An Evangeliarium, from the monastery of Altaich, near Straubing, in Bavaria, now in the Munich Library, in which the figures of Christ in the act of benediction, and of St. Mark, are remarkable, and where the whole technical process is very clean.

An Evangeliarium, also in the Munich Library, from the Niedermünster monastery at Regensburg. At the beginning of the MS. we find various allegorical subjects, of a mystic character, with rich tendril-like ornament and numerous inscriptions. One of these, representing the victory over death by the sacrifice of Christ, is remarkable. In the centre Christ is represented on the Cross, his feet fastened to a board with two nails, in red drapery, with the royal crown and priestly stole. Somewhat lower at each side of the cross stand, on the left, Vita, a female figure having a crown adorned with a cross and rich drapery, her face and hands raised upwards; on the right, Mors, pallid in colour, with matted hair, the countenance half-veiled, a deep wound in the neck, the body half nude, and the clothing mean, sinking down with broken lance and scythe. A dragon, which grows out from the foot of the cross, appears to bite this figure in the arm. On both sides are smaller figures; above are Sol and Luna, veiled. On the right is the New Covenant, a female figure crowned, with the standard of victory, and the cup of the Sacrament on the crown. On the left is the Old Covenant, her countenance concealed by the border, the scroll of the Law and the sacrificial knife in her hands. Below, on the right, are the uprisen dead; on the left, the rent veil of the Temple. Further on in the MS., before each Gospel, there is a representation of its evangelist, with the appropriate symbol above the figure, and underneath, according to the allegorical notion already mentioned, one of the four rivers of Paradise, here represented in the form of a nude male figure, with two horns and a large water urn. The painting of all these subjects is very neat, and in the drawing a certain knowledge of form is already perceptible.

Specimens of that style of outline, above mentioned, are seen in a Psalter in the Library of St. Galle (No. 21), adorned by Notger, abbot of St. Galle, surnamed Labeo, or Teutonicus, with pictures which are very rude for the period.

The Netherlandish miniatures executed at this time agree in essential respects with those of Germany, only that a more or less shining surface shows the mixture of gum with the colours. The miniatures in the second part of a Vulgate in the British Museum (additional, No. 17,738) are an example of this. Some only of the colours, the vermilion and the green, are given in their full force. The symbolic subject, fol. 2, b, especially shows a skilful artist.

Another specimen is supplied by the Commentary of St. Gregory on the book of Job, in the Imperial Library, Paris (Sorbonne, No. 267), in which the motives are of great vivacity. As the pictures throughout about half the work are unfinished, their technical processes are more plainly seen. The outlines are very cleverly drawn with the pen, then the requisite local colours laid on, and finally the details added in a darker tone with a brush.

CHAPTER II.

THE BYZANTINE-ROMANESQUE EPOCH.

1150—1250.

DATING from the middle of the twelfth century, and continuing uninterrupted till the middle of the thirteenth, a great advance is seen throughout Germany and the Netherlands in all the arts, including that of painting, which from monastic hands gradually passes into those of the laity. The field of ecclesiastic subjects became largely extended, and that system of placing the type and countertype from the Old and New Testament in juxtaposition first fully developed. In the literary elaboration of the floating traditions of Charlemagne, King Arthur and his Round Table, and of the Song of the Niebelungen, the romantic feeling of this period first found expression, and was also rendered available in the department of pictorial representation. In this service were enlisted all the outward forms of life —armour, weapons, the costume of noble knights and ladies—all taken from models immediately within the painter's reach. Side by side with those fantastic modes of conception, of which, in ecclesiastical subjects, the frequent treatment of the Apocalypse is an example, flourished also those humorous ideas which found so rich and picturesque an expression in the grotesque sculpture of Romanesque churches, and in the drolleries of the miniatures. The system of representing the occupations of each month in the calendar gave further occasion for the introduction of scenes from daily life. Finally, the representation of animals, as illustrations of Aristotle's Natural History, and also of those writings treating of the chace, and especially of the science of falconry, became very popular. As respects, however, the conception of ecclesiastical subjects, Byzantine art exercised even in this period considerable influence, though in a different style from that formerly adopted. Instead of continuing the mummified forms of that school, the painters of the day began to recognise the excellence which lay in its original inventions, and succeeded in animating them with their own peculiar feeling. In the movements a sense of beauty and grace is frequently apparent, and Byzantine meagreness yields to a certain fulness of facial forms. Only in particular subjects, such as the Crucifixion, did the unfortunate conception of later Byzantine art continue to be adhered to. As regards the narrow and stiff folds of the drapery, and the dramatic and often violent character of the motives, the sculptures which adorned both the exterior and interior of the Romanesque churches exercised a very effective influence. The expression of emotions by means of gesture was also successfully cultivated, and the costumes more and more taken from common life. The treatment, in which body colours were preferred, was carried to great mastery and precision. Till towards the year 1200, the colours as a rule are, like the Byzantine pictures which served as models, much broken with lighter tints; after that time the colours, like the later Byzantine pictures, are forcible and frequently dark. The coloured backgrounds also, hitherto used, are almost invariably replaced by a gold ground. In the predominance of decided and generally black outlines, and in the scumbling of the colours, a new principle is traceable. At the same time the Teutonic spirit of art is still more originally and independently seen in the pictures with pale outlines, filled up with generally very slight colouring. With few exceptions, the painting of this epoch is represented only by miniatures in MSS., of which I proceed to describe a few of the most remarkable:—

THE HORTUS DELICIARUM.

A Psalter, in the library of Prince Wallerstein, at Mahingen, not far from Nördlingen, which belongs to the beginning of this period, shows in the occupations of the months, illustrating the calendar, various animated features taken from life—for instance, in March the sower; in September the gathering, treading, and pressing of the grape; and the tapping of the beer in November. At the same time the religious subjects still evince a strong Byzantine tendency, only that the Virgin in the Nativity, and the Christ showing his wounds, have something grand and noble in character. The tone of colouring is bright.

The splendid MS. of the Hortus Deliciarum (a collection of extracts from the fathers, ecclesiastical writers, and other works), executed in the latter part of the twelfth century, in the convent of Hohenburg, in Alsace, but at present in the Public Library of Strasburg. It is adorned with a large number of miniature illustrations of the text, and thus contains, with subjects from sacred history, some of an allegorical character, and others which represent scenes from real life. The latter display fully the costume and fashions of the time in great variety. The conception for the most part, particularly in the tedious allegories, is rather poor, and requires numerous marginal explanations to elucidate its meaning; nevertheless, in the figures of the saints (which are represented in the early Christian manner), there is a dignified grandeur and repose, and occasionally surprising boldness and meaning in the ideas of the artist himself. Amongst the most remarkable is a figure of Superbia, a female in rich attire and flowing drapery, seated on horseback, on a lion-skin, and poising her lance.

A peculiar school of miniature illustration appears to have been formed at this time in the convents of Upper Bavaria; most of the drawings with which the MSS. are illustrated are only in pen and ink, but the flesh is generally distinguished from the drapery, and even different parts of the latter are distinguished from each other, by tints of red and black ink. In the figures themselves there is seldom more colouring, but the grounds are always filled in and enclosed with borders of different colours.¹ Of these works we may first mention the MS. of the German Æneid, by Henry von Veldeck, written about the year 1200, which was brought from Bavaria, and is now preserved in the Royal Library at Berlin. The drawings represent in a long series the events narrated in the poem. They in general deserve attention from the care bestowed upon the costume and other details, but in all that regards feeling for form and grace they are far inferior to the Hortus Deliciarum; in the deformity of many of the figures they even remind us of the MSS. of Bamberg already described. Still they possess a peculiar interest as steps in the history of German art. There is here unfolded, in the movements of the hands in particular, a complete language of gesture, equally well adapted to convey the expression of tranquil intercourse or of passionate energy. Thus, for example, when the solitary complaints of love, or the sorrow for the death of the loved one, are to be depicted, grief and suffering are admirably expressed by a convulsive wringing of the hands.

Far more important are the drawings of another MS. of the same time and school, containing the beautiful German poem of Werinher, deacon of the convent of Tegernsec, on the Life of the Virgin, which has passed from the collection of Herr v. Nagler into the Royal Library of Berlin.² With respect to excellence of form, these drawings are nearly equal to those of the Hortus Deliciarum, and in single parts they surpass them in quiet grace and naïveté. This is particularly shown in those in which the expression of a serene and happy tone of mind is the chief object, as, for instance, in a group of the Blessed, in a Vision of the Virgin. Others, in which the artist represents passionate, and especially sorrowful feelings, are of the highest excellence. In spite of the insufficiency of his means, he has exhibited in the positions, gestures, and cast of drapery, a

---

[1] See Kugler's Essay, 'Die Bilderhandschrift der Eneidt in der Königl. Bibliothek zu Berlin.' Museum, 1836, No. 36–38.

[2] See Kugler's dissertation, De Werinhero, sæculi xii. monacho Tegernseensi, &c.

tragic pathos so peculiarly expressive as to excite our greatest astonishment, when we consider the early epoch of art at which the work was executed. The best of these drawings are—one that represents the Damned (also in a Vision of the Virgin), in which they are bound together by glowing chains, and are driven hither and thither by inward torments; and another, of which the subject is the lamentation at Bethlehem of the mothers after the massacre of their children; in this one woman rends her garment, another cowers on the ground and supports her head on her hand, a third wrings her hands, a fourth with a passionate movement raises her hands and appears to appeal to Heaven against the horrible outrage.

As a further step of progress, in connection with the foregoing, we may mention the drawings by Conrad, a monk of the convent of Scheyern, who was distinguished as the author of many learned works, and lived about the middle of the thirteenth century. The Royal Library of Munich contains several of the works which he embellished with drawings, amongst which a book of the Gospels, and another of the Lessons, are particularly important.[1] At the beginning of the latter MS. are several large subjects from the Apocalypse; then two remarkable legends in smaller drawings —one containing the history of Bishop Theophilus, the earliest German version of Faust; and lastly, a number of illustrations of sacred history. The lines are not drawn with the certainty and precision of those before described; but, on the other hand, the desire of imitating the forms of nature is still more evident, the movements are still freer, the cast of the drapery follows more easily the movements of the figure, and its outline has at once softness and dignity.

One of the most interesting illustrated MSS. of this period, but of another school, is the Psalter, written about the year 1200 for the Landgrave Hermann of Thuringen, formerly in the convent of Weingarten, but now in the King's private library at Stuttgart.[2] The miniatures are

---
[1] Munich Library. Cod. Lat. Membr. c. p. No. 7, b. c.; No. 13, a. Museum, 1834, No. 21, p. 165.
[2] Museum, No. 13, p. 97. See Dibdin, 'A Bibliographical and Antiquarian Tour in France and Germany,' vol. iii. p. 158.

highly finished, and executed with great neatness. The style essentially resembles that of the time, but the figures have an air of more solemn dignity, while at the same time their severity is often pleasingly softened by an expression of mild and simple grace. Here we find in single heads (especially in those of Christ) traces of ideal beauty, the more surprising, since in other works of the time all the heads are still stiff, and without grace. At the beginning of this MS. is a calendar, in which each month is ornamented with a figure of its patron saint, and characterised by a country scene. Representations of this kind must have been very rare at so early a period; the costume and occupations throughout belong to the North, and consequently testify that the drawings are the productions of a native school. Then follow, in the Psalms themselves, various subjects, such as the Baptism of Christ, his Death, Descent into hell, Ascension, &c. &c. The feeling in these is excellent, particularly in that which represents the Virgin and John, in a simple attitude of thoughtful sorrow, standing at the feet of the crucified Saviour. After this comes the Litany, over which, in the upper part of the page, are half-length portraits of saints and princes; those of the Landgrave Hermann and his wife Sophia are the first, and in these we see an example, remarkable for so early a period, of an attempt at individual likeness already crowned with signal success.

A rich and interesting MS., an Evangeliarium, written about 1200, is in the Cathedral Library at Trèves. It is remarkable for an elaborate and very original representation of the Root of Jesse and other symbolical pictures, which are rendered in a curious style, with numerous inscriptions. Antique personifications also—for instance, of river gods—occur still here.

A Psalter, written about the same time as the foregoing, and probably in the Rhine country, now in the City Library at Hamburg, No. 85. The beautiful and original motives which appear here are evidences of what German art could do in this early period. We may instance the way in which the Child is caressing the Virgin in the Presentation in the

Temple; also the large picture of the Madonna and Child, occupying an entire page, which, in the meditative expression conveyed by the action of the Child, recalls the grandeur of Guido da Siena.

An Evangeliarium, also about 1200, probably written in Mayence, now in the Library at Aschaffenburg, No. 3. This, as regards number of pictures, of which the Sermon on the Mount is remarkable, and for excellence of art, is one of the most important documents of this time.[1]

A Psalter, in the Library at Bamberg, No. 232, and unquestionably executed in that city about the first half of the thirteenth century, is of a darker scale of colour. With the exception of a few examples which recall Byzantine types, the fourteen large pictures are of admirable composition, generally original motives, and very skilful technical execution.[2]

The few wall pictures still remaining of this period are sometimes very peculiar in invention, full of symbolical meaning, and of happy motives. The execution, however, does not extend beyond a rather coarse outline, with slight rendering of lights and shadows. Nor is it to be supposed that the large number of such specimens of art as have perished, and of which evidence still survives,[3] should have materially differed from these. I add a few examples of the most important still existing. On the walls of the cathedral of Worms are several faded paintings in the Byzantine style, among which a gigantic Madonna, in one of the transepts, is remarkable; it reaches half way up to the vault of the nave. The twenty-four ceiling compartments in the former monastery of Brauweiler, three leagues from Cologne, which were possibly executed about 1200, represent the power of Faith to overcome the world, from a passage in the 11th chapter of the Epistle to the Hebrews.

---

[1] 'Kunstwerke und Künstler in Deutschland,' vol. i. p. 377, &c.
[2] Ibid., vol. i. p. 103, &c.
[3] See notice of the paintings in the Monastery of Benedictbeuren in Bavaria, in Fiorillo's 'Geschichte der bildenden Künste in Deutschland,' vol. i. p. 178, &c. Bishops Burcard of Halberstadt, Otto of Bamberg, and Uffo of Merseburg had the walls of their cathedrals decorated with paintings. See Hotho's 'Malerschule Hubert's van Eyck,' vol. i. p. 42.

In the centre of the whole is the colossal bust picture of Christ. In the other compartments appear those who, by the triumph of their faith, obtained the promises, such as Mary Magdalen and the Thief on the Cross; hose who suffered for their faith, such as Daniel and St. Thecla; and those who fought for their faith, such as Samson and St. Hyppolitus, both of whom are distinguished by great beauty of motive.

The fact that painting flourished at an early period in Cologne is shown by a passage in the poem of Parzival, by Wofram of Eschenbach,[1] written about the year 1200. The only examples surviving may be seen in the Baptistery of St. Gereon, Cologne, where SS. Barbara and Catherine, and a reposing angel, are especially remarkable. These were probably executed soon after the erection of the church in 1227.

Another important memorial of art, dating from about 1200, are the paintings which cover the whole length, above 100 feet, of the wooden roof of St. Michael's church at Hildesheim. They are in three series. In the centre series are Adam and Eve, Abraham, the four kings of Israel, Moses, and the Virgin: at the sides the Patriarchs, Prophets, and Saints. These figures, which are in strict architectonic arrangement, and the decorations surrounding them, show a very respectable grade of art, and are harmonious in colouring and of general clearness of effect. An admirable plate of this, in chromo-lithography, with text by Dr. Kraatz, is to be had at Storch and Krahmer's, Berlin.

Of still more importance are the paintings in the choir

---

[1] The lines are thus quoted by Passavant, p. 403:—

"Als uns die aventiure gicht
Von Chölne noch von Mastricht
Dechein sciltere entwurf'en baz
Denn' als er ufem orse saz."

That is to say—

"As our tale runs,
No painter of Cologne or Mästricht
Could have painted him more comely
Than as he sat upon his horse."

and in the left aisle of the transept of the cathedral at Brunswick. They are, however, unfortunately deprived of their original character by means of an unskilful restoration. On the walls of the choir, in figures larger than life, and arranged according to symbolical allusion, are the Sacrifice of Cain and Abel, the Death of Abel, the Sacrifice of Isaac (typifying the Redemption through the death of Christ), Moses and the Burning Bush, and the Raising of the Brazen Serpent. On the ceiling the scheme of Redemption is more clearly given in the Root of Jesse. The cupola in front of the choir represents the Lamb of the New Covenant, with scenes from the Life of Christ,—from the Nativity to the day of Pentecost,—and the twelve Apostles. The figures of eight Prophets connect these scenes with the Old Testament. On the ceiling of the transept, by a better hand, are Christ and the Virgin enthroned, figures above lifesize, with two colossal Angels and the twenty-four Elders. On the east wall are Christ in Limbus, and the Ascension; opposite, in well-known allusion to the Last Judgment, the parable of the Wise and Foolish Virgins. Judging from the purely Romanesque character of these pictures, and of the decorations belonging to them, they were decidedly executed before the year 1250.

To the termination of this period we may also attribute the wall-paintings in the old chapel of the Castle at Forchheim, a small fortress lying between Bamberg and Erlangen. The chief picture represents the Adoration of the Kings; the others consist of the Last Judgment, the Annunciation, and Prophets. The conceptions and single motives are good, but belong to traditionary art; the execution is somewhat rude.[1]

Some interesting paintings have lately come to light in the restoration of the splendid cathedral of Bamberg, on occasion of its being freed from its covering of plaster of many hundred years old. They are in the niches of one of the transept-walls of St. Peter's choir, and must undoubtedly belong to the beginning of the thirteenth century. Easel

---

[1] 'Kunstwerke und Künstler in Deutschland,' vol. i. p. 146, &c.

pictures, in the Byzantine style, are very rare in Germany. As one example of such, we may mention a painting representing Christ enthroned on a rainbow, with four saints at his side, which is in the Provincial Museum of Münster, and was taken from the convent of St. Walburg at Soest.[1]

Some works connected with painting, and in this style, though in other materials, are also preserved, such as the paintings on glass which fill the south window of the nave in Augsburg cathedral, and are composed of figures of saints. One of the most important of these examples of the successful efforts made in art towards the end of this period is furnished by the fragments of tapestry preserved in the abbey church of Quedlinburg, woven about the year 1200 by the abbess Agnes herself, with the assistance of her nuns, to adorn the walls of the choir of that church. The subjects are allegorical, and represent the marriage of Mercury with Philology (after Marcianus Capella). The original drawings were evidently by different hands; while some are in the common style of the day, others contain single figures of such beauty of form, and so much symmetry in the limbs, with a cast of drapery so grand, and arranged with so much artistic knowledge, yet so entirely free from the peculiarities of the ancient Christian models, that we may imagine we here see art approaching to full perfection. In the cathedral at Halberstadt there are also tapestries in the Byzantine style, but they are far ruder in the drawing than those of Quedlinburg.

At this epoch also painting in Bohemia exhibits a similar character. The strong Byzantine influence especially is here accounted for by the fact that St. Methodus, the apostle of Bohemia, was himself a painter. Examples are seen in the National Museum at Prague, in the form of the MS. of a Latin Dictionary,[2] dated MCII. and signed Miroslaw, and in the pictures of a Bible in the library of Prince Lobkowitz at Prague, executed about 1250. In this last the tendency to abstract personifications is seen. Thus

---

[1] Becker, 'Ueber die altdeutschen Gemälde aus dem ehemaligen Augustiner-Nonnen-Kloster St. Walburg zu Soest.' Museum, 1835, No. 47, p. 374.

[2] See 'Kunstblatt' of 1850, p. 130.

Darkness (Tenebre) is represented by two sleeping figures —Light by a small figure with a torch in its hand.[1]

The art of painting, as practised in the Netherlands, judging from the existing though not numerous MSS. with miniatures, agrees essentially with that of Germany at this period. At the same time Byzantine tradition assumes more the upper hand here, which is owing doubtless to the fact that Counts of Flanders occupied the throne of Constantinople during the so-called Latin Empire. In freedom and animation of early Byzantine motives, and in drawing and technical development, some of these exhibit great excellence. I give the following examples:—

A Missal in the British Museum (addit. No. 16,949), probably written between 1150 and 1200. Technical skill and beauty of colouring are particularly remarkable here.[2]

A Psalter in the Royal Library at the Hague. This is a very rich and important specimen, especially for scenes from life in the calendar, and for the extraordinary beauty of the Romanesque decorations. It belongs doubtless to the same time.

The chief example, however, known to me is a Psalter in the Imperial Library at Paris (Suppl. Français, No. 1132 bis), written about 1200. In the numerous and admirably-executed pictures with which this work is decorated, appears (for instance, in the same page containing Christ, the Virgin and Apostles, &c.) an adherence to Byzantine motives, combined with features taken from life. This is also seen in the Annunciation to the Shepherds, and in a combat of horsemen. Drolleries also occur in the initials.[3]

Another specimen, worthy to be named with the foregoing, is a MS. containing the greater part of the Vulgate, in the same library (MSS. Latins, No. 116). This, though

---

[1] Kunstblatt, 1850, p. 148.
[2] 'Treasures of Art in Great Britain,' vol. i. p. 122.
[3] 'Kunstwerke und Künstler in Paris,' p. 311. Having been misled by Italian miniatures of the 14th century in the latter part of the MS., and by the Byzantine influence also prevailing in Italy from 1200–1300, I have erroneously described this MS. as Italian.

much less rich in contents, gives very favourable evidence of the high grade of art at this time in the Netherlands.

Unfortunately, no specimens either of wall or of easel pictures have been, to the best of my knowledge, preserved in the Netherlands. This is to be more regretted in the town of Maestricht, the artists of which, according to the above-mentioned poem of Parzival, by Wolram von Eschenbach, enjoyed a great reputation.

BOOK II.

THE TEUTONIC STYLE.

FIRST EPOCH, 1250—1420.

INTRODUCTION.

THE general introduction of Gothic architecture which took place from this time in the Netherlands and in Germany, exercised here, and in all countries where it was consistently carried out, a very unfavourable influence on the development of monumental painting. The fact that this mode of building necessarily broke up the surface of the walls into columns and windows deprived the art of wall painting of its required space. The great height of a Gothic building also rendered the roof, as well, a useless field. On the other hand, the stunted forms under which Gothic architecture appeared in Italy preserved to the Italian painters those walls and ceilings which offered the fundamental condition of the development of high monumental art in that country. Wanting this, the artists of the Netherlands and Germany were restricted to the production of altar pictures, which came more and more into vogue. Nor even in this field did they enjoy full liberty. The centre compartment—the only space adapted by its size for a comprehensive composition of life-sized figures—was generally engrossed by sculpture, while the wings, which were the only portions left for the painter, were, by their long and narrow forms, so unfavourable to pictorial art, that they are usually seen divided into two, and thus only adapted for the execution of figures on a very small scale.

CHAPTER I.

THE PERIOD WHEN PAINTING WAS PRINCIPALLY RESTRICTED TO THE ILLUMINATION OF OUTLINES.

1250—1350.

THE art of this period indicates in so far an improvement on that of the foregoing, that we observe a greater effort at independence, to the abandonment partially of the Byzantine models, and entirely of Byzantine styles of colouring and treatment. The length of time required, however, for the development of a new style will account for the pictures of this epoch, which must be considered as one of transition, being decidedly inferior in point of art to those of the preceding time. In the motives of the earlier pictures of this time a mixture of the forms of Romanesque and Gothic sculpture prevails; in those of a later period Gothic feeling alone is seen. The attitudes have a conventional twist, which often gives rise to an ugly prominence of the body. A similar peculiarity is observable in the draperies, which, in the earlier examples, though those are more developed than in the period before them, still adhere to a parallel tendency; in later works, however, they assume a more forced form, with widely separated and often meagre folds. Another feature shows itself in the representations of the Almighty, of Christ, and of the Virgin, where the antique costume, which long tradition had hallowed, is frequently no longer preserved. Angelic beings also from this time are seen clothed in a mantle over their hitherto straight tunics. The heads are generally still of typical form; in the earlier time of an oval shape, broad above and contracted below, with wide-open eyes, narrow, pointed noses, and somewhat large mouths drawn down at the corners; in the later period the oval assumes greater fullness, the nose is short, and the mouth small. Outward coarseness and vulgarity is now expressed by caricatures with large crooked noses; spiritual depravity by a distorted laugh; and sorrow, especially, by the drawing down of the corners of the mouth. Occasionally also the attempt at individuality of feature is already seen. In point of colouring the abandonment of tradition entails bright and gaudy hues, among which vermilion and a powerful blue play the chief parts. As the black outlines of this time are somewhat meagrely treated, the colour of the cheek only given by red spots, and the shadows of the draperies simply rendered by a darker local tint, these pictures, which are drawn with great certainty of hand, have the effect of very gaily illuminated pen-drawings. After the year 1300 the dawning feeling for greater harmony of colour is seen in the use of more broken tints—for instance, bluish-pink, brownish, greenish, &c.; also in a more careful design and a more delicate distribution of lights and shadows. These examples have already more the effect of paintings. The spaces are only indicated. In the forms of architecture the Romanesque and Gothic alternately prevail; trees are quite conventional in shape, the backgrounds are gilt, and, in the miniatures, also panelled in pattern. In these latter also, as in the former period, we occasionally see simple pen-drawings displaying much originality.

As every new movement in painting, from this time forward, proceeds from the Netherlands, and as their flourishing political state contrasts conspicuously, from the year 1250, with the wars and disorders in Germany, I shall henceforth commence my observations always with Netherlandish examples.

The earliest dated specimen known to me, showing the effort at greater independence, is the MS. of a Vulgate, in two folio volumes, in the library of the Seminary at Liege. The pictures in the initials, heading each book, evince, it is true, no very skilful artist, but are important as showing by the date, 1248, how early this style of art began to be practised in the Netherlands.

Close upon the last mentioned in time, though far superior in art, are the here and there illuminated pen-drawings in a MS. of the French History of Alexander the

Great (No. 11,040) preserved in the Library of the old Dukes of Burgundy at Brussels. The numerous battles are represented with the weapons and in the fashion of the painter's time, of which they give a very animated and intelligent picture. The beautiful and youthful head of Alexander in the picture of his interment has something poetical.

That single cases long continued to occur in which the old solid treatment in body colour was seen combined with the new style, is proved by the MS. of a Psalter in the same library (No. 8070) executed about 1300, the portion drawn by the pen being treated with a certain breadth and great freedom, while the heads have often much expression. In the conception also of many of the animals a surprising truth is evident, and the various drolleries introduced are so delightful that Teniers and Jan Steen seem anticipated in them.

Another remarkable evidence of the state of painting in the Netherlands, towards the conclusion of this period, is afforded by the miniatures executed, according to an inscription, by "Michiel van der Borch," in 1332, in the MS. of a Bible in Flemish rhymes, by Jacob von Maerland, in the Westrenen Museum at the Hague.[1] The motives of the figures are very speaking and dramatic. For instance, in the Creation of Eve the sleep of Adam is very correctly expressed, and the Eve very pretty. At the same time the forms are frequently of marvellous fullness, as seen in the picture of the drowning of the Israelitish children. The folds of the draperies are also treated with unusual breadth. In the Nativity we see the announcement of that realistic mode of conception in which the Netherlands were destined to precede all other countries.

As regards wall painting, one specimen at all events of this period has been preserved in the former refectory of the old Biloque Hospital at Ghent. It represents, in colossal figures, the Saviour enthroned, blessing the Virgin, who sits opposite to him with raised and clasped hands. Behind them,

[1] See a complete account in an Essay by me in the German 'Kunstblatt' of 1852, No. 28.

on a much smaller scale, are three angels holding a canopy. The whole is enclosed in a framework of a very usual Gothic form. Judging from the developed style of this period, the execution of this was probably not earlier than 1300. Both from the size and the decided character of the motives, this work is one of considerable effect. At the same time the treatment is slight, and the feet and hands very feeble in drawing. At the sides, and only in outline, are the figures of John the Baptist with the Lamb, pointing to Christ, and of St. Christopher with the Child.

Although the art of Northern Germany shows a certain Netherlandish influence, yet there, and still more in Southern Germany, we observe the forms to be more clumsy, the outlines ruder and coarser; the heads also are too large, and a prevalence of short noses is seen from an early time.

A specimen of this Netherlandish influence is afforded by the MS. of a Psalter in the Ambras collection at Vienna, probably executed in some Westphalian convent not long after the year 1300. Within 84 circles are a series of pictures from the Creation of the World to the Last Judgment, the outlines of which are, it is true, meagre, but rendered with a rare precision of pen. Of the same kind are the miniatures in the MS. of the Romance of 'Wilhelm von Oranse,' written for the Landgraf Henry of Hesse in the year 1334, and now in the Electoral Library of Cassel. They are remarkable for animated though unskilful movements, for an occasional attempt at expression in the faces, and also for a good cast of drapery.

In the choir of the Cathedral of Cologne, on the wall surrounding the stalls, are a number of wall paintings—those on the Gospel side showing scenes from the life of St. Peter, and of Pope Sylvester; those on the Epistle side, incidents from the life of the Virgin, and from the legends of the Three Kings. The proportions are good, the motives lively, the draperies in good taste, but the heads still very conventional and of little expression. The thick reddish outlines, and the very small indication of shadow, place these pictures on a very low scale of development. As they were doubtless executed on the occasion of the dedication of the choir in 1322, and as, from the circumstance of the choir being considered the holiest place in the cathedral, the best painters were probably chosen; as also Cologne was one of the chief central points of art in Germany, we can have no better opportunity than these pictures afford us for forming conclusions regarding the state of painting in that country; and these conclusions are far from favourable. Below these paintings are all kinds of little drolleries, which, though mannered and coarse in execution, are of spirited invention.

Two easel pictures also in the Cologne Museum—a small altarpiece of a Crucifixion, and the Apostles Paul and John—lead to the same unfavourable verdict on this form of art.

I will mention only one more instance of wall painting, which occurs towards the end of this period, on a low space in the Ehinger House at Ulm. The figures of men seated two and two probably represent the prophets. A man with a dog, and a woman with a monkey, upon the entrance gate, are very animated. Although these have been subjected to later restorations, yet it is easy to perceive the low stage of art and homely treatment which characterised them.

As regards the application of painting to secular subjects, two MSS. containing the songs of the Troubadours are interesting. At the head of each poem its contents are usually embodied in an appropriate form of occupation. Not that any portrait-like attempt at individuality is here seen—on the contrary, the type of the period prevails in somewhat rude a form. The black outlines are broad and bold, with a certain readiness of hand, and the colouring very slight and coarse. These works exhibit just that style of drawing which served as a model to the woodcut of the next century. The earliest of these MSS., executed about 1280, and formerly in the convent of Weingarten in Suabia, is now in the private library of the King of Würtemberg at Stuttgart. It betrays only a moderate artist, though the motives of the figures are often animated. More important is the other manuscript, of about the year 1300, which formerly belonged to Rüdiger Manesse at Zürich, and is now in the Paris Library.[1] The motives of the figures resemble, for the most part, those in the former manuscript, to which they are so similar, that either they have been copied from it, or both have been taken from a common model. In the Paris manuscript, however, the size is larger, and the technical execution rather more worthy of an artist, while the feeling for the peculiar circumstances of each subject is more delicate, and the style in which they are conceived and treated has greater truth and spirit. Sometimes the poet is represented alone, and sometimes with his ladylove, it may be in the character of a hardy huntsman, or of an armed knight. In some the meditative feeling and reflection of the poet are admirably expressed, as in the figure of Henry of Veldeck, who sits amongst flowers and birds, thoughtfully resting his head upon his hand; or in that of Reinmar der Zweter, who is placed on an elevated seat, and dictates to two secretaries busily occupied at his side. The portrait of the Hardegger is very gracefully treated. He lies under a tree, a falcon on his wrist; his head supported on the lap of his mistress, who is bending tenderly over him. The movements, indeed, particularly in difficult attitudes, are not always easy or natural, and of this defect the last-named drawing affords an instance; yet, for the most part, the feeling for form is rather purer, and the drapery generally falls in beautiful and well-chosen lines.[2] Larger works of another kind, with the general type of the German style more or less strongly marked on them, are not numerous; such as painted glass for church-windows, and tapestry. A piece of the latter of remarkable dimensions may be observed in the church of St. Elizabeth at Marburg, the principal subject of which is taken from the history of the Prodigal Son.

[1] Professor von der Hagen, of Berlin, has published many of the illuminations of this manuscript, under the title 'Bildersaal altdeutscher Dichter,' Berlin, 1856. T. A. Stargardt.'
[2] Museum, 1834, No. 5, p. 35; No. 11, p. 82.

It is probable that art in Bohemia advanced beyond that of Germany at this time. This is strikingly attested by the miniatures in a Passionale executed for Kunigunde, sister of King Ottocar II. of Bohemia, and Abbess of the convent of St. George at Prague, painted in 1316 by Colda, a Dominican friar, and now in the University Library at Prague. The animation of the actions; the fine taste shown in the large folds of the drapery, which is cast, it is true, after the model of Gothic sculpture; and the good drawing, are all surprising considering the period. The sleeping figure of Adam, in the Creation of Eve, may in all respects be compared with Giotto's cotemporary figures. Various inventions of attractive character may be designated as nationally Bohemian. For instance, the representation of the Magdalen, who, in presence of SS. John and Peter, announces to the Virgin, who is resting on a bed, the Resurrection of Christ; also the intensity of feeling in the meeting of Christ and his mother after the Resurrection, &c.[1]

CHAPTER II.

DEVELOPMENT OF PAINTING IN ITS MORE INDEPENDENT CHARACTER.

1350—1420.

From about the year 1340 that artistic feeling which we have observed dawning as early as 1300 advances more and more towards development. The meagre and hard black outlines are replaced by those of a broader and softer description drawn with the brush, and more in unison with the rest of the treatment; the transitions from lights to shadows become more delicate and melting; harmoniously broken tints dispel the crude and gaudy colouring hitherto practised, and herald the coming of a more refined feeling. At the same time blue and vermi-

---

[1] German Kunstblatt, 1850, p. 155, &c.

lion are longest retained in their former unbroken force. Nor was this awakening feeling for truth and nature content to continue the same unattractive type of heads. A new and happier form, founded on observation of life, began at this time to make itself known. The oval of the face became more delicate, and the mouths and noses—the latter only retaining somewhat the hooked form in a male head—assumed a very pleasing character, in which the prevailing religious spirit of the period, spiritual purity, manly dignity, and, still more, feminine gentleness, began to be expressed in simple but distinct signs. In figures representing profane persons more variety adopted from nature is also perceptible, together with lively expression. These improvements are accompanied by more elevated and subdued action, and the drapery exhibits a more refined and picturesque taste and a softer flow of lines. As regards, however, the drawing of the nude, this, upon the whole, remains in a backward state—the forms are generally spare, and the feet too small, though the hands are often of happy action. One peculiar and very prevalent branch of painting, which was carried out at this time to a climax of great dexterity, consists in pictures executed in chiaroscuro. Gold grounds become more limited in extent, and the space of the background more and more copiously expressed by buildings either of Romanesque or Gothic character, by trees and hills of still conventional forms, and by the introduction of all kinds of house utensils. Even as early as the commencement of this period gold grounds are often replaced by the indication of a blue sky; indeed, as early as towards the year 1360 landscape backgrounds of very creditable character begin to occur. To all appearance this new impulse in art, and especially the development of the space of the background, proceeded from the Netherlands. In the extreme rarity of pictures of a larger size, the destruction of which has been accounted for in our preface, the inquirer about art in the Netherlands must content himself chiefly with the evidence furnished by miniatures, of which happily a rich store exists.

At the head of this period, and in many respects combining also the previous period, may be placed a Picture Bible in the Imperial Library at Paris (MSS. Français, No. 6829 bis), containing no less than 5124 pen drawings, washed with Indian ink, and representing in numerous succession the types and antitypes from New and Old Testament, executed in every respect by a very intelligent artist.[1] In close affinity with these are the miniatures of a missal, executed by the Presbyter Lorenz of Antwerp, in 1366, at Ghent, and now in the Westrenen Museum at the Hague.[2] These also show traces of the preceding period; the outlines, however, are already soft and rendered with the brush, the forms truer to nature, the soft fold of the drapery tenderly blended. In some pictures, for instance in the Nativity, the Byzantine form of conception is still retained; single motives, however, show the observation of nature.

A very important evidence, as regards the latter part of this period, is afforded by the miniatures in a MS. of the travels of Marco Polo, and six other well-known travellers, now in the Imperial Library at Paris (MSS. Français, No. 8392), which, there is reason to believe, were executed from 1384 to 1405, for Philip the Bold Duke of Burgundy.[3] Here we see the form of art peculiar to this time already fully developed; the cheerful and harmonious colouring especially is characteristic of that feeling for colour which was ultimately the excellence of Netherlandish art: on the other hand, the drawing is proportionably inferior. The marvellous narratives of these travellers opened here a rich field for those fantastic representations—men carrying their heads before their chests, &c.—which so well suited the genius of the time.

Next in point of time we may quote the Prayer-book of Margaret of Bavaria, who married, in 1389, John, son of Philip the Bold, surnamed "Sans peur,"—now in the British Museum (Harleian, No. 2897). The greater num-

---

[1] 'Kunstwerke und Künstler in Paris,' p. 327.
[2] German Kunstblatt, 1852, No. 28.
[3] 'Kunstwerke und Künstler in Paris,' p. 331, &c.

ber of the miniatures, which are very beautiful, are by Netherlandish hands.[1] Among these may be mentioned those referring to King David, fol. 28 b, 42 b, and 72 b. To a hand of more realistic tendency may be assigned the Preaching of St. Ambrose, fol. 160 a; and finally to one of more idealising character, the Unbelief of St. Thomas, fol. 164 a, and the principal picture, the Ascension, fol. 188 b.

Of still higher importance is a Prayer-book in the Bodleian (Douce, 144), which, according to an inscription it contains, was finished in 1407. This work, by the number and extent of the compositions, and the great advance of art it exhibits, in which several different hands may be distinguished, is peculiarly fitted to compensate for the scantiness of larger pictures. I can only point out a few of the most remarkable pieces. The occupations of the month, and the signs of the Zodiac, in the Calendar; the Virgin, to whom an angel is bringing bread and wine, fol. 10 a; the Annunciation, fol. 28 a; the Visitation, fol. 52 a; and two processions, 105 a, and 108 and 109. Here a delicate feeling for individuality is already perceptible, with an animation and truth, for instance, in the singing chorister boys, not surpassed by the celebrated work of that subject by Luca della Robbia. The Crucifixion, fol. 111 a: although the Christ is too tall here, yet the whole conception is elevated, and the sorrow of the fainting Virgin as earnestly as it is beautifully expressed. Finally the Virgin nursing the Child, fol. 123 a.[2]

A few years later in time and not less important in art are the miniatures of another Prayer-book in the British Museum (additional No. 16,997), by a Netherlandish artist. The following are the most admirable:—The Annunciation, in which three singing angels show a high stage of development—the Adoration of the Shepherds—the Descent of the Holy Ghost—All Saints—the Virgin reading—the four Fathers of the Church—both the St. Johns—the cele-

---

[1] 'Art Treasures in Great Britain,' vol. i. p. 124.
[2] Ibid., vol. iii. p. 75, &c.

bration of the Mass—and especially the Crucifixion, and the Assumption of the Virgin, which, both in arrangement and style of art, show a great artist.[1]

Another MS., also in the British Museum, viz. the Poems of Christina of Pisa (Harleian, No. 4431), contains various good pictures by Netherlandish painters, and which as specimens of the conception of secular subjects, and also of subjects borrowed from mythology, are very remarkable. Among them are, a pretty young woman kneeling before a man, and the Marriage of Peleus, in which the feast is spread on three tables of the form of the time.[2]

Fortunately a few specimens of the church pictures of this period have survived, which, with the exception of the last we are about to mention, do not come up to the standard of their time as representations of a larger scale of painting.

The first, originally painted for the Tanners' Hall in Bruges, is now in the cathedral of that town. The subject is the Crucifixion, figures about two-thirds the size of life. The Christ is rather long and meagre, but not badly drawn. He is already lifeless. On the right is St. John, with the Virgin fainting; she is of very noble form, supported by two holy women. On the left, of violent and rather clumsy motive, is the Centurion, in silver armour, with a guard, a priest, and a monk. At the sides in niches are SS. Barbara and Catherine. The expression of the heads is lively, the colouring of the flesh feeble, and the modelling poor; the background is gilt, with a pattern.

The second picture, also the Crucifixion, was formerly in the church of St. John at Utrecht, and is now in the Museum at Antwerp, No. 14. It includes only the figures of the Virgin and St. John, with the kneeling portrait of the Archdeacon Heinrich von Ryn, who died in 1360, and upon whose monument, in St. John's church, this picture was erected. The Christ is of similar conception to that above described, but exhibits a less skilful artist. The portrait also is characterised by no signs of individuality.

---

[1] 'Treasures of Art,' &c. vol. i. p. 125.   [2] Ibid., p. 126.

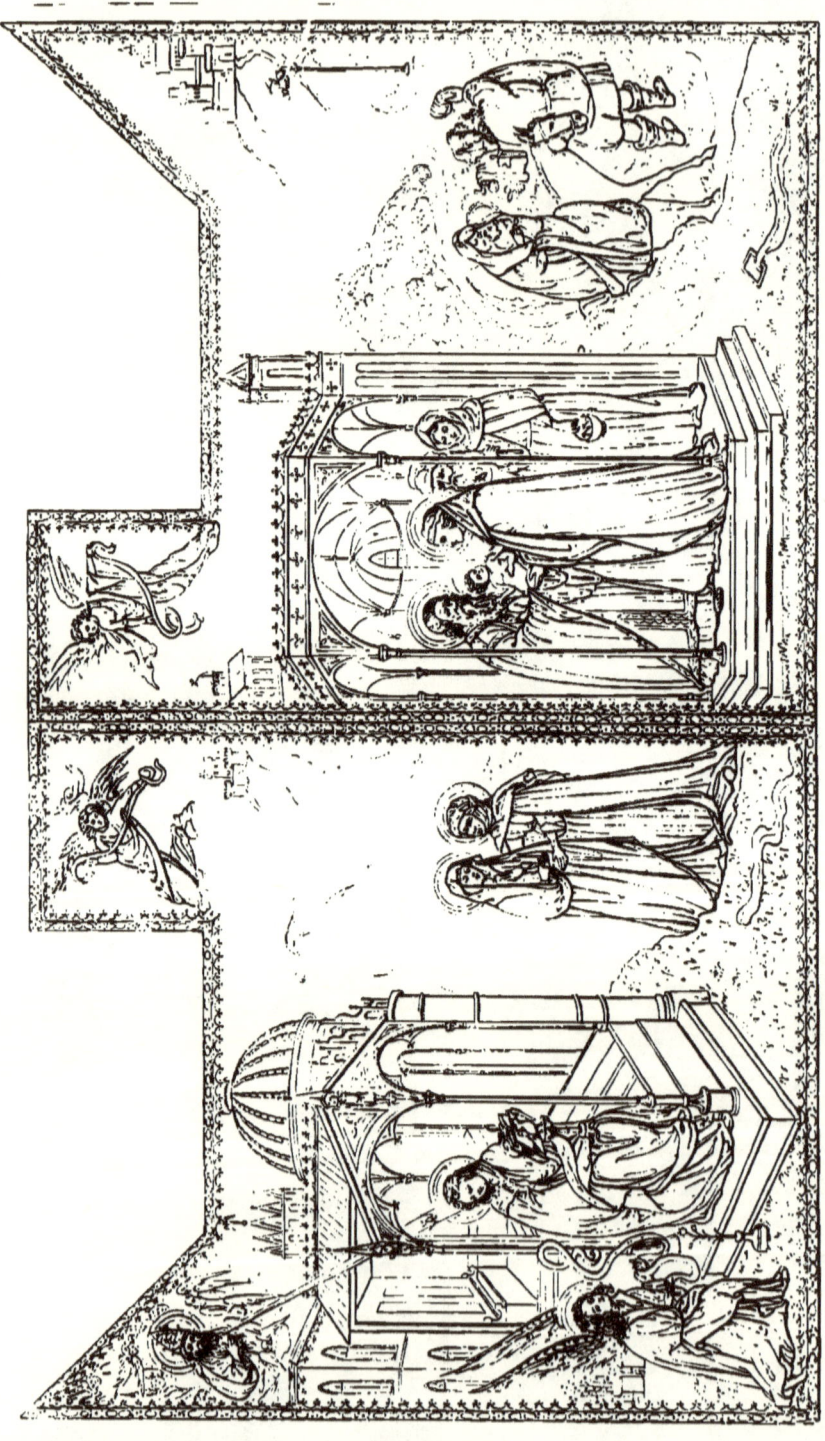

PICTURES ON AN ALTARCHEST AT DIJON.

PICTURES ON AN ALTAR-CHEST AT DIJON

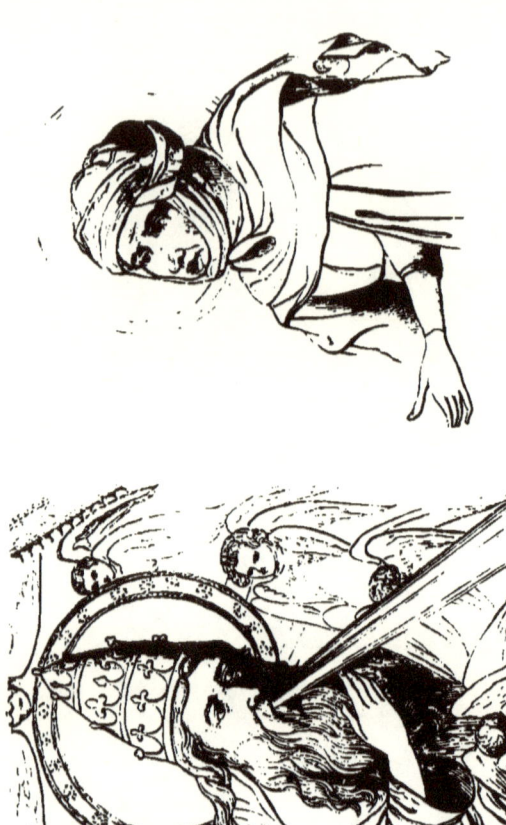

PICTURES ON AN ALTAR-CHEST AT DIJON

FIGURES ON AN ALTAR-CHEST AT DIJON. Page 30. No. 4

The best parts are the gestures and expression of sorrow of St. John. The ground is here also gilt, with a pattern.

The third and most important relic of this kind are the pictures on the outside of the wings of a large altar-chest in the Museum at Dijon, executed by order of Philip the Bold, between 1392 and 1400, for the Chartreuse which he built at Dijon. They are probably the work of one MELCHIOR BROEDERLAM, known as his painter, and represent, as the first woodcut shows, the Annunciation, the Visitation, the Presentation, and the Flight into Egypt. They occupy the boundary-line between the style of this period and the realistic feeling of that which succeeds it. The forms of the heads, see the other woodcuts, are still roundish and soft, and occasionally, as in those of the Virgin and Simeon in the Presentation (which is the most successfully treated), exhibit a delicate feeling for beauty, and at the same time an individuality of character. The Joseph in the Flight into Egypt is even coarsely realistic. The folds of the drapery are still soft, but the colours have assumed a clearness and power which borders on gaudiness. In the fullish forms no study of nature is yet perceptible; the backgrounds, rocks and trees, are still of conventional form, and the skies of gold ground.

It is in Bohemia, as regards Germany, that the style of this period is soonest seen to arrive at complete development. This part of Germany, which was distinguished in the arts even in the previous period, now made considerable progress under the reign of the art-loving Emperor Charles IV. (reigned 1348-78), who did his utmost in order to advance his favourite Bohemia in this respect. Many a miniature in still existing MSS. gives very favourable evidence of the state of art in Bohemia, of which they are better exponents than a number of chiefly ruined wall and panel pictures. The painters principally employed by the Emperor were THEODORICH OF PRAGUE, NICOLAUS WURMSER of Strasburg, and one KUNZ. The chief locality of their labours was the castle of Karlstein in the vicinity of Prague, the favourite residence of Charles IV. To decide what is the particular work of each of these painters among the surviving pictures which adorn the church of our Lady,

the chapel of St. Catherine, and the church of the Holy
Cross, or Royal Chapel, would, considering the vagueness
of all traditions, and the various restorations they have suffered, be extremely difficult. Those which are generally
attributed to Theodorich of Prague afford us a standard of
conclusion. These consist of 125 half-length figures,
larger than life, of saints, teachers, and rulers of the Church,
executed in tempera on panel, and decorating the church of
the Holy Cross. They show an excellent painter in the
forms of art belonging to the beginning of this period.
The heads of the men consist of two rather monotonously
repeated types, though evincing a successful aim at earnestness and dignity. At the same time the forms are somewhat broad and ungraceful, and in the over-large noses
with their broad ridges may be recognised a native Bohemian peculiarity. The female heads, on the other hand, are
of nobler and more refined forms. The wide-open eyes are
characteristic of the Bohemian school. The intentions of
the figures are usually good, the hands full in form and
well put in action; the draperies, in the well-known type,
with large folds softly modelled in broken colours. In the
colouring of the heads a certain alternation may be perceived. Some are of a tender, coolish red, others more warmly
tinted; a light grey prevails in the half-tones and shadows.
The fused treatment degenerates often into great softness.
The accessories frequently exhibit a happy aim at truth of
nature, as, for instance, the desk, bookstand, and pens in
the picture of St. Ambrose, which formed one of this series,
though now in the Imperial Gallery at Vienna; two others
have also been transferred to the University Library at
Prague. An affinity to these pictures is seen in an altarpiece in the Gallery of the Estates of Bohemia at Prague,
from the Provost's house at Raunitz on the Elbe, containing the Virgin and Child adored by the Emperor Charles
IV. and his son Wenceslaus, and SS. Sigismund and
Wenceslaus in the upper part; and below, the patron
saints of Bohemia, SS. Procopius, Adalbert, Vitus, and
Ludmilla, with the donor of the picture, Oczko von
Wlassim, archbishop of Prague. The heads of the saints

are elevated in form and pure in expression. Considering also the date of the picture, 1375, the portraits are of surprising individuality. A Crucifixion, with the Virgin and St. John, originally also executed for the castle of Karlstein, and now in the Imperial Gallery at Vienna, is a somewhat feebler work by the same master, to whom Van Michel, the well-known editor of the Catalogue of that collection in the time of Joseph II., most arbitrarily assigned the name of Nicolas Wurmser.

The paintings in the Castle of Karlstein are obviously by four different hands. One of them, TOMMASO DA MODENA, the author of the existing remnants of an altarpiece in several compartments, inasmuch as he belongs to the Italian school, concerns us only so far as he exerts a very decisive influence in the form of heads, and in other respects, over two of the other painters. A second hand may be traced in the following works: Scenes from the Apocalypse, in the church of our Lady, the Virgin being represented as the winged woman with the Child; of grand and elevated conception. Also the Virgin again, of still finer invention, fleeing before the seven-headed dragon, which is admirably rendered. Another large picture, not so easy of interpretation, is probably the Adoration of Antichrist. In the church of the Holy Cross, also from the Apocalypse, are, the Almighty enthroned in the Mandorla, surrounded by choirs of angels, the seven stars in the one hand, the book with seven seals in the other; the Adoration of the Lamb by the 24 elders; the Annunciation; the Visitation; the Adoration of the Three Kings; Christ with Martha and Mary; the Magdalen anointing the feet of Christ; Christ as the Gardener; and the Raising of Lazarus. These in great measure ruined pictures (query, by Wurmser?) show a painter of ample power of invention, refined feeling for composition and beauty, and skilful treatment. To the third hand the following, in the church of our Lady, may be ascribed:—Charles IV. delivering to Blanka his wife the cross which he had received in Rome from the Pope; the same monarch presenting his son Wenceslaus with a ring; and again in prayer. The author of these subjects (query,

Kunz?) appears as a very skilful portrait-painter. The graceful forms and action of his hands are especially remarkable. By the fourth master are the portraits of the Emperor Charles IV., and Anne of the Palatinate, his fourth wife, both holding a cross, over the entrance to the St. Catherine's chapel. Within the chapel is the Virgin, of quite Giottesque form of face, giving her hand to the Empress Anne, and the Child giving his hand to the Emperor. The painter has been most successful in the portraits, especially in that of the Empress.

The wall paintings in the chapel of St. Wenceslaus in the Cathedral at Prague are so over painted as to offer no means of forming an opinion. The most important picture of the whole school is said to be in the church of the fortress of the Wissèhrad at Prague.

A large mosaic, on the south side of the exterior of the Cathedral of Prague, remains still to be noticed. It is divided into three compartments; in the middle is Christ in a glory, surrounded by angels, six Bohemian saints below him, and still lower the donors, Charles IV. and his wife; on the left is the Virgin with several saints, and below is the Resurrection. On the right is seen John the Baptist, with saints, and underneath are the condemned. The style of this work is again rather rude, and only worthy of notice, as a whole, on account of its execution in mosaic, which rarely occurs in Germany.

On the other hand, a number of MSS. with miniatures give ample materials for judgment, and show more properly the peculiarity and great significance of the Bohemian school at this period. At the same time, many of these specimens agree in various respects so entirely with cotemporary French and Netherlandish miniatures, that there can be no doubt that Charles IV., who, at an earlier time, resided long in Paris, must have summoned French painters to Prague, or Bohemian painters to Paris. It will suffice here to mention a few of the most remarkable MSS. with miniatures.

Two Prayer-books belonging to Archbishop Ernest of Prague, died 1350 : one of them in the library of Prince

Lobkowitz at Prague; the other and richer one, in which the artist designates himself by the name of Sbinko de Trotina, in the library of the National Museum of that city. Both serve to prove that the style of art characteristic of this period was fully, and consequently very early, developed.

The MS. of an Essay on the Doctrines of Christian Truth, executed in 1373 by Thomas Stitney, and now in the University Library at Prague (xvii. A b), shows how early the Bohemians began to treat the common events of daily life with vivacity, taste, and feeling for beauty. The most remarkable pictures are of a youth and a beautiful girl (fol. 37 b); several young women dedicating themselves as the Brides of Christ (fol. 44 b); and a woman praying (fol. 124 a).[1]

Next in order may be mentioned the miniatures in the German translation of the Bible executed by order of the Emperor Wenceslaus, reigned 1378–1400, now in the Imperial Library at Vienna.

The admirable miniatures also in a missal belonging to Sbinko Hasen von Hasenburg, appointed Archbishop of Prague 1402, and who died as Archbishop of Presburg in 1411, now in the same library, show that the school continued to advance in excellence till towards the conclusion of the period. I may mention the Adoration of the Kings, and the Baptism of Christ, as particularly excellent.

An Evangeliarium, written by a priest of the name of Johann von Troppau, for Albrecht II., Archduke of Austria, and adorned with very fine miniatures—now in the Library at Vienna—serves to prove that the Bohemian school had also taken root in the province of Moravia, then a dependency of Bohemia.[2] The same may be said of Silesia, then similarly situated, which is evidenced by two pictures proceeding from a convent in Silesia, now in the Berlin Museum; the one (No. 1221) the Mocking of Christ,

---

[1] See further account of these three MSS. in the German Kunstblatt of 1850, No. 37.
[2] Ibid., No. 38.

the other (No. 1219) the Crucifixion. Both exhibit a skilful master, who may have flourished about 1400.

But in Austria also this style of art attained a peculiar development. A brilliant example of this is afforded by the miniatures in the MS. of a German translation of Durandus' Rationale Divinorum Officiorum, in the Imperial Library. These were commenced for the same Duke Albert II., and completed for his nephew Archbishop William. The miniatures, which may be safely assigned to the period between 1384 and 1403, are equal, in point of art, to the best Bohemian paintings, but are distinguished from them by greater force of colour and decision of forms. The best of them combine good arrangement and drawing with delicate heads and a blooming flesh-tone. The Last Supper, and the Last Judgment, are especially remarkable. The portraits of the above-mentioned princes, which occur in various parts, show a happy aim at individuality.

The style of this period in Germany is seen to attain its noblest form in the last decades of the 14th, and first of the 15th century, in the city of Cologne. That spiritual calm, peaceful bliss, and untroubled moral purity which religion alone engenders, is expressed in a rare degree in the Cologne school. In perfect agreement with this character are the harmoniously broken colouring, the tender tints of the flesh, the moderate nature of the modelling, and the soft and fused style of the execution. The weak side of this school, in which powerful expression and dramatic subjects were least affected, was the deficiency of knowledge as to the anatomical structure of the human frame. The difficulty of assigning the artist's name to the surviving specimens of Cologne art is far greater than in the Bohemian school. From a passage in the Limburg Chronicle, 1380, which runs thus—" In this time there was a painter in Cologne of the name of Wilhelm; he was considered the best master in all German Land; he paints every man, of whatever form, as if he were alive "—from this passage the custom arose of attributing the best pictures in Cologne and the vicinity, of this period, to MEISTER WILHELM. And true as this conjecture may be in some instances, we must not forget that there is no certainty as to the real origin of one single picture. The earliest among those assigned to him is probably the wall picture in St. Castor at Coblentz, in the Gothic niche over the monument to Kuno von Falkenstein, Archbishop of Treves, who died in 1386. It represents the Crucifixion, with the Virgin, SS. John, Peter, and Castor, and the kneeling figure of the Archbishop. The forms of SS. Peter and Castor recall, in point of treatment, the previous epoch. The Virgin and St. John express their grief chiefly by lively gestures. The individuality of the Archbishop is still of very moderate character. The considerable restorations diminish the value of this relic, and greatly impede all opinion as to its original character.

Far more worthy of the great name of Meister Wilhelm are some portions of the numerous pictures which once adorned the altarpiece and wings in the church of St. Clara, and which are now in the chapel of St. John in the Cathedral. These comprise the Nativity, the Annunciation to the Shepherds, the Bathing of the Infant, the Adoration of the Kings, the Presentation in the Temple, the Flight into Egypt, and the scenes from the Passion in the centre compartment.[1] The other portions are by a less important hand, only partially related to Meister Wilhelm.

In connexion with these works may be mentioned a picture in the Berlin Museum (No. 1224). This consists of 34 compartments, representing scenes from the life of Christ and the Virgin, from the Annunciation to the Last Judgment, of animated and often admirable composition, delicate tone of colouring, and light and spirited treatment.

Next in order comes a small altarpiece with wings, in the Museum at Cologne. The head of the Virgin, who is caressed by the Child, exhibits in the fullest extent the purity of character, sweetness of expression, and softness and delicate tone of flesh peculiar to this school. The

[1] See Hotho's 'Malerschule Hubert's van Eyck,' vol. i. p. 240; with whose statement I entirely agree.

figures of SS. Catherine and Barbara have also the tenderness characteristic of the same. Greatly resembling this is a small altarpiece, No. 1238, in the Museum at Berlin, with the Virgin and Child and four female Saints in the centre compartment, and SS. Elizabeth of Hungary and Agnes on the wings.

A picture of St. Veronica with the Sudarium, at Munich, Cabinets No. 13, furnishes a very fine example of this master, a more careful execution and warmer colouring being combined with the same purity and tenderness of feeling.

Passing over several other works attributed with more or less justice to Meister Wilhelm, I will only observe that the number of pictures in and about Cologne—for instance, in a closed chapel in the Cathedral at Aix-la-Chapelle, evidently painted in his manner—are considerable. At Cologne these specimens are chiefly to be found in the Museum, and in the chapel of the Hôtel de Ville. A small Crucifixion also, in the collection of the late Mr. Dietz, is particularly remarkable. Others, originally in Cologne, have accompanied the Boisserée collection to Munich; some also have made their way to the chapel of St. Maurice at Nuremberg. The Garden of Eden, in the Prehn collection in the Frankfort Library, is a small but very attractive picture. The cheerful and naïve form of conception is in strict unison with the tender execution and gay colouring. The fact that the influence of this master extended to Guelders, the neighbouring province of Holland, is evident by the miniatures in a Dutch Prayer-book, belonging to Maria, Duchess of Guelders, of the year 1415, now in the Royal Library at Berlin.

The most beautiful specimen of this early German art I know in England is a small altarpiece with wings, containing numerous figures of very elevated style and tender execution. It belongs to Mr. Beresford Hope.[1]

A close affinity with the Cologne school is also distinctly seen in the style of art which prevailed in Westphalia. I need only instance those pictures of SS. Dorothea and

---

[1] 'Galleries and Cabinets, &c., in Great Britain,' p. 190.

Ottilia, originally from Soest, now in the Town Museum at Münster. They show a master of elevation and refinement, nearly related to Meister Wilhelm in style, but more independent in character, and in many respects more advanced.

A large picture, formerly in St. Michael's church at Lüneburg, now in the public gallery at Hanover, consisting of numerous, and in parts interesting paintings of about the commencement of the 15th century, shows that, without being dependent on the school of Cologne, the style of this period had spread also into the region of Lower Saxony.

Next to Prague and Cologne, the city of Nuremberg may be considered as a central point of art. The fine sculptures by Schonhofer which adorn the exterior and interior of the porch of the church of our Lady, and which were completed in 1361, evidently assisted much in this local development. Without deviating from the general character of this period, greater knowledge and observation of the human figure are apparent here than in the Bohemian and Cologne schools; modelling and colouring are also both more powerful.[1] Unfortunately, however, no painters' names have descended to us with their works, and only in a few instances does an inscribed date afford an accurate standard of their time.

An altarpiece, founded by a member of the noble family of Imhof—the chief portions in the gallery of the church of St. Lawrence—may be adjudged to the last decade of the 14th century. The centre compartment of the inner side contains the Coronation of the Virgin, and the wings four Apostles. The head of the Virgin, with downcast eyes, is of unusual beauty of form; her figure also slender and of elevated character, and the folds of her blue drapery of much purity of taste. The conception of the Saviour, who is crowned and looking at his mother, is serious and dignified. The flesh-tones of the Virgin are delicate, those of

---

[1] See further in 'Künstler und Kunstwerke in Deutschland,' vol. i. p. 165, &c., and 247, &c. Also Hotho, as above, vol. i. p. 291, &c.: and v. Rettberg 'Das Kunstleben Nurnberg's.'

the Christ of a warm brownish tint with whitish lights. The reverse of the altarpiece represents in the centre compartment a Pietà with the Virgin and St. John, and on the wings four other apostles. In point of merit it nearly equals the front side. The expression of past suffering in the head of the dead Christ is especially fine; the nude is but weakly rendered. The eight apostles are variously and worthily characterised. This portion of the altarpiece is in the castle at Nuremberg.

But a little later in date are the four wings of an altarpiece, which, according to tradition, was executed for the Deichsler family in 1400, and placed in the now demolished church of St. Catherine at Nuremberg. Now in the Berlin Museum, No. 1207-1210. They represent the Virgin, who, here also, is very delicately formed, and the Child, the latter very meagre; St. Peter Martyr, of great energy of character, and glowing colour; St. Elizabeth of Thüringen, of mild and delicate aspect; and John the Baptist. In the lively action of the last-named saint is seen the energy which characterises Gothic sculpture, while the warmly coloured head with the aquiline nose shows a burning eagerness to bear witness to Him whose symbol, a weakly drawn lamb, is upon his arm. In the drawing of hands and feet these pictures are less advanced.

The fact that the style of art peculiar to Nuremberg was generally diffused throughout all Franconia is proved by a picture on the monument of Berthold, Bishop of Eichstadt, in the church at Heilsbron, who died in 1365. The Virgin, who is very fine in form and expression, approaches that on the altarpiece belonging to the Imhof family, and, even if not executed immediately after the Bishop's death, belongs decidedly still to the 14th century. The portrait was probably rather individualised by a restoration which took place in 1497.

In Suabia also the style of this period attained a very respectable development. We see this in various pictures, belonging to the latter part of this time, which are preserved in the always accessible Royal collection, formerly belonging to M. Abel, in the palace of Ludwigsburg near Stuttgart.

Two large pictures on panel, the one containing the Evangelists Mark and Luke with St. Paul, the other St. John the Evangelist with SS. Dorothea and Margaret, formerly in the church of Almendringen, near Ehringen, bear evidence of an excellent hand. The same may be said of two other large panel pictures from the monastery of Heiligkreutzthal in Upper Suabia, representing the Entombment, and the Procession of the Three Kings.

Finally we may mention another direction taken by art, differing from all the preceding as respects greater truth of nature and drawing, though with less expression of feeling, and which is evidenced by three fragments of pictures in the Berlin Museum—the Marriage of St. Catherine, No. 1232; two angels holding a tabernacle, No. 1231; and St. Peter, No. 1220. The locality, however, whence these pictures proceed is unfortunately unknown.

BOOK III.

THE TEUTONIC STYLE.

SECOND EPOCH, 1420—1530.

COMPLETE DEVELOPMENT OF THE TEUTONIC FEELING FOR ART
IN THE SPIRIT OF THE MIDDLE AGES.

CHAPTER I.

THE BROTHERS VAN EYCK.

THE Netherlandish school, which, in the previous periods, had greatly distinguished itself in the art of painting, was also the first completely to work out its peculiar Teutonic element. This element manifested itself in the endeavour to express that spiritual meaning which these artists so strongly felt, through the medium of the forms of real life; rendering these forms with the utmost distinctness and truth of drawing, colouring, perspective, and light and shadow, and filling up the space with scenes from nature, or objects created by the hand of man, in which the smallest detail was carefully given. The great importance of such a development of the realistic feeling in painting, which had never been sufficiently acknowledged, may be thus explained. To it we owe the purest evidence of that peculiar enthusiasm, both for art and Christianity, with which the Teutonic race was imbued. As respects the Italians—the great leaders in art among the Romanesque nations—the relation to art, as well as to the Christian religion, appears of a totally different character. The national peculiarity of their ecclesiastical painting rests, namely, on very different grounds from those on which that of the truly Teutonic Netherlanders was based. The antique Roman race constituted the foundation of the population of Italy. Those Germanic hordes who poured into the peninsula contributed but a portion to this population, and were gradually absorbed with it into a new form of unity. The Teutonic feeling for art, and its conception of Christianity, became therefore strongly modified by the prevailing classic element. In addition to this the existence of numerous monuments of antique art in the country exercised from time to time a strong influence upon all artistic development. But though the combination of these conditions happily resulted in the finest productions of Christian art, yet, when compared with the antique, and especially with Greek art, they exhibit no such thorough originality as that displayed by the painting of the early Netherlandish schools, but must be rather considered as a happy cross between antique and Teutonic feeling. In the circumstance, therefore, that early Netherlandish art, in its freedom from all foreign influence, exhibits to us the contrast between the natural feeling of the Greek and of the German races in the department of art—these two races being the chief representatives of the cultivation of the ancient and the modern world—and exhibits this contrast in a purity and distinctness not traceable in any other form; in this circumstance consists the high significance of this school when considered in reference to the general history of art. While it is characteristic of the Greek feeling to idealize not only the conceptions of the ideal world, but even that of portraits, by the simplification of forms, and the prominence given to the more important parts of a work of art, the early Netherlanders, on the other hand, conferred a portrait-like character upon the most ideal personifications of the Virgin, the Apostles, Prophets, and Martyrs, and in actual portraiture aimed to render even the most accidental peculiarities of nature. While the Greeks expressed the various features of outward nature—such as rivers, fountains, hills, trees, &c.—under abstract human forms, the Netherlanders endeavoured to express them as they had seen them in nature, and with a truth which extended to the smallest details. In opposition to the ideal, and what may be called the personifying tendency of the Greeks, the Netherlandish race developed a purely realistic and landscape school. In this respect the other Teutonic nations are found to approach them most nearly, the Germans first and then the English.

The schools of art characteristic of both the other Romanesque nations—the French and the Spanish—must be considered as subordinate when compared with those of Italy and the Netherlands; inasmuch as they were alternately and strongly influenced by each, occasionally both influences holding the balance with happy equality, but oftener the one prevailing over the other.

The high development of the realistic feeling, as it first appears before us in the pictures of the brothers Van Eyck, was for a long time looked upon as a perfect riddle. It may, however, be mainly accounted for by the fact that the works of the generation preceding them were completely destroyed in the iconoclastic storm which raged in the Netherlands in the 16th century. In order, therefore, to account, as far as possible on historical grounds, for the marvellous perfection exhibited by the Van Eycks, I have been obliged to recur to the sculpture and to the miniatures antecedent to them. Nor has my research been unsuccessful. From the inspection of a number of monumental reliefs in the possession of M. Dumortier at Tournay, I have convinced myself that the school of sculpture existing there during the middle ages very early pursued a realistic direction, and towards the middle of the 14th century had already made considerable progress.[1] The life-sized stone statues executed in 1396 for Philip the Bold of Burgundy, by CLAES SLUTER, and which decorated the fountain of the Chartreuse at Dijon, show even a development of the realistic tendency and a knowledge of nature which places them on a par with the pictures by the Van Eycks.[2]

---

[1] The monument to Colard de Seclin, Doctor of Rights, inscribed 1341, is particularly important, as showing that not only was a great individuality already given to portraits, but that the features of the infant Christ, who in some respects was evidently studied from nature, partook also completely of a portrait-like character.

[2] See article by me in the German 'Kunstblatt' of 1856, No. 27. This also contains an account of sculpture by the same Claes Sluter on the monument to Philip the Bold, now in the Museum at Dijon.

They represent the figures of Moses (whence the fountain is called "Puits de Moyse"), David, Jeremiah, Zechariah, Daniel, and Isaiah. We gather from this that sculpture in the Netherlands, as well as in Italy, took the lead of painting; and as we are historically informed that the painters of Italy studied from Lorenzo Ghiberti's celebrated bronze doors of the Baptistery at Florence, so we may safely conclude that a similar course was pursued in the Netherlands. The earliest evidence of this is found in various miniatures executed in 1371 by one JOHN OF BRUGES, painter to King Charles V. of France, which decorate a translation of the Vulgate now in the Westrenen Museum at the Hague.[1] At the commencement of the volume appears the rather large portrait of Charles V. taken in profile, with a figure kneeling before him, also in profile, who, we are informed by a dedication in French verse in the MS., was one Jehan Vaudetar, who presented this Bible to the King. Both heads are portraits of thorough individuality and tender flesh-tones. A few small historical subjects also, fol. 467— the Nativity, the Adoration of the Kings, and the Flight into Egypt—further evidence the existence of Netherlandish painters who, a generation before the Van Eycks, had, even in this department of art, attained great proficiency. The animated and free motives and truthful forms we meet with here were obviously taken from nature, as also the drapery and style of modelling. The express designation of "Pictor" applied to John of Bruges, while the mere worker on miniatures was called "Illuminator," shows us, however, that he must have painted pictures on a large scale. Considering too that HUBERT VAN EYCK, who according to the common acceptation was born in the year 1366, probably at Maaseyck, a small town not far from Maestricht, must have been settled before the year 1412 in Bruges,[2] there is no doubt of his being acquainted with the works of the admirable master above mentioned, and of their influence upon his art. Just as little can it be doubted

---

[1] See article by me in the 'Deutsches Kunstblatt' of 1856, p. 268, &c.
[2] In 1412 he was a member of the brotherhood of the Virgin with Rays. See Carton, 'Les Trois Frères v. Eyck,' p. 93.

that he must have seen the sculpture in the neighbouring town of Tournay, and that this also assisted in the development of his mind. But while, on the one hand, he carried the realistic tendency, already existing in such masters as John of Bruges, to an extraordinary pitch of excellence, it is evident that in many essential respects he adhered to the more ideal feeling of the previous period, imparting to this, by the means of his far richer powers of representation, greater distinctness, truth of nature, and variety of expression. Throughout his works is seen an elevated and highly energetic conception of the stern import of his labours in the service of the Church. The prevailing arrangement of his subject is symmetrical, holding fast the early architectonic rules which had hitherto presided over ecclesiastic art. The later mode of arrangement, in which a freer and more dramatic and picturesque feeling was introduced, is only seen in Hubert van Eyck's works in subjection to these rules. Thus his heads exhibit the aim at beauty and dignity belonging to the earlier period, only combined with more truth of nature. His draperies unite its pure taste and softness of folds with greater breadth; the realistic principle being apparent in that greater attention to detail which a delicate indication of the material of the drapery necessitates. Nude figures are studied from nature with the utmost fidelity: undraped portions are also given with much truth, especially the hands; only the feet remain feeble. That, however, which is almost the principal quality of his art, is the hitherto unprecedented power, depth, transparency, and harmony of his *colouring*. To attain this he availed himself of a mode of painting in oil which he himself had perfected. Oil painting, it is true, had long been in use, but only in a very undeveloped form, and for inferior purposes. According to the most recent and thorough investigations[1] the improvements introduced by Hubert van Eyck, and which he doubtless only very gradually worked out, were the following.

---

[1] See Sir Charles Eastlake's 'Materials for a History of Oil-painting.' London, 1847. Longman. Chap. VIII.-XI.

THE TRIUMPH OF THE CHURCH.
In the National Museum, Madrid.

First he removed the chief impediment which had hitherto obstructed the application of oil-paint to pictures properly so called. For, in order to accelerate the slow drying of the oil colours, it had been necessary to add a varnish to them, which consisted of oil boiled with a resin. Owing to the dark colour of this varnish, in which amber, or more frequently sandarac, was used, this plan, from its darkening effect on most colours, had hitherto proved unsuccessful. Hubert van Eyck, however, succeeded in preparing so colourless a varnish that he could apply it, without disadvantage, to all colours. In painting a picture he proceeded on the following system. His outline was drawn on a *gesso* ground, so strongly sized that no oil could penetrate the surface. The under painting was then executed in a generally warm brownish glazing colour, and so lightly that the light ground was clearly seen through it. He then laid on the local colours, thinner in the lights, and, from the quantity of vehicle used, more thickly in the shadows; in the latter availing himself often of the under painting as a foil. In all other parts he so nicely preserved the balance between the solid and the glazing colours as to attain that union of body and transparency which is his great excellence. Finally, in the use of the brush he obtained that perfect freedom which the new vehicle permitted; either leaving the touch of the brush distinct, or fusing the touches tenderly together, as the object before him required. Of three works which are now, and doubtless with perfect justice, attributed to him, but one is historically authenticated. As the other two, however, as historic evidence will show, must have been earliest executed, I will advert to them first. The one now in the National Museum in S. Trinidad at Madrid,[1] see woodcut, represents in a rich and original manner a subject early treated by Christian art, viz. the Triumph of the New over the Old Testament, or that of the Christian Church over the Synagogue, by the sacrifice of Christ. As this picture,[2] consi-

[1] In 1786 this picture was in the chapel of St. Jerome at Valencia; and later, in the convent of Parnal in Segovia.
[2] Although I have not seen this picture, yet I adopt Passavant's opinion as

dered as a work of art, stands in strict connection with the chef-d'œuvre of Hubert van Eyck, of which more hereafter, and which was probably commenced in 1420, its execution may be adjudged from about 1415 to 1420. It is throughout imbued with the spirit of the ecclesiastical art of the middle ages. The figure of the Almighty[1] is seen enthroned under a gorgeous Gothic canopy, terminating in a pointed tower, holding a sceptre in the left hand, and in the act of benediction with the right. At the sides are the Virgin reading on the right, and St. John the Evangelist writing on the left. On the arms of the throne are the attributes of the four Evangelists; at the feet of the Almighty the Immaculate Lamb, whom he made an offering for the sins of the world. Below, this offering is seen in the form of a stream of water, in which the sacramental wafers are floating, flowing into a little flower-garden where six angels are celebrating the glory of God on different instruments. Beyond these, on each side, are singing angels under Gothic canopies, also terminating in lesser pointed towers. A scroll in the hands of one of the angels, on the left, contains the inscription which sets forth the meaning of the stream of water as follows: " Căn :—fons ortorum, puteus aquarum viventium "—referring to the text in the Song of Solomon, ch. iv. verse 15: " A fountain of gardens, a well of living waters." The water flows finally into a Gothic fountain which rises in the centre of the foreground, and which, with the usual allegorical allusion, is decorated with a pelican feeding her young with her blood. On the right are the ranks of the Blessed, victorious through Christ, headed by the Pope standing, bearing a tall crozier with the

---

to its being a work by Hubert van Eyck (see 'Christliche Kunst in Spanien,' p. 196, &c., Leipsic, 1853, published by Weigel) with the greater confidence for the following reason:—M. Passavant states that it agrees in every respect with the well-known St. Bavon picture, and this assertion is carried out in character of heads, drawing of hands, and taste of drapery, by an admirable tracing of the picture in Madrid, now in the Cabinet of Engravings at Berlin. On the other hand, M. Cavalcaselle, in his 'Early Flemish Painters' (see p. 92), attributes it to Jan van Eyck. The accompanying woodcut is taken from that work.

[1] I differ from both Passavant and Cavalcaselle, who conceive this figure to represent the Second Person of the Trinity.

standard in his left hand, and with the right directing the attention of the Emperor, who is kneeling in adoration, to the fountain, as the source of all salvation. Behind both are other clerical and lay personages. On the left, in front, is the High Priest standing, his eyes bound, holding a broken standard in his right hand, with his left endeavouring to prevent a kneeling Jew from paying adoration. Besides these are eight more Jews in lively actions of horror and despair. In the three principal upper figures, and in the angels, a deep religious expression is seen combined with a pure feeling for beauty; in the lower figures a keen portrait-like character prevails. The momentary and dramatic actions of some of the Jews are especially admirable. The colouring of this picture, which, independent of the upper projection, is 5 feet 6 inches high, is harmonious and clear, and the very careful execution masterly in the highest degree.

The second picture is that of St. Jerome extracting a thorn from the front paw of the lion, who is seated on his hind feet before him,[1] now in the Gallery at Naples. The head of the Saint is very dignified, his brown drapery of broad forms and pure taste, the reddish-brown flesh-tones of extraordinary power and depth. The various objects in the space also, the Cardinal's hat, books—one of which is open—bottles, &c., are of astonishing truth.[2]

The chief work by Hubert van Eyck, however, and one authenticated by an inscription upon it, is the large altar picture, consisting of two rows of separate panels, once in the Cathedral of St. Bavon at Ghent. It was painted for Judocus Vyts, Seigneur of Pamele, and Burgomaster of Ghent, and his wife Elizabeth, of the then distinguished family of Burlut, for their mortuary chapel in that cathedral. For this purpose Hubert van Eyck probably removed to

[1] This picture was formerly most arbitrarily assigned to Colantonio di Fiore, whose authenticated works are painted in the conventional Giottesque forms. I recognised it as by the hand of Hubert van Eyck during my stay in Naples in 1841. See 'Kunstblatt' of 1847, p. 162, &c.
[2] An outline of this picture is seen in D'Agincourt's 'Histoire de l'Art par les Monuments'—Peinture, plate 132. The editors of the new edition of Vasari attribute it to Jan van Eyck. Note to p. 163, Introduction, vol. i.

Ghent, about the year 1420, where in 1422 he became a member of the Brotherhood of our Lady.[1] When the wings were opened, which occurred only on festivals, the subject of the upper centre picture was seen, consisting of three panels, see woodcut, on which were the Triune God—the King of heaven and earth—and at his side the Holy Virgin and the Baptist: on the inside of the wings were angels, who with songs and sacred music celebrate the praises of the Most High: at the two extremities, each inside the half-shutters which covered the figure of God the Father, were Adam and Eve, the representatives of fallen man. The lower central picture shows the Lamb of the Revelation, whose blood flows into a cup; over it is the dove of the Holy Spirit; angels, who hold the instruments of the Passion, worship the Lamb, and four groups, each consisting of many persons, advance from the sides; they comprise the holy martyrs, male and female, with priests and laymen; in the foreground is the fountain of life; in the distance the towers of the heavenly Jerusalem. On the wing pictures, other groups are coming up to adore the Lamb; on the left, those who have laboured for the kingdom of the Lord by worldly deeds—the soldiers of Christ, and the righteous judges; on the right, those who, through self-denial and renunciation of earthly good, have served him in the spirit—holy hermits and pilgrims; a picture underneath, which represented hell, finished the whole.

This work is now dispersed: the centre pictures and the panels of Adam and Eve only being in Ghent. The lower picture of hell was early injured and lost, and the others form some of the greatest ornaments of the gallery of the Berlin Museum.[2]

---

[1] Carton, 'Les Trois Frères van Eyck,' p. 36.

[2] "The pictures here exhibited as the works of Hemmelinck, Messis, Lucas of Holland, A. Dürer, and even Holbein, are inferior to those ascribed to Eyck in colour, execution, and taste. The draperies of the three on a gold ground, especially that of the middle figure, could not be improved in simplicity, or elegance, by the taste of Raphael himself. The three heads of God the Father, the Virgin, and St. John the Baptist, are not inferior in roundness, force, or sweetness, to the heads of L. da Vinci, and possess a more positive principle of colour."—*Life of Fuseli*, i. p. 267. This is a very remarkable opinion for the period when it was written.

THE ALTARPIECE OF THE ADORATION OF THE LAMB.

Painted by John and Hubert van Eyck for the Church of St. John (now St. Bavon) at Ghent, in 1432.

The three figures of the upper centre picture are designed with all the dignity of statue-like repose belonging to the early style; they are painted too on a ground of gold and tapestry, as was constantly the practice in earlier times: but united with the traditional type we already find a successful representation of life and nature in all their truth. They stand on the frontier of two different styles, and, from the excellences of both, form a wonderful and most impressive whole. In all the solemnity of antique dignity the Heavenly Father sits directly fronting the spectator—his right hand raised to give the benediction to the Lamb, and to all the figures below; in his left is a crystal sceptre; on his head the triple crown, the emblem of the Trinity. The features are such as are ascribed to Christ by the traditions of the Church, but noble and well-proportioned; the expression is forcible, though passionless. The tunic of this figure, ungirt, is of a deep red, as well as the mantle, which last is fastened over the breast by a rich clasp, and, falling down equally from both shoulders, is thrown in beautiful folds over the feet. Behind the figure, and as high as the head, is a hanging of green tapestry, adorned with a golden pelican (a well-known symbol of the Redeemer); behind the head the ground is gold, and on it, in a semicircle, are three inscriptions, which again describe the Trinity, as all-mighty, all-good, and all-bountiful. The two other figures of this picture display equal majesty; both are reading holy books, and are turned towards the centre figure. The countenance of John expresses ascetic seriousness, but in the Virgin's we find a serene grace, and a purity of form, which approach very nearly to the happier efforts of Italian art.

On the wing next to the Virgin, see woodcut, stand eight angels singing before a music-desk. They are represented as choristers in splendid vestments and crowns. The brilliancy of the stuffs and precious stones is given with the hand of a master, the music-desk is richly ornamented with Gothic carved work and figures, and the countenances are full of expression and life; but in the effort to imitate nature with the utmost truth, so as even to enable us to distinguish with certainty the different voices of the double quartett, the spirit of a holier influence has already passed away. On the opposite wing, St. Cecilia sits at an organ, the keys of which she touches with an expression of deep meditation: other angels stand behind the organ with different stringed instruments. The expression of these heads shows far more feeling, and is more gentle: the execution of the stuffs and accessories is equally masterly. The two extreme wings of the upper series, the subjects of which are Adam and Eve, see woodcut, are still in Ghent, but are inaccessible to the traveller, being kept strictly locked up, as it is reported from a feeling of decorum. The attempt to paint the nude figure of the size of life, with the most careful attention to minute detail, is eminently successful, with the exception of a certain degree of hardness in the drawing. Eve holds in her right hand the forbidden fruit. In the filling up, which the shape of the altarpiece made necessary over these panels, there are small subjects in chiaroscuro: over Adam, the sacrifice of Cain and Abel; over Eve, the death of Abel—death, therefore, as the immediate consequence of original sin.

The arrangement of the lower middle picture, the worship of the Lamb, see woodcut, is strictly symmetrical, as the mystic nature of the allegorical subject demanded, but there is such beauty in the landscape, in the pure atmosphere, in the bright green of the grass, in the masses of trees and flowers, even in the single figures which stand out from the four great groups, that we no longer perceive either hardness or severity in this symmetry. The wing picture on the right, see woodcut, representing the holy pilgrims, is, in the figures, less striking than the others. Here St. Christopher, who wandered through the world seeking the most mighty Lord, strides before all, a giant in stature, whilst a host of smaller pilgrims, of various ages, follow him. A fruitful valley, with many details showing a surprising observation of nature, is seen through the slender trees. The cast of the folds in the ample red drapery of St. Christopher, as in the upper picture, reminds us still of the earlier style. The whimsical and singular

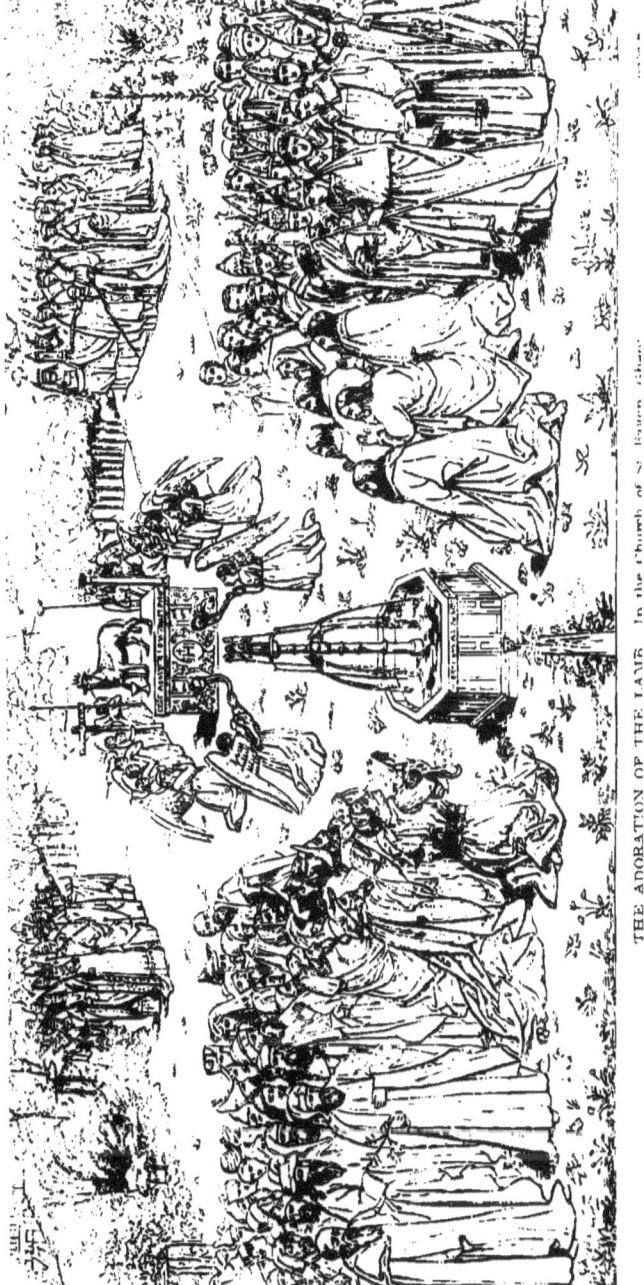

THE ADORATION OF THE LAMB. In the Church of S. Bavon, Ghent.

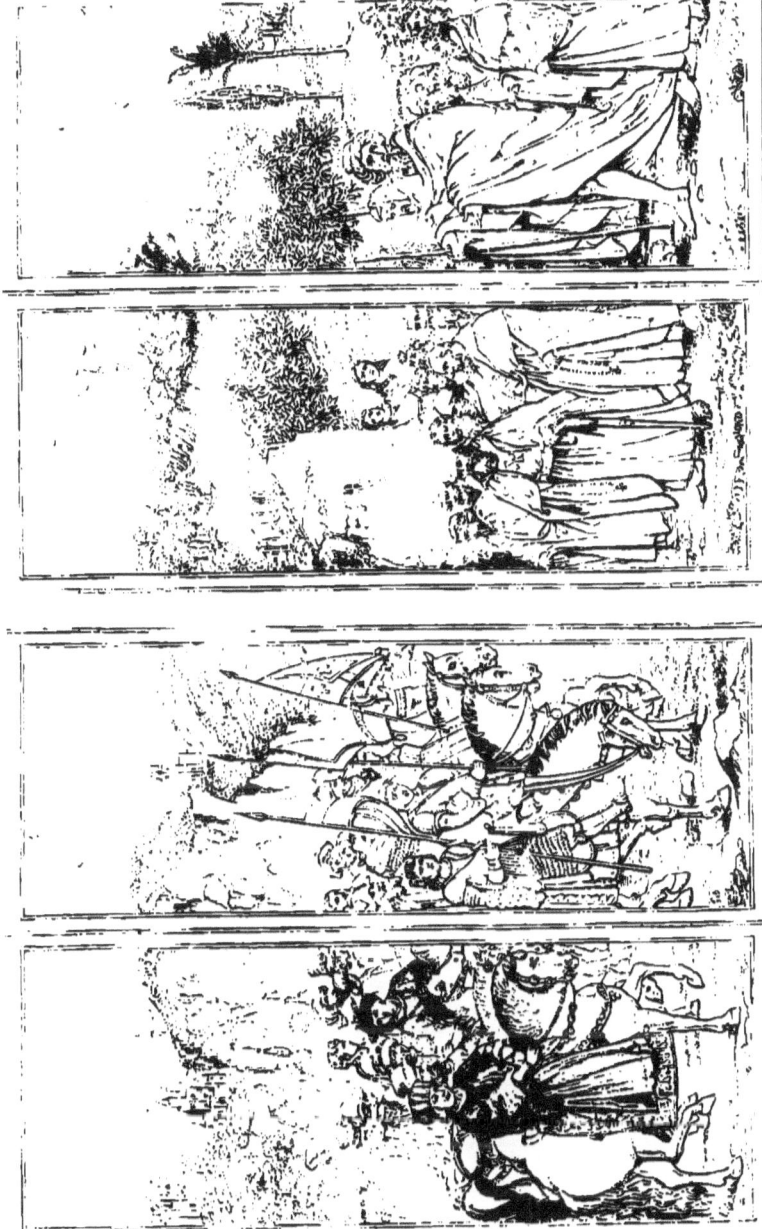

expression in the countenances of the pilgrims is also very remarkable. The picture next to the last described is more pleasing; it represents the troop of holy anchorites passing out of a rocky defile. In front are St. Paul the Hermit and St. Anthony, the two who set the first example of retirement from the world; and the procession closes with the two holy women who also passed the greater part of their lives in the wilderness, Mary Magdalen and St. Mary of Egypt. The heads are full of character, with great variety of expression: on every countenance may be traced the history of its life. Grave old men stand before us, each one differing from the other: one is firm and strong, another more feeble; one cheerful and single-minded, another less open. Some inspired fanatics wildly raise their heads, whilst others with a simple and almost humorous expression walk by their side, and others again are still struggling with their earthly nature. It is a remarkable picture, and leads us deep into the secrets of the human heart—a picture which in all times must be ranked amongst the master-works of art, and which to be intelligible needs no previous inquiry into the relative period and circumstances of the artists who created it. The landscape background, the rocky defile, the wooded declivity, and the trees laden with fruit, are all eminently beautiful. The eye would almost lose itself in this rich scene of still life, if it were not constantly led back to the interest of the foreground.

The opposite wing pictures differ essentially in conception from those just described: see woodcut. Their subject did not in itself admit such varied interest, and it is rather the common expression of a tranquil harmony of mind, and of the consciousness of a resolute will, which attracts the spectator, combined at the same time with a skilful representation of earthly splendour and magnificence. Inside the wing to the right we see the soldiers of the Lord on fine chargers, simple and noble figures in bright armour, with surcoats of varied form and colour. The three foremost with the waving banners appear to be St. Sebastian, St. George, and St. Michael, the patron saints of the old Flemish guilds, which accompanied their earls to the crusades. In the head of the St. George the painter has strikingly succeeded in rendering the spirit of the chivalry of the middle ages—that true heroic feeling and sense of power which humbles itself before the higher sense of the Divinity. Emperors and kings follow after him. The landscape is extremely beautiful and highly finished, with rich and finely-formed mountain ridges, and the fleecy clouds of spring floating lightly across. The second picture (the last to the left) represents the righteous judges; they also are on horseback, and are fine and dignified figures. In front, on a splendidly caparisoned grey horse, rides a mild, benevolent old man, in blue velvet trimmed with fur. This is the likeness of Hubert, to whom his brother has thus dedicated a beautiful memorial. Rather deeper in the group is John himself, clothed in black, with his shrewd, sharp countenance turned to the spectator. We are indebted to tradition for the knowledge of these portraits.

Both these wing pictures have the special interest of showing us, by means of armour, rich costumes, and caparisons, a true and particular representation of the Court of Burgundy in the time of Philip the Good—when it was confessedly the most superb court in Europe.

The upper wings, when closed, see woodcut, represented the Annunciation, and this was so arranged, that on the outer and wider ones (the backs of the two pictures of angels singing and playing) were the figures of the Virgin and the angel Gabriel—on the inner narrower ones (that is, on the back of the Adam and Eve) a continuation of the Virgin's chamber. Here, as was often the case in the outside pictures of large altarpieces, the colouring was kept down to a more uniform tone, in order that the full splendour might be reserved to adorn with greater effect the principal subject within. The angel and the Holy Virgin are clothed in flowing white drapery, but the wings of the angel glitter with a play of soft and brilliant colour, imitating those of the green parrot. The heads are noble and well painted: the furniture of the room is executed with great truth, as well as the view through the arcade which forms the back-

Outer Shutters of the great Van Eyck picture at Berlin

ground of the Virgin's chamber, into the streets of a town, one of which we recognise as a street in Ghent.

In the semicircles which close these panels above, on the right and left are the prophets Micah and Zechariah, whose heads have great dignity, but are somewhat stiff and unsatisfactory in their attitudes. In the centre (corresponding with the figures in chiaroscuro over Adam and Eve) are two kneeling female figures represented as sibyls.

The exterior portion of the lower wings contains the statues of the two St. Johns. These display a heavy style of drapery, and there is something peculiarly angular in the breaks of the folds, imitated perhaps from the sculpture of the day, which had also already abandoned the older German style. This peculiarity by degrees impressed itself more and more on the style of painting of the fifteenth century, and the drapery of the figures in the Annunciation already betrays a tendency towards it. The heads exhibit a feeling for beauty of form which is rare in this school. John the Baptist, who is pointing with his right hand to the Lamb on his left, is appropriately represented, as the last of the Prophets, as a man of earnest mien and dignified features, with much hair and beard. John the Evangelist, on the other hand, appears as a tender youth with delicate features, looking very composedly at the monster with four snakes which, at his benediction, rises from the chalice in his hand.

The likenesses of the donors are given with inimitable life and fidelity. They show the careful hand of Jan van Eyck, but already approach that limit within which the imitation of the accidental and insignificant in the human countenance should be confined. The whole, however, is in admirable keeping, and the care of the artist can hardly be considered too anxiously minute, since feeling and character are as fully expressed as the mere bodily form. The aged Judocus Vyts, to whose liberality posterity is indebted for this great work of art, is dressed in a simple red garment trimmed with fur; he kneels with his hands folded, and his eyes directed upwards. His countenance however is not attractive, the forehead is low and narrow, and the eye without power. The mouth alone shows a certain benevolence, and the whole expression of the features denotes a character capable of managing worldly affairs. The idea of originating so great a work as this picture is to be found in the noble, intellectual, and expressive features of his wife, who kneels opposite to him in the same attitude, and in still plainer attire.

Unfortunately Hubert van Eyck was not permitted to complete this grand work in all respects with his own hand. He died on September 16, 1426, and was buried in the family vault of the Vyts, below their chapel in the cathedral. Only at the request of Judocus Vyts was Jan van Eyck, the younger brother and scholar of Hubert, prevailed upon to finish the picture in the incomplete parts.[1] A close comparison of all the panels of this altarpiece with the authentic works of Jan van Eyck shows that the following portions differ in drawing, colouring, cast of drapery, and treatment, from his style, and may therefore with certainty be attributed to the hand of Hubert:—Of the inner side of the upper series, the Almighty, the Virgin, St. John the Baptist, St. Cecilia with the angels playing on musical instruments, and Adam and Eve; of the inner side of the lower series, the side of the centre picture with the apostles and saints, and the wings with the hermits and pilgrims, though with the exception of the landscapes. On the other hand, of the inner side of the upper series, the wing picture with the singing angels is by Jan van Eyck; of the inner side of the lower series, the side of the centre picture of the Adoration of the Lamb, containing the patriarchs and prophets, &c., and the entire landscape; the wing with the soldiers of Christ and the Righteous Judges, and the landscapes to the wing with the hermits and pilgrims; finally,

---

[1] This appears from the following inscription of the time, on the frame of the outer wing:—

"Pictor Hubertus ab Eyck, major quo nemo repertus
Incepit; pondusque Johannes arte secundus
Frater perfecit, Judoci Vÿd prece fretus."

The discovery of this inscription, under a coating of green paint, was made in Berlin in 1824, when the first word and a half of the third line, which were missing, were fortunately supplied by an old copy of this inscription, found by M. de Bast, the Belgian connoisseur.

the entire outer sides of the wings, comprising the portraits of the founders, and the Annunciation. The Prophet Zechariah and the two Sibyls alone show a feebler hand.

About one hundred years after the completion of this altarpiece, an excellent copy of it was made by Michael Coxis for Philip II. of Spain. The panels of this work, like those of the original, are dispersed; some are in the Berlin Museum, some in the possession of the King of Bavaria, and others in the remains of the King of Holland's collection at the Hague. A second copy, which comprises the inside pictures of this great work, from the chapel of the Town-house at Ghent, is in the possession of J. L. Lemmé, Esq.

Till within a very recent period the name of JAN VAN EYCK has almost obscured that of Hubert. For although there is no doubt that the elder brother was the first to develop the new mode of painting, yet the fame of it did not extend beyond Belgium and across the Alps until after the death of Hubert, when the just celebrity it acquired throughout Europe was speedily transferred to Jan van Eyck. As early as 1455 Jan was commemorated in the writings of Facius, the Italian scholar, as the greatest painter of the century, while the name of Hubert was not even mentioned.[1] Giovanni Santi also, in his well-known poem, alludes only to the "Gran Jannes." It was Jan van Eyck to whom Antonello da Messina resorted in Bruges, in order to learn the new style of painting; he alone also is mentioned by Vasari in his first edition of 1550—Hubert, not till the second edition of 1568, and then only very incidentally. Vasari was copied by most of the writers who succeeded him, and only recently has fitting attention been paid to Van Mander, who, as early as 1604, gives, in his book on painters, a detailed account of Hubert. Although we have no certainty regarding the date of Jan van Eyck's birth, yet it may be with great probability assigned to the year 1396. In his portrait, introduced in the wing of the

---

[1] 'De Viris Illustribus,' p. 46: "Johannes Gallicus nostri sæculi pictorum princeps judicatus est." See other evidence of the same kind in favour of Jan van Eyck in 'Early Flemish Painters,' p. 47, &c.

Upright Judges, which could hardly have been painted earlier than 1430, he appears as a man of 35 years old at most. In addition to this there is indubitable evidence that he died in 1441,[1] consequently in about his 46th year, which again corresponds with the fact that he died comparatively young.[2] Thanks to modern investigation, some circumstances, at least, of his life have been discovered. In 1420 he showed the guild of painters in Antwerp a head painted in oil, which excited such a sensation, that more than a century afterwards the upper classes of Antwerp presented the guild with a goblet with a representation of the event.[3] Jan van Eyck was then probably in the service of John of Bavaria, who, as Bishop of Liege, 1390-1418, acquired the name of "sans pitié," and who afterwards, by marriage, became the Duke of Luxembourg.[4] Four months later he died. The painter then entered the service of Philip the Good, Duke of Burgundy,[5] with a salary of 100 livres, where he continued till his decease. He so won the confidence of the Duke as to be sent on secret missions, by which his artistic labours must have been occasionally much interrupted. Two journeys of this kind in 1426 would hardly leave him the leisure to work at the great undertaking of his brother's altarpiece. In 1428 also it must have stood still, Jan van Eyck being obliged to accompany the ambassadors de Lannoy and de Roubaix to Portugal, in order to paint the portrait of Isabella of Portugal, who was betrothed to the Duke. It was not until the close of the

---

[1] M. de Stoop, of Bruges, has discovered the account of the funeral expenses of Jan van Eyck in the church of St. Donatian. See a more particular indication of the year, Carton, ' Les Trois Frères van Eyck,' p. 42, &c.

[2] See 'Historie van Belgis,' by Marcus van Vaernewyck, edition of 1649, p. 119 ; and the poem in praise of Lucas de Heere, teacher of Van Mander, at the passage, "Van dezer wereldt vrough dees edel Bloeme schiedt." Other evidence for assigning his birth to about 1396 is contained in Carton's work above mentioned, p. 27, &c.

[3] See 'Notice sur l'Académie d'Anvers, 1824,' by van Kirchoff. Compare ' Early Flemish Painters,' by Cavalcaselle, p. 45.

[4] The facts that Jan van Eyck was in the service of this very prince, whose territory included the town of Maaseyck, and that his daughter after his death became a nun in the convent of Maaseyck, tend to fix this as the place whence the family proceeded.

[5] See Count Léon de Laborde, ' Les Ducs de Bourgogne,' and the whole passage as quoted in ' Early Flemish Painters,' p. 50.

year 1429, when he had returned to Bruges, and, in the following year bought himself a house, that he was probably enabled to continue his labours on the great picture without interruption, so as to render the work fit for public inspection, on the 6th May 1432.[1] Fortunately the world possesses various authentic pictures by Jan van Eyck, in which his original powers are more easily recognised than in the part he executed of the great altarpiece, where he doubtless accommodated himself with true fraternal piety both to the composition and general style of his master and brother. His own works also show a very different originality from that which characterised Hubert. He possessed neither that enthusiasm for the rich significance of the ecclesiastical art of the middle ages, nor that feeling for beauty in human forms or in drapery, which belonged to the elder brother. His feeling, on the other hand, led him to the closest and truest conception of individual nature. In the head of the Saviour he adhered to the early Byzantine type, but all his Virgins and saints have a thoroughly portrait-like character, and are even occasionally ugly in form, and without any particular elevation of feeling. His realistic treatment also was carried out with admirable mastery in the stuffs of which his draperies were formed, in the backgrounds, and in every possible detail. Only in the overloading of his drapery with sharp and angular folds in ideal figures has he obviously imitated the sculptors who preceded him. His hands also, on these occasions, are often too narrow. Where, however, he had only to paint portraits—a task which quite coincided with the tendency of his mind—he attained a life-likeness of conception and a truth of form and colouring in every part, extending even to the minutest details, such as no other artist of his time could rival, and which art in general has seldom produced. As regards his participation in the merit of the improved mode of oil-painting, I entirely agree with Mr. Cavalcaselle, that he probably found his far older brother already in possession of the advantages he had developed, though Jan van Eyck may, by his own practice

---

[1] Count Léon de Laborde, 'Les Ducs de Bourgogne,' vol. i. p. 225, and 'Early Flemish Painters,' p. 52, &c.

of the art, have brought them to greater perfection.[1] In the management of the brush he possessed obviously a greater facility than Hubert, by which also he was enabled to render the material of every substance with marvellous fidelity. Here, as in his flesh-tones, the colours are seen alternately blended with tenderness, or, as in freely growing hair, lightly thrown on to the panel. In the aim at roundness of modelling, the highest lights of the flesh-tones approximate to white, and in the shadows to a powerful and sometimes rather heavy brown, broken with yellow. The brown in Hubert's shadows, on the contrary, has a reddish tendency. The distinctness of his sight, and the wonderful precision of his hand, inclined Jan van Eyck to a moderate and occasionally very small scale of size. The pleasure he took in the imitation of every form of nature led him in some instances to desert the class of ecclesiastical subjects, as for example in the Otter-hunt,[2] and in the Bath-room,[3] both of these being early cited as admirable pictures, though they have now disappeared. Finally, he so loved to represent landscapes with distant views that he not only introduced such in the background of his historical pictures, but an example is known in which a similar landscape constituted the whole of his subject.[4] Besides the pictures by him now in England, I will only quote those which are easy of access. In these I endeavour to observe a chronological order. Others of less importance I omit altogether.

The earliest picture known to be by Jan van Eyck is the consecration of Thomas á Becket as Archbishop of Canterbury, in the collection of the Duke of Devonshire at Chatsworth, inscribed with his name and the year 1421. Although this picture contains some fine heads, and is of great power

---

[1] 'Early Flemish Painters,' by Cavalcaselle, pp. 44 and 46. According to the date, 1417, inscribed on an oil picture by Pieter Christophsen, in the Städel Museum at Frankfort, it appears that the new art of oil painting was already then in vogue, when Jan van Eyck could hardly have been more than twenty years of age.
[2] 'Anonimo,' by Morelli, p. 14.   [3] See Facius.
[4] The representation of the world, which, according to Facius, he executed for Philip the Good, was essentially nothing more than the representation of a landscape, which was especially renowned for the indication of towns and villages, and for the illusion produced by perspective.

of colour, yet a certain inferiority in feeling and execution shows it to be a youthful production of the master.[1]

St. Francis kneeling before a mass of rock and receiving the stigmata; the lay brother before him with his hand covering his face. This small picture, which is at Lord Heytesbury's seat, Heytesbury, in Wiltshire, is remarkable for its solid and delicate execution, and for the depth and fullness of its warm tone. The fact that Lord Heytesbury purchased it from a medical man in Lisbon renders it probable that this work was executed by the master during his stay in Portugal in 1428-29.[2]

Next in chronological succession follow those wings of the altarpiece at Ghent, now in the Berlin Museum, which were the work of Jan van Eyck. I am the more inclined also to attribute to him the landscapes in the wings of the Hermits and Pilgrims, otherwise painted by Hubert, and in which southern vegetation, such as the orange, the stone pine, the cypress, and the palm, are rendered with great fidelity, from the fact that Jan van Eyck alone, from his voyage to Portugal, had had the opportunity of seeing these objects in nature.

The Virgin and Child seated under a penthouse. Inscribed " Completum anno domini MCCCCXXXII per Johannem de Eyck, Brugis," with his motto, " Als ich chan," in other words " as well as I can."[3] The head of the Virgin in this little picture is of unusually noble character, the folds of the drapery very sharp and angular. This picture is at Ince Hall, near Liverpool.

The Virgin enthroned, giving the breast to the Child. Her features are pleasing, but of no spiritual character. The Child, who is clumsy in body, is less attractive. The sharp and admirably rendered folds of the Virgin's drapery hide the form too much. This picture, which, from its former possessor the Duke of Lucca, was called the Madonna di Lucca, is now in the Städel Institute at Frankfort.

[1] 'Treasures of Art,' vol. iii. p. 349.
[2] 'Galleries and Cabinets of Art in Great Britain,' p. 389.
[3] According to Carton, ' Les Trois Frères van Eyck,' part of a Dutch motto, " Als ik kan, niet als ik wil."

The portrait of a man, in the National Gallery, No. 222. Signed "Johēs de Eyck me fecit año MCCCC33, Oct. 21," and his motto as above. This picture is of marvellous truth and vivacity, and equal precision and mastery of execution.

In the National Gallery, also, No. 186, are the portraits of Jan van Eyck and his wife, probably married to him in 1430. They are dressed in holiday attire, and are represented standing, hand in hand, in a small room, with numerous accessories. At their feet is a terrier dog. Signed "Johannes de Eyck fuit hic 1434." No other picture shows so high a development of the master's powers. Besides every other quality peculiar to him which we have already mentioned, and which it possesses in fullest measure, we observe here a perfection of general keeping and of chiaroscuro which no other specimen of this whole period affords. It is no wonder that the Princess Mary, sister of Charles V., and Governess of the Netherlands, should, as Van Mander relates, for this picture, have bestowed a post of 100 guldens a year upon a barber to whom it belonged.[1]

The Virgin with the Child on her arm, to whom St. Barbara is presenting the donor, an ecclesiastic in white robes. The background, landscape and architecture. This remarkable work is, in point of fact, a delicate miniature in oil, and follows the preceding picture very closely in time. At Burleigh House, seat of the Marquis of Exeter.

Nearly related in every respect to the last mentioned is a picture in the Louvre, No. 162, representing the Virgin crowned by an angel, with the Child on her lap, and adored by the donor Rollin, chancellor of Philip the Good,[2] who kneels before her. The features of the Virgin are pretty, but of little spirituality of character, the Child of unusual elegance for the master, the angel very beautiful, and the portrait of the donor of astonishing energy and animation.

[1] Van Mander, p. '126. His statement that these two persons were in the act of betrothal by a third person, called "*Fides*," proves nothing, as he speaks of the picture evidently from hearsay.

[2] We gather this from a passage in Courtépée's 'Descrip. Hist. et Topogr. du Duché de Bourgogne,' quoted by Cavalcaselle in 'History of Early Flemish Art,' p. 97. According to this the picture was formerly in the sacristy of Notre Dame at Autun.

The mantle of the Virgin is in numerous sharp breaks. The landscape background, which exhibits a town lying upon a river, and distant snow mountains, contains the richest and most incredible amount of detail that the master has bequeathed to us.

Next in succession we may take a picture, inscribed 1436, in the collection of the Academy at Bruges, which, in its different parts, is of very unequal merit. The Virgin, seated under a canopy, is of unusual ugliness, and the Child, who is playing with a parrot, has the features of a little old man. The head also of the St. George, standing on the left of the Madonna, has no spiritual expression whatever. On the other hand, St. Donatian, standing opposite to him, though of very portrait-like character, is incomparably more dignified. But the most admirable figure is that of the kneeling donor, the Canon, George de Pala, who is presented by St. Donatian. The decided character of his very individual features borders on hardness.[1] This work, with figures about two-thirds life-size, is the largest we know by the master.

The portrait of Jan de Leeuw, in the gallery of the Belvedere at Vienna, with the same date inscribed, has the same certainty of forms, and is unusually grey in the shadows.

Another portrait, of much analogy to the last, is also in the Belvedere Gallery. It is there called, though in my opinion erroneously, the portrait of Judocus Vyts in advanced years.

The picture of St. Ursula seated before a rich Gothic tower—her attribute—is in the Museum at Antwerp, dated 1437. It is especially interesting as showing how Jan van Eyck treated chiaroscuro. Although executed with the point of the brush, it has all the effect of a careful pen-drawing.

The head of Christ as Salvator Mundi, 1438, in the Berlin Museum, shows us how closely he adhered in his principal forms to the early, bearded, eastern type, at the same time developing his warm and powerful colouring, and

[1] See engraving of this picture, in which, however, little attention has been paid to the heads, in Carton's 'Les Trois Frères van Eyck,' p. 72, where also the elaborate inscriptions on the frame are fully given.

peculiar mastery over detail, as for instance in the painting of the beard.

The portrait of his wife, who was, however, by no means attractive in feature, in the Academy at Bruges, painted in 1439, is a specimen of marvellous delicacy and decision of carrying out. It is also truer in colouring, though less warm, than his other portraits.[1]

To his more highly finished pictures belongs finally a small altarpiece in the Dresden Gallery. The centre represents the Virgin seated with the Child in a rich chapel of Romanesque architecture: the inner sides of the wings contain St. Catherine, and St. George, who is presenting the donor; the outer sides the Annunciation in chiaroscuro.

Finally, I must mention the embroidered ecclesiastical robes, preserved in the Imperial Treasury at Vienna, the cartoons for which, I am convinced, proceeded from Jan van Eyck. These robes were executed for Philip the Good, for the Festival instituted by him in honour of the Order of the Golden Fleece. A figure of the Almighty, a Baptism of Christ, and some Saints are imbued with Jan van Eyck's feeling.

The brothers van Eyck had a sister, by name MARGARET VAN EYCK, who is said to have been a skilful painter, but to whom no work can with certainty be assigned. She died also before her brother Jan, and was buried, like Hubert, in the cathedral at Ghent.

It is only within the last ten years that the discovery of a third brother, of the name of LAMBERT VAN EYCK, has been made. A notice in the church books of the cathedral of Bruges, dated 21 March, 1442, states that, on the petition of Lambert van Eyck, brother of the celebrated painter Jan van Eyck, the Chapter had granted permission, with consent of the bishop, to have the body of the same removed from the outer precincts of the cathedral, where it had lain, to a spot within the edifice near the font.[2] This fact of a third

---

[1] On the upper border of this picture is the inscription, "Conjux meus Johannes me complevit 1439, 11 Juni." On the lower border, "Etas mea triginta tria annorum. ALS IXH XAN."

[2] Respecting this and all other records of Lambert van Eyck, see the often cited Carton, 'Les Trois Frères van Eyck,' p. 54, &c.

brother would have been of little consequence, but for a passage in the archives of Lille, from which it appears that he was also a painter.[1] If this was really the case, an unfinished picture, mentioned in an almost cotemporary account of Jan van Eyck, may probably be by him. According to that account, this picture was painted in 1445 for Nicolas of Maelbecke, abbot and dean of the monastery of St. Martin at Ypres; was placed above the grave of the donor in the church of the monastery, he having died in 1447; was taken by the last Bishop of Ypres into his palace at the invasion of the French, towards the close of the last century; and after being long in the hands of M. Bogaert, a bookseller at Bruges, came finally by purchase into the family of Van der Schrick, at Louvain.[2] It consists of a centre and two wings. In the first, the Holy Virgin, as Queen of Heaven, splendidly crowned, with long flowing hair, and a wide, richly ornamented purple mantle, holds the infant Christ in her arms; before her kneels the donor of the picture, and the background consists of ancient church architecture, through which we look out on a rich and animated landscape. The wings contain four subjects from the Old Testament, in part only sketched, which must be taken to relate to the mystery of the Nativity, in the spirit of the ancient Christian symbols. The subjects are—Moses and the Burning Bush, Gideon with the Angel and the Miraculous Fleece, the Closed Gate of Ezekiel, and Aaron with the Budding Rod. On the outside of the wings there is the Virgin, in chiaroscuro, with the Child, appearing to the Emperor Augustus and the Tiburtine Sibyl, who explains to him the meaning of the vision.

[1] An account-book of the expenses of Duke Philip the Good states, " A Lambert de Heck, frère de Johannes de Heck, peintre de Monseigneur, pour avoir été, à plusieurs fois, devers mon dit seigneur, pour aucunes besognes que mon dit seigneur voulait faire faire." As the same account-book contains the same expressions regarding the painter Huc de Boulogne, it is probable that by the term " besognes " pictures of an inferior order were understood. I share this opinion with Carton, and with Count Léon de Laborde.

[2] Passavant declares this picture to be a copy, but Dr. de Merseman, a thorough investigator of art at Bruges, has proved that this is the same work which was formerly in the church at Ypres. See Carton's ' Les Trois Frères van Eyck,' p. 62, &c. The improbability of a copy having been made of this, in many parts, only just begun work, speaks for itself.

E

The principal portions, namely the Virgin and the Donor, are too feeble in drawing and execution of the flesh parts for Jan van Eyck, nor could he really have taken part in the picture, since his death is known to have taken place in 1441. At the same time, there is such affinity in all accessories, in the hair and crown of the Virgin, and especially in the rich landscape, to Jan van Eyck's works, that there can be no doubt of its having proceeded from the atélier of a cotemporary master. The old record too, which names Jan van Eyck as the originator of the work, is so far in favour of Lambert from the fact that it was deeply interested in attributing it to the more celebrated of the brothers.[1] Several of the smaller figures show so striking an accordance with the two Sibyls and the prophet Zechariah in the Ghent altarpiece, that I am also inclined to attribute these, the weaker portions of that great work, to the hand of Lambert. For the same reasons it is probable that he was the author of the repetition of the great picture in the Academy at Bruges, which in every way approaches so near the original, and is now No. 11 in the Museum at Antwerp.

CHAPTER II.

SCHOOL OF THE BROTHERS VAN EYCK TILL NEAR THE CLOSE OF THE 15TH CENTURY.

THE influence of this realistic tendency in art thus completely carried out, as well as of the new and admirable mode of applying oil-paint, extended to every country in Europe where art was practised with any success. In the Netherlands themselves it was of course most felt; after them in Germany; and then in France, England, Italy, Spain, and Portugal. We need only examine its progress in the two first-named countries.

Among the Netherlandish scholars and followers of the Van Eycks, of whom any record has been preserved, some appear to have been gifted with considerable powers,

[1] See my article in the 'Kunstblatt' of 1849, Nos. 16 and 17.

though none attained the excellence of their great precursors. Although a number of works representing this school still exist in the various countries of Europe, yet, compared with the actual abundance of them at one time, they constitute but a scanty remnant. And more scanty are the notices we possess regarding the lives and circumstances of these painters; the documentary researches, however, of the last ten years have elicited a few fresh facts and dates.[1]

The three following painters may be considered as fellow-scholars of Jan van Eyck under his brother Hubert.

PIETER CHRISTOPHSEN,[2] alias son of Christopher. Judging from a picture, dated 1417, in the Städel Museum at Frankfort, No. 402, representing the Virgin and Child enthroned, with SS. Jerome and Francis at the sides, this painter must have been born at latest in the last ten years of the 14th century, and, therefore, may be considered to have been a scholar of Hubert van Eyck. The broad and beautiful cast of the draperies in this picture, as well as the style of colouring, show a feeling borrowed from that master. The head of the Virgin, however, and still more that of the Child, are incomparably inferior to Hubert in sense of beauty. To this earlier time belong also four small panel pictures in the Madrid Gallery, No. 454, representing the Annunciation, Visitation, Nativity, and Adoration of the Kings. The Gothic portals in which they are enframed are decorated with subjects in chiaroscuro.[3] The later works of Pieter Christophsen are in some respects feebler. His heads are sometimes wanting in earnest religious feeling; his drawing, especially of the feet, is weak, and

---

[1] The most distinguished of these inquirers have been Count Léon de Laborde, at Paris; M. Wauters, the keeper of the records at Brussels; the Abbé Carton, at Bruges; Edward van Even, keeper of the records at Louvain; and many other Belgian gentlemen, whose names are mentioned in the Introduction to the Catalogue of the Antwerp Museum of 1857, p. ix., &c.

[2] So called from the inscription " Petrus XPR" on his pictures. Vasari twists this into the names of Pietro Crista. In the archives of the cathedral of Cambray (see Count de Laborde's above-mentioned work, Introduction, p. cxxv. *f.*) he is designated Petrus Cristus, of Bruges.

[3] See Passavant's 'Christliche Kunst in Spanien,' p. 129; and Cavalcaselle's ' Early Flemish Painters,' p. 119.

his execution meagre. Of this class are his picture of St. Eligius selling a ring to a bridal couple, dated 1449, from the Guildhall of the Goldsmiths at Antwerp, now in the possession of Mr. Oppenheim, the banker, at Cologne; and two wings, inscribed 1452, formerly belonging to an altarpiece at Burgos, afterwards removed to Segovia, and now in the Berlin Museum, No. 529 A and B—the one representing the Annunciation and Nativity, the other the Last Judgment.[1] They must always excite interest, however, by their astonishing force and freshness of colour, and their careful execution. In close succession to these is a Virgin and Child, to whom St. Anna is giving a pear, in the Dresden Gallery, No. 1613, and there designated "School of Van Eyck." On the other hand, the master is more favourably seen in the portrait of a Lady, niece to the celebrated Talbot, in the Berlin Museum, No. 532.[2]

JUSTUS VAN GHENT, mentioned by Vasari as one of the first oil-painters of the Van Eyck school,[3] was, according to an old MS. record in the Flemish tongue, a scholar of Hubert.[4] No tidings are given, however, either of his earlier life or of his birth; but considered as scholar to a master who died in 1426, his birth can hardly be placed later than 1400. From the fact, also mentioned by Vasari, and confirmed by historical evidence,[5] of his having painted a large picture for the high-altar of the church of the Fraternity of Corpus Christi at Urbino, in 1474, it is evident that he was not only alive at that time, but still highly appreciated as a painter. The picture, still in the same church, also shows that to a certain degree he deserved his reputation. The composition representing Christ standing in the act of giving the chalice to the Apostles

---

[1] See further an article by me in the 'Deutsches Kunstblatt' of 1854, p. 65.
[2] On the cotemporary but now lost frame was an inscription telling the name of the painter and that of the person portrayed.
[3] Sienese edition, vol. i. p. 177, and vol. xi. p. 64, where he is called Giusto da Guant.
[4] See De Bast, 'Messager des Sciences,' Gand, 1824, p. 133. Although there called Iudocus, I am convinced that the same individual is meant.
[5] Pungileoni, 'Elogio Storico di Giovanni Santi,' p. 64, &c. Urbino, 1822.

kneeling around, is arranged with considerable artistic discrimination. With the exception of the Christ, whose striding position and head are unsuccessful, the motives are free and speaking, and show, in their earnest and dignified character, an affinity to the Apostles and Hermits, by Hubert van Eyck, in the St. Bavon picture. The same may be said of the forms of the well-drawn hands, with which also the other portions of the figures, which are three-fourths life-size, correspond. Finally, the brownish, though less deep and transparent, flesh-tones coincide with those of his master. The portraits of Federigo di Montefeltro, Duke of Urbino ; of Caterino Zeno, envoy from the Venetian republic ; and of an aged man, probably the painter himself, are very true and living. The predella, containing allegorical representations of the Holy Sacrament, no longer exists. Another picture mentioned in this Flemish MS.—a Decollation of the Baptist, in the Cathedral of Ghent—was destroyed by the Iconoclasts ; also two pictures by him, the Crucifixion of St. Peter, and the Beheading of St. Paul, which, in the year 1763, were still in the church of St. James, in the same city, have disappeared.[1]

An important position among the scholars of the Van Eycks is occupied by DIERICK STUERBOUT. This painter was born at Haarlem, about the year 1391,[2] and was consequently designated by Vasari,[3] and later by Van Mander,[4] as DIERICK VAN HARLEM. He probably received his first instructions from his father, also called Dierick Stuerbout —a name frequently contracted into "Bout" alone. As the father, however, who was especially known for the development of his landscape backgrounds,[5] was no longer

---

[1] 'Early Flemish Painters,' p. 157.
[2] This appears from the record of a judicial case at Brussels, dated December 9, 1467, where he was summoned as a witness, and where his age is given as about seventy-six. See Notice by Wauters, in the 'Chronicle of the Historical Society at Utrecht,' Series ii., year vi., p. 268.
[3] Vasari, vol. xi. p. 68, the Sienese edition.
[4] Ibid. p. 129 b.
[5] For this we have the testimony of Johannes Molanus, a respected writer, who died 1585, in his MS. description of Louvain, discovered in the library of the ancient Dukes of Burgundy, in 1835, the publication of which will

living in 1400,¹ the son must early have been put to school to some other painter. The best school at that time in the Netherlands was the atelier of Hubert van Eyck; and as the works of no other cotemporary painter in the Netherlands show so great an affinity in character of heads and colouring with those portions of the St. Bavon altarpiece which are decidedly by Hubert's hand as the pictures by Stuerbout, there is little doubt that he must have owed his higher culture in art to the teaching of this great master. The fact of his having resided some time in his native city Haarlem, as a master-painter, appears from Van Mander's testimony, who indicates the house which he had occupied.² At a later period he migrated to Louvain, though when this removal took place is not precisely known. The fact, however, that his brother, a less known painter, of the name of Hubert, was established in Louvain in 1438,³ where, according to the same Molanus we have quoted, he received the office of painter to the city in 1454,⁴ makes it probable that Dierick must also have established himself there by that time. At all events, he was living in Louvain in 1461, in which year he was appointed "Portraiteur" to the city; and in 1462 he there executed a picture.⁵ In the ensuing years he was employed by the Brotherhood of the Holy Sacra-

shortly ensue. Landscape, as a distinct branch of art, belongs first to the sixteenth century; but the fact that in historical delineations in Holland figures were at a very early period treated on a small scale, and the space around carefully carried out, is proved by certain early Dutch miniatures. See 'Kunstwerke und Künstler in Paris,' p. 340, &c.

¹ See the same Molanus, same place.
² Cavalcaselle states, 'Early Flemish Painters,' p. 311, that he lived there many years. This, however, is not said by Van Mander.
³ For information on this and every point concerning Dirk Steuerbout see the instructive pamphlet by Edward van Even, 'Niederlandische Konstenaers,' Amsterdam, 1858.
⁴ This office, according to the above-named pamphlet, p. 17, consisted only in the execution of ornaments. Another brother, Albert by name, was also settled in Louvain.
⁵ This appears from a Latin inscription on a picture existing at Haarlem in Van Mander's time, and of which we have only his Dutch translation, as follows:—" Duysent vier hundred en twee et tsestien Jaer nac Christus gheboort, heeft Dirk, de te Haerlem is ghebooren my te Lowen ghemaeckt, de euwighge rust moet hem ghewerden." This picture consisted of figures the size of life, Christ in the centre, and SS. Peter and Paul on the wings.

ment to paint two pictures for two chapels in St. Peter's church, which had come into their possession since the year 1433. For the smaller chapel he executed an altarpiece, with the martyrdom of St. Erasmus in the centre, and SS. Jerome and Bernard on the wings; for the larger chapel also an altarpiece, with the Last Supper in the centre, and on the wings four compartments, one above the other, with emblematical representations of the Lord's Supper, taken from the Old Testament. The last altarpiece, on which he laboured several years, receiving from time to time small instalments of payment, was completed in the year 1467.[1] In the year after, he finished two pictures ordered by the magistracy of Louvain for the council-chamber in the well-known Town-hall, the building of which was terminated in 1460. They consist of life-sized figures, and represent events calculated to admonish the judges of the strict fulfilment of their office. These were taken from a legend in the Chronicle of Gottfried of Viterbo, written in the 12th century, relating how the Emperor Otho III. had, on the false testimony of his empress, a guilty and disappointed woman, executed one of the nobles of his court. The wife of the murdered man, however, proved, by the ordeal of fire, the innocence of her husband; the empress was condemned to the flames.[2] For these pictures the painter received the then considerable sum of 230 crowns, a proof how highly his works were esteemed; while the satisfaction of the magistracy was further shown by the immediate commission to execute two more works. The one, an altarpiece with wings, 6 feet

[1] That both these altarpieces, designated in the church as the works of Memling, and by me attributed to Justus van Ghent, are by the hand of Steuerbout, is evident from the following passage in Molanus:—" Theodorici filii opus sunt in ecclesia D. Petri duo altaria venerabilis sacramenti quæ multum ex arte commendantur." The fullest confirmation of this passage has been extracted by M. Edward van Even from the financial records of the Brotherhood of the Holy Sacrament for the last-named picture. Even the painter's receipt, of the year 1467, has been found. It runs thus: "Je Dieric Bouts kenne mi vernucht (sic) en wel betaelt, als van den werc dat ic ghemackt hebbe den heiligen sacrement."
[2] This appears from a record in the Annals of Louvain, first published in the 'Messager des Sciences,' &c., p. 18, 1832, and afterwards by Cavalcaselle, in 'Early Flemish Painters,' p. 290.

high and 4 feet wide, representing the Last Judgment, was destined for the council-chamber of the Sheriffs, and was completed in 1472; the other, intended to take its place in a collection of pictures which the city authorities proposed forming in the Town-hall, consisted of four pieces, ranging 12 feet in height, and, forming altogether a length of 26 feet, would have been the largest known work of this school. The artist contracted to paint both pictures for 500 crowns; but before completing the second compartment of the last great work, death interrupted his labours in 1479.[1] The greater part of the pictures thus recorded being still in existence, I am not only enabled to form a deliberate opinion as to the master's style of painting, but also, with this standard, to identify other works by his hand. In his treatment of religious subjects the feeling of devotion which pervades the whole early Netherlandish school is accompanied by the expression of a repose, solemnity, and slight melancholy, which imparts a peculiar charm. In the arrangement of his subject the sense of the picturesque so predominates over that of the symmetrical, as often to give an arbitrary and scattered look to his compositions. At the same time separate actions have generally something angular and stiff, which shows itself especially in the position of the legs; the proportions are also often too long and meagre, the legs again being particularly in fault, and the forms too slender. On the other hand, the character of the heads is very various, of much animation and individuality, generally full of meaning, and occasionally displaying a delicate feeling for beauty. The drawing is very able, and the hands always in good action. In point of drapery no painter of this school approaches so near to Hubert van Eyck, or is so exempt from the angularity of folds peculiar to Jan van Eyck. His distinctive merits, however, consist in his colouring, in his landscape backgrounds,

---

[1] Regarding his death, and also the price awarded to the unfinished work by Hugo van der Goes, of which more hereafter, see the same work by E. van Even, p. 14. See also the passage describing these pictures in the Louvain Annals, 'Early Flemish Painters,' p. 291.

and in the style of their execution. For depth, power, and fulness of colouring, no other painter in the whole school can indeed be compared with him. His red and green draperies, for instance, are so melting and transparent as only to be likened to garnets and emeralds. This effect in the green extends even to the trees and plants of his landscape backgrounds, which, in their greater softness and depth of tone, and slightly more developed aërial perspective, assign to him the highest place among his compeers. It is evident that the example of his father, whose excellence in this direction has been mentioned, must have influenced him. We know for certain that a picture by Dierick, representing events from the life of St. Bavon, was, as late as 1609, in the possession of a Mr. T. Blin, at Haarlem. Here the environs of the city were given with such detail, that even a well-known hollow tree then existing could be identified.[1] Finally, in the treatment of the whole picture he displays a breadth and softness, compared with which the works of his in other respects superior fellow-scholar, Rogier van der Weyden the elder, appear—namely, in the execution of rich stuffs—to be somewhat hard and meagre. The number of works attributed to Stuerbout are by no means inconsiderable. My limits, however, only allow me to mention those most characteristic of the master, and also most accessible to the reader.

His probably earliest production known to me are two small wings containing eight events from the legend of St. Ursula, in the chapel of the hospital *des Sœurs Noires* at Bruges, and there wrongly given to Memling. These pictures, which are of great delicacy, were perhaps executed before the death of Hubert van Eyck in 1426, and therefore before the painter's return to Haarlem. The exterior of the wings also, with the four Evangelists, the four Fathers of the Church, and the Annunciation, in chiaroscuro, are well deserving notice. Next in period may be

[1] The description of this picture is found in a note to the French translation of Guicciardini's 'Account of the Netherlands,' published in Amsterdam, in 1609, by Pieter van Berge. See Edward van Even, p. 29, &c.

taken two works belonging to a larger altarpiece. One of these, representing Judas and his troop taking our Lord, is in the Munich Gallery, Cabinets, No. 58. The composition is rich and animated, but the meagreness of the forms, angularity of the motives, and a certain hardness of outline, assign it to the earlier period of the painter. At the same time his admirable individuality of heads is already pronounced in this work, also the variety of his flesh-tones, and the power and depth of his colouring. The other—the Ascension—wrongly attributed to Memling, is in the chapel of St. Maurice at Nuremberg, No. 23. The dignity expressed in the head of the Saviour is still an attractive feature, but it is otherwise too much restored.

To these pictures probably succeeds, in point of time, his smaller altarpiece in the cathedral of Bruges: the centre containing the Martyrdom of St. Hippolitus, who is torn to pieces by four horses; and the wing, the King by whom the Saint was condemned, with four other figures, and the now partly obliterated portrait of a man and his wife, the founders of the picture. The expression of grief in the Saint is very elevated; the flesh of a brownish tone, and well modelled. But the horses, considering the time, are the most remarkable portion, being well formed, and of much vivacity of action. The landscape background already bears witness to his peculiar excellence in that line. The centre picture has been unfortunately much retouched.

In close approximation to this last work is the small altarpiece, with the Martyrdom of St. Erasmus, already alluded to, in St. Peter's at Louvain, and which was probably executed in 1463 or 1464. The drawing of the Saint's body shows an evident improvement upon the last picture. The disagreeable effect of the peculiar martyrdom of this Saint, whose bowels were wound out upon a windlass, is much diminished, though somewhat at the expense of the truth usually observed by the school in such scenes, by the absence of blood, and of all distortion of the features. Some of the heads are less warm and clear than usual, but the modelling is throughout excellent. The drapery of St. Jerome, in the wing, may be considered, in cast, colouring, and making out, one of the most beautiful efforts of the whole school. The landscape of the background is one of the finest examples of the master's hand.

Immediately following may be placed the larger altarpiece, completed in 1467, which is in the same church at Louvain, and the centre of which represents the Last Supper. In every portion of this work the painter appears at the very zenith of his art. The figures of Christ and his Disciples are distributed with great artistic judgment round a quadrangular table, and exhibit an admirable variety in action, character, and expression. The noble head of the Saviour forms a striking contrast to that of Judas, which is distinguished by its jet black hair and malignant expression. I had on former occasions conjectured the head of one of the subordinate figures to be the portrait of the painter. Herr van Even, who is of the same opinion, has, in the pamphlet alluded to, given an outline from a tracing of the head, which is that of an elderly man of fine features, but rather morose expression. The wings to this picture are not less fine. Two of them, Abraham and Melchisedec, and the Gathering of the Manna, are in the Munich Gallery, Cabinets, Nos. 44 and 55; two others, Elijah in the Wilderness fed by an Angel, and the first celebration of the Passover, in the Berlin Museum, Nos. 533 and 539. The Gathering of the Manna has suffered much by fresh glazings, but it has, in common with the fourth-mentioned subject, a very beautiful landscape.

The two pictures from the legend of the Emperor Otho, though the largest and the latest by the master (executed 1468), are by no means the most satisfactory of his works. The angular motives, over-long proportions, and meagre limbs—in short, the weak points of the painter—are much more conspicuously seen in figures the size of life than in his smaller productions. At the same time, the vivacity of the heads, the warm and vigorous colouring, though here and there defaced by cleaning, and the thorough execution, suffice to give these pictures no inconsiderable value as works of art. They were preserved in the Town Hall at Louvain until 1827, when they were purchased for

10,000 florins by William I. of Holland, from whom they were inherited by William II., in whose collection they remained until 1830. At the sale of his pictures by the Dowager Queen they were bought by Mr. C. J. Niewenhuys, and are in his house at Brussels. Although the influence of this great painter, as regards his cotemporary artists, was not so universal as that exercised by Rogier van der Weyden the elder, of which more hereafter, yet it must have been considerable, though now very difficult to trace.[1] It is unmistakeably seen, however, in the person of Hans Memling. This painter owed to Stuerbout not only the depth and clearness of his colouring, but also that peculiar enamel and softness in which he excels his own master, Rogier van der Weyden the elder. It is for this reason that most of Steuerbout's pictures have been attributed to Memling.

The painters next described may with certainty be considered the scholars of Jan van Eyck.

Of these, ROGIER VAN DER WEYDEN THE ELDER attained by far the most celebrity. As late as the year 1846, however, he was known only by the appellation of Roger of Bruges. In that year his name was first discovered by M. Wauters, the keeper of the Archives at Brussels, to be Rogier van der Weyden, and his birthplace Brussels.[2] He was born probably within the last ten years of the 14th, certainly not later than the beginning of the 15th century, his reputation as a great master being already so firmly established by the year 1430, that Pope Martin V., who died 1431, presented a small altarpiece by him to Juan II., King of Spain.[3] This work, which bears evidence of a consummate master's hand, is now in the Muséum at Berlin. In the earlier years of Rogier van der Weyden, when he was still under the tutelage of Jan van Eyck at Bruges, he executed a number of pictures in tempera, of

---

[1] His brothers, and several sons, all painters, appear to have been of a very subordinate class.

[2] See the first quarter number of the 'Messager des Sciences Historiques,' Brussels.

[3] See Passavant's article in the 'Kunstblatt' of 1843; also mine in the 'Deutsches Kunstblatt' of 1854, p. 57.

figures the size of life.[1] As early as 1436, however, he filled the honourable post of official painter to the city of Brussels. The chief work executed by him in this character was an altarpiece for the apartment dedicated to the administration of Justice in the Hôtel de Ville at Brussels. According to the custom of the time, it set forth examples of stern observance of the law, for the admonition of those placed in authority. The principal picture shows how Herkenbald, a judge in Brussels in the 11th century, executed his own nephew, convicted of a grave crime, but who would otherwise have escaped the penalty of the law, with his own hands; and how the sacramental wafer which, on the plea of murder, was denied to him by the priest, reached the lips of the upright judge by means of a miracle. The wings contained an example of the justice of the Emperor Trajan. These much admired works, which were seen by Albert Durer on his visit to the Netherlands,[2] were still in their original places as late as the 17th century. They probably perished in the burning of the Hôtel de Ville, at the siege of Brussels, by the French, in 1695. For private individuals of distinction Rogier van der Weyden also carried out considerable works; for instance, a large altarpiece, probably executed between 1440 and 1447, for the chapel of the hospital at Beaune, in Burgundy, founded by Nicolas Rollin, chancellor to Philip the Good, and which is still in an apartment of that institution.[3] In 1449 he went to Italy, where he painted an altarpiece for Lionello d'Este, Lord of Ferrara, representing in the centre a Descent from the Cross, and on one wing the Expulsion of Adam and Eve from Paradise, which excited the greatest admiration.[4] In 1450 he was present at the celebration of the Jubilee at Rome.[5] Nor did he leave Italy without visiting Florence,

[1] Van Mander, fol. 126 b.
[2] 'Reliquien von Albrecht Dürer,' Nürnberg, 1826, p. 81.
[3] See Passavant, 'Kunstblatt,' No. 59, and an article by me in the 'Deutsches Kunstblatt,' 1856, p. 239.
[4] 'Colucci Antichità Picene,' tom. xv. p. 143. Cyriacus of Ancona there calls him " Pictorum decus."
[5] Facius, same work, p. 45.

and becoming acquainted with the Medici, as is proved by a picture now in Frankfort, of which a description will follow later. After his return to Brussels he executed a picture for Peter Bladolin, treasurer to Philip the Good, which was placed by that dignitary on the altar of a church in the town of Middelburg, founded and completed by him in 1450,[1] and which is now in the Berlin Museum. Another larger work, painted from 1454 to 1459, for Bishop John of Cambray,[2] has unfortunately disappeared. On the 16th June, 1464, Rogier van der Weyden died, and was buried in the cathedral of Brussels.[3]

Although it is proved by abundant evidence that Rogier van der Weyden was the scholar of Jan van Eyck, yet his works show also the decided influence of Hubert. Indeed he is much nearer related in the moral tendency of his art to the elder than to the younger brother, and was doubtless well acquainted with Hubert, who did not die till 1426. Like him he treated those subjects suggested by the symbolic feeling of the Church during the middle ages, with the greatest enthusiasm. As regards also the purer taste of his drapery he approximates nearer to Hubert than to Jan. The latter, however, he resembles in the masterly carrying out of the realistic feeling, and not less in the deficiency of a sense of beauty, which sometimes pervades his works. Indeed the too exclusive aim at truth led Rogier van der Weyden occasionally to represent the tasteless and the disagreeable. Thus his nude is meagre, his fingers too long, his feet, especially in his earlier works, ill formed. His colouring, on the other hand, though not equal in depth and warmth to that of his master, is nevertheless of astonishing vigour and power; his flesh-tones in his earlier period golden, and only in his later time somewhat cooler. Of his existing pictures I can only mention the finest, and those in the order in which they may have been painted.

[1] 'Messager des Sciences et des Arts en Belgique,' 1835, p. 333-348.
[2] Count Léon de Laborde's 'Les Ducs de Bourgogne,' tom. i., Introduction, p. 58.
[3] See Sweertius, 'Monumenta Sepulcralia Brabantiæ autor,' p. 284; also Water's Registre des Sépultures, 'Messager des Sciences Historiques,' 1845, p. 145.

The small triptych altarpiece, presented by Pope Martin V. to the King of Spain,[1] and brought in recent times by General Armagnac from Spain to France, now No. 534 A of the Berlin Museum, represents the Nativity, a Dead Christ in the lap of the Virgin, and Christ appearing to his Mother after his Resurrection. These are intense in feeling, powerful in colour, and of miniature-like execution, but meagre in the limbs. Painted borders to the pictures, in the manner of Gothic portals, contain numerous other subjects in chiaroscuro.

An altarpiece, with three scenes from the life of John the Baptist, representing his Birth, the Baptism of Christ, and his Decollation, now in the Berlin Museum, No. 534 B. These pictures were formerly in Spain.[2] They are enframed in borders, like those just described, with which they also closely agree in the whole style of execution.

A triptych, in the collection of the Marquis of Westminster in London; half-length figures, and painted doubtless as a sepulchral monument. In the centre, Christ in the act of benediction; in his left hand the globe: of very stern and almost forbidding character, and, what is unusual, with black hair. On his right is the Virgin — a noble head — adoring him: on the left John the Evangelist; a fine head, of great depth of colour, holding the chalice in his left hand. On the right wing is John the Baptist, of very earnest character, pointing with his right hand to Christ. On the left wing the Magdalen, with a dignified expression of repentance, holding the box of ointment. This important work approaches, in point of warmth and depth of colouring, very near to the foregoing pictures.[3]

The Last Judgment, in the hospital at Beaune. This is the most comprehensive example of the master that has

[1] It was formerly wrongly conjectured to be the travelling-altar of Charles V. See Passavant's 'Christliche Kunst in Spanien,' p. 130.
[2] For the reasons why I do not agree with Passavant and Cavalcaselle in considering these pictures to have belonged to the Chartreuse at Miraflores, and for a further description, see 'Deutsches Kunstblatt,' 1854, p. 58.
[3] See more detailed description in 'Treasures of Art,' vol. ii. p. 161, &c. In the Gallery itself it is wrongly imputed to Memling.

descended to us. Our illustration will show how strictly his composition adheres to the forms of tradition; while at the same time the formally symmetrical arrangement of the upper part is broken by the vivacity and freedom of the motives. The heads, especially those of John the Baptist and some of the Apostles, are unusually elevated in character for him; the expression also of sympathy is very touching. The papal figure behind the Apostles, in the right wing, is Pope Eugenius IV.; the crowned individual next him, Philip the Good; and the crowned female opposite, on the left wing, probably Philip's second wife, Isabella of Portugal. The lower part, which is divided from the upper by strata of clouds, is upon the whole somewhat empty, and has also been much disfigured by over-painting. The head of the Archangel Michael is fine, but his figure too long. On the outer sides, see woodcut, are the kneeling portraits of Rollin the founder, and his wife Guignonne de Salin; both of great excellence. The chiaroscuro figures of SS. Sebastian and Anthony, treated like statues, and the similarly painted Annunciation, are by the hand of an assistant.

Next in period to the last picture we may place that now in the Städel Institute at Frankfort, which was doubtless painted for Pietro and Giovanni de' Medici, and which represents their patron-saints of the same names, and those of the house of Medici, SS. Cosmo and Damian, surrounding the Virgin and Child. The execution of this picture is of the tenderest finish, and, compared with the foregoing, shows an improvement in drawing.

The altarpiece with wings, executed for Peter Bladolin, is in the Berlin Museum, No. 535. In the centre is the Nativity, with the kneeling donor, and angels of great beauty, some of whom kneel close to the Infant, while others hover over the roof of the stable. On the one side is the Annunciation of the Redeemer to the Ruler of the West—the Emperor Augustus—by means of the Tiburtine Sibyl; on the other the Annunciation to the Rulers of the East—the Three Kings, who are keeping watch on a mountain, where the Child appears to them in a star. The arrange-

THE LAST JUDGMENT. By Rogier van der Weyden the Elder

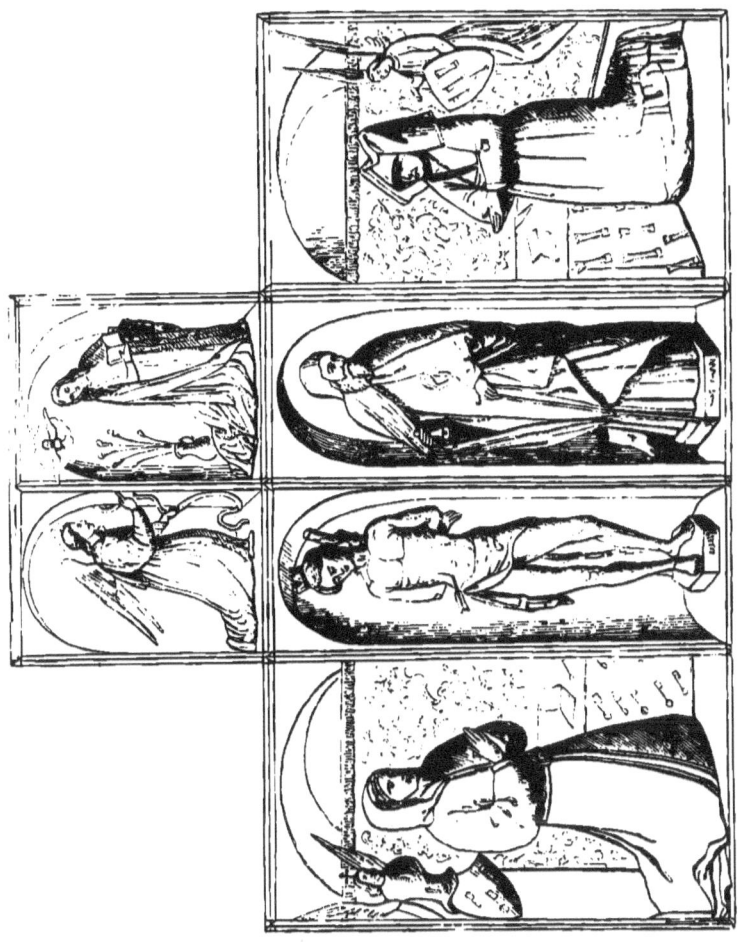

OUTER SHUTTERS OF LAST JUDGMENT 1 y Rogier van der Weyden the Elder

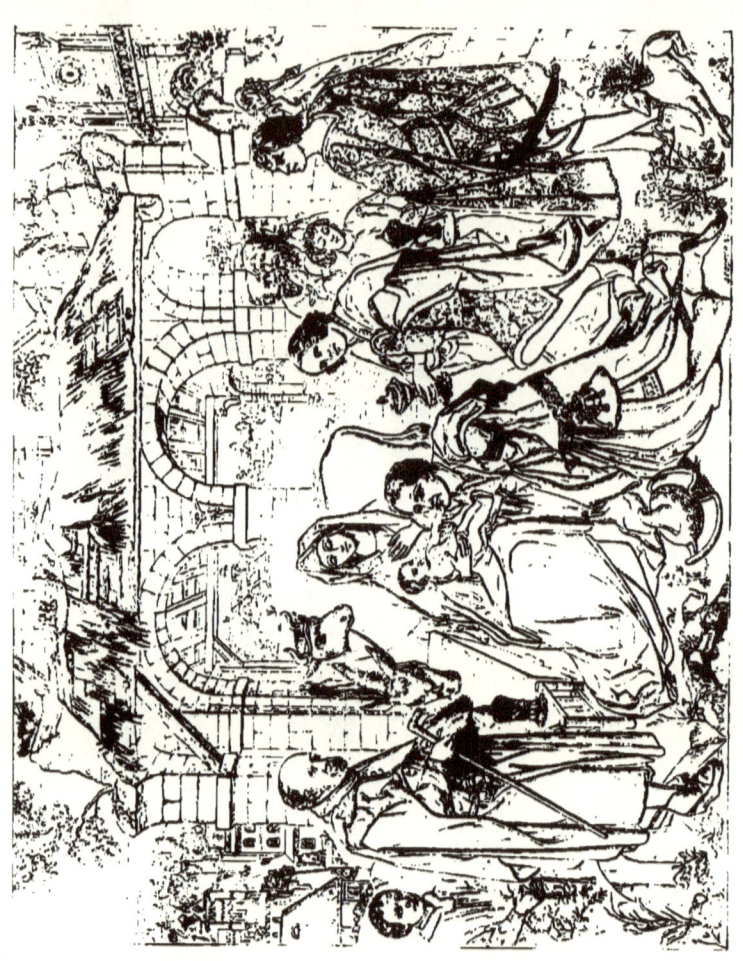

ment of this portion is peculiarly grand, and the heads highly characteristic. This is one of the most remarkable and best preserved examples of Rogier van der Weyden.

The Adoration of the Kings, with the Annunciation, and the Presentation in the Temple, in the wings, is now in the Munich Gallery, Cabinets, Nos. 35, 36, 39, and wrongly designated as a Jan van Eyck. This was probably painted for the church of St. Columba in Cologne, and was afterwards in the Boisserée collection: we subjoin an illustration. This is one of the largest and finest works by the master. The figure of the Virgin in the Presentation is very noble, and perhaps the most successful rendering of this Handmaid of the Lord that has descended to us by the painter. The woodcut only gives the centre picture. Unfortunately, both flesh and draperies have been rendered very glaring in colour, by means of the glazings which the Boisserées employed so abundantly.

St. Luke painting the Virgin — also in the Munich Gallery, Cabinets, No. 42. The head of the Virgin is here of a portrait-like character, and of no beauty of feature. The Child also is meagre and unattractive. On the other hand, the head of St. Luke, though also portrait-like, is very agreeable; the landscape of great transparency; and the colouring of astonishing power.

The Descent from the Cross, in the Gallery of the Hague, No. 55, and wrongly designated as Memling, is a rich composition, with heads of highly pathetic expression and admirable execution. It is rather cooler in the flesh-tones.

The Seven Sacraments, formerly on the altar of a church at Dijon, now in the Antwerp Museum, No. 30. On the centre and larger panel, by way of figure of the Last Supper, is the Crucifixion seen in a Gothic church. On the right wing are the Sacraments of Baptism, Confirmation, and Penance; on the left the Consecration of the Priesthood, Marriage, and Extreme Unction. The motives and heads are speaking and animated, but the colouring is cooler, and the shadows less transparent, than usual.

Among the later works of the master the following specimens may be included:—Three narrow wing-pictures, with figures almost life-size, formerly in the Belgian monastery of Flemalle, now in the Städel Institute, and representing — 1st. The Virgin nursing the Child: the maternal expression is admirably given, and the white drapery of masterly modelling. 2nd. St. Veronica, with the Sudarium, on which the black but very noble countenance of Christ is impressed. 3rd. The Trinity: the Almighty holding the dead, stiff, and meagre body of the Saviour, which is admirably executed in chiaroscuro.

The fact that Rogier van der Weyden, like his master Jan van Eyck, also painted miniatures, is proved by the picture heading a Hennegau chronicle, by Jacques de Guise, in the Library of the old Dukes of Burgundy at Brussels. It represents Jacques de Guise presenting this MS. on his knees to Philip the Good of Burgundy, who is surrounded by his son Charles the Bold and the grandees of his court. In point of animation and individuality of heads, keeping, power of colour, and freedom of treatment, this miniature is one of the finest which this Belgian school produced.[1]

No painter of this school, the Van Eycks even not excepted, exercised so great and widely extended an influence as Rogier van der Weyden the elder. Not only were Hans Memling—the greatest master of the next generation in Belgium—and his own son, also named Rogier, his scholars, but innumerable works of art of other kinds were brought forth in the country,—miniatures, various block-books (the Biblia Pauperum, the Speculum Salvationis, the Song of Solomon), and old engravings,—in which his form of art is recognisable. It was under the auspices of this master that the realistic tendency of the Van Eycks pervaded all Germany; for it is quite intelligible that their more universal reputation only took place after the death of Jan van Eyck, when the great consideration in which Rogier van der Weyden was held throughout

[1] I was the first to recognise this as the work of Rogier van der Weyden. See 'Kunstblatt' of 1847, p. 177. Passavant and Count Léon de Laborde agree in my verdict. There is a lithograph of this miniature engraved in the 'Messager,' &c., of 1825.

Europe induced German artists to visit his atélier at Brussels. Martin Schongauer, for instance, the greatest German master of the 15th century, is historically known to have been a scholar of Rogier. The same may be said of the painter Frederick Herlen, who came from Nordlingen in Suabia, and his works equally show that he was taught by Rogier. I shall have occasion also to mention his influence in the works of other German artists.

HUGO VAN DER GOES, a painter born and resident in Ghent,[1] is mentioned even by Vasari, under the name of "Hugo d'Anversa," as a scholar of Jan van Eyck. He executed in Bruges, and probably during his years of apprenticeship, many of those large pictures in tempera[2] with which it was then the custom to adorn the walls of rooms. He was also employed on similar decorations[3] for the entry of Charles the Bold into Bruges, on occasion of his marriage with Margaret of York. Of his oil pictures, only the one mentioned by Vasari[4] is historically authenticated. This was ordered by Tommaso Portinari, agent for the house of Medici, in Bruges, for the high altar of the church of the Hospital of S. Maria Nuova at Florence, founded by his ancestor Folco Portinari, and now hangs on the left wall of the choir of that church. The middle picture represents the Adoration of the Shepherds, figures almost lifesize. In the centre is the Virgin kneeling, and taken almost in front; the tips of her fingers touching each other: on the right is Joseph; opposite to him three Shepherds adoring; also numerous angels. In the landscape background are the Annunciation to the Shepherds, and other figures. On the wings, which now hang on the opposite wall, are the portraits of Tommaso Portinari, and two little sons, presented by their patron saints, SS. Matthew and Anthony, and those of the founder's wife and daughter, presented by their patron saints, SS. Margaret and Magdalen. In the heads generally, which are portrait-like,

---

[1] Schaye's 'Archives de Louvain.'
[2] Vaernewyck's 'Historie van Belgis,' folio 132 b.
[3] 'Early Flemish Painters,' p. 128.
[4] Vasari, vol. iii. p. 268, Sienese edition.

a feeling of earnestness and severity is seen, and at the same time a deficiency in the sense of beauty. The drapery also has not only a sharp and snapt character, but the arrangement of the chief folds is stiff and hard. The scale of colour is clear, but at the same time it is the coolest I know by the scholars of the Van Eycks. The local flesh-tones are partly pale, partly a coolish red; the shadows grey. He is the earliest master of this school who painted blue draperies, broken with green, combining further with this mixture an orange colour, which is far from enhancing the general harmony. In other respects Van der Goes possesses the highest qualities of his school. His portraits are true to nature and animated, his drawing is good and conscientiously carried out in every part, and his execution is solid. A small portrait of this same Tommaso Portinari, by his hand, is in the Pitti Palace.

Of the other pictures usually given to this master, those most in accordance with his principal work at Florence are the following:—An Annunciation, in the Berlin Museum, No. 530, and the same subject in the Munich Gallery, Cabinets, No. 43. The red tone of the flesh in the last is caused by a modern glazing. All the other works attributed to his hand differ more or less from the example above described.[1]

Various important works, which he executed for the Netherlands, perished by the hands of the Iconoclasts; such as survived having disappeared since. He also occasionally drew cartoons as designs for glass-painting; one of which, in the church of St. James at Ghent, was so fine as to be pronounced by Van Mander a design by Jan van Eyck.[2]

Hugo van der Goes died in the year 1478, in the convent of Rooden, in the vicinity of Brussels, to which he had retired in his later years.[3]

GERARD VAN DER MEIRE, member of a family at Ghent which produced several painters.[4] In a document dating

---

[1] Some of the most important pictures wrongly given to him will be described in the notices on other masters.
[2] Van Mander, folio 127 b.
[3] Sweertius Monum. Sepulcral. Brabantiæ autor, 1613, p. 323.
[4] 'Catalogue of Antwerp Museum,' 1857, p. 24, &c.

from the end of the 15th century he is denominated a scholar of Hubert van Eyck:[1] considering, however, the fact of his having been admitted into the Brotherhood of St. Luke at Ghent in 1452, twenty-six years after Hubert's death, the truth of this statement may be questioned;[2] the more so as the only picture which tradition assigns to him by no means gives evidence in its favour;—we allude to a large altarpiece in a chapel of the cathedral of Ghent, the Crucifixion, a composition of thirty-one figures in the centre; on one wing the Raising of the Brazen Serpent, with seventeen figures; on the other, Moses striking the Rock, with twenty-six figures. These compositions show little skill; the motives are stiff and lame; the heads generally monotonous in character, and without modelling; the drapery with sharp breaks; the proportions too long; and the figures, especially of Christ and the thieves, very meagre. A few of the heads, however, such as the Virgin and the Centurion, are of elevated expression; and the rocky landscape, with the snow mountains in the distance, even beautiful. The clear and somewhat crude general effect is partly attributable to overcleaning. A few better preserved portions, such as the Moses, and the two male figures standing behind him, show the power and depth of the original colouring. Judging from the whole style, this painter has far more analogy with Jan van Eyck. This picture also could hardly have been executed earlier than 1480. The painter also is mentioned as late as 1474, as a member of the fraternity of St. Luke's. All other pictures attributed to him are of uncertain evidence. At all events, those in the Antwerp Museum bearing his name are not by him.

Cotemporary with Rogier van der Weyden, but it appears in less dependence on the style of the Van Eycks, there flourished in Haarlem a painter of the name of ALBERT VAN OUWATER, who founded there an original Dutch school. Van Mander[3] mentions him as a capital master, who par-

[1] 'Messager des Sciences et des Arts,' Ghent, 1824, p. 132.
[2] 'Catalogue of Antwerp Museum,' 1857, p. 24, &c.
[3] See folio 128 b.

ticularly excelled in the drawing of hands and feet, and in the rendering of drapery and landscape. His especial excellence in the latter department, and the fact of his being the founder of the very early school of landscape-painting in Haarlem, appear from the circumstance that several of his landscapes were preserved in the house of Cardinal Grimani[1] in the 16th century. Unfortunately, no picture by him can now be positively identified. A Pietà in the Imperial Gallery at Vienna,[2] which Passavant ascribes to the master,[3] is at all events an excellent picture of the early Dutch school: the composition is devoid of style, and most of the heads ugly, but of intense feeling and expression; the proportions are long, the execution of the utmost solidity.

A scholar of Ouwater, GEERTGEN VON ST. JANS, so called from a monastery of the Knights of St. John at Haarlem, where he resided, was, according to Van Mander, a very distinguished painter, whose talent was admired by Albert Durer on occasion of his visit to Haarlem. He died, however, at the early age of twenty-eight.[4] The only authenticated pictures by him are two wings of an altarpiece mentioned by Van Mander, and now in the Vienna Gallery,[5] Nos. 31 and 34,—the one representing a Pietà; the other, three legends referring to the bones of John the Baptist—namely, to their interment in the presence of Christ, the burning of them by Julian the Apostate, and the removal of some of them to the chief seat of the Knights of St. John, St. Jean d'Acre, in 1252. The heads have throughout a portrait-like appearance, and are animated, though, with the exception of some of the Knights of St. John, who are elevated in character, the forms are

---

[1] 'Anonimo,' by Morelli, p. 76, and p. 220, &c.
[2] There attributed to Jan van Eyck; Catalogue, p. 224, No. 10.
[3] 'Kunstblatt' of 1841, p. 39.
[4] Van Mander, folio 129.
[5] According to a short notice on the back of the second picture, they were presented to Charles I. by the States-General in 1635, and probably bought with other pictures by the Archduke Leopold, at the sale of the Royal Gallery. The Pietà was engraved by T. Matham, with a notification of the master's name.

ugly. The figures, which are smaller in proportion to the landscape than in most of the pictures of the Van Eyck school, are over-slender and meagre, but of very good drawing. A heavy brown tone predominates in the flesh. The darkening of the otherwise admirably modelled draperies renders the general effect somewhat heavy and spotty. The execution of detail, which extends equally to all accessories, is marvellous. Great attention is paid to the making out of the landscape. Judging from the style of art, these pictures may be assigned to about 1460-70.

The greatest scholar[1] of Rogier van der Weyden the elder was indubitably HANS MEMLING.[2] All that is known of him with historical certainty is, that in 1477-78 he was in great poverty;[3] that up to 1487, when perhaps under better circumstances, he laboured at his art in Bruges, and more especially for the Hospital of St. John in that town; and that he died before the year 1499.[4] In him the school attains the highest delicacy of artistic development; while at the same time, in feeling for beauty and grace, he was more gifted than any painter subsequent to Hubert van Eyck. Compared with the works of his master, his figures are of better proportions and less meagreness of form; his hands and feet truer to nature; the heads of his women are sweeter, and those of his men less severe; his outlines

[1] The name "Ausse," or "Havesse," both Italian perversions of the name which Vasari (Siena edition, vol. i. p. 177; vol. iii. p. 312; vol, xi. p. 63) mentions as a scholar of Rogier of Bruges, is without doubt intended for Hans Memling, which is further proved by the resemblance between the works of each.

[2] Also erroneously called Hemling. The reasons I have assigned on former occasions, and lastly in the 'Kunstblatt' of 1854, p. 177, for adopting the name Memling as the true reading, have been finally confirmed by a document published by M. Carton, at Bruges, in which it appears that in 1483 Master *Jan van Memmelinghe* took a scholar of the name of Passeier van der Meersch. The occurrence of the same name also in a catalogue of deceased painters closes the question. See 'Catalogue of Antwerp Museum' of 1857, p. 37.

[3] See Carton, 'Annales de la Soc. d'Emulation de Bruges,' tom. v., 2nde Série, No. xxxiv. p. 331, &c. The story of Memling's having been taken into the Hospital of St. John at Bruges, in the character of a sick soldier, after the battle of Nancy, which was first promulgated by the superficial and incorrect writer Descamps, is not entitled to any credit.

[4] In an index of the property of the Company of "Librariers" at Bruges, dated 1499, an altar-picture is thus described: "Ghemaect by der hand van *weylen* Meester Hans." See Carton, as last quoted.

are softer; in the modelling of his flesh parts more delicacy of half-tones is observable; and his colours are still more luminous and transparent. In aërial perspective also, and chiaroscuro, his works show an improvement. On the other hand, he is inferior to Rogier van der Weyden the elder in the carrying out of detail—for instance, in that of the materials of his draperies—and in the rendering the full brilliancy of gold. In the earlier time, when he occasionally worked on the same panel with his master,[1] the pictures of the two are difficult to distinguish. Of no other painter of this school have so many first-rate works descended to us. I proceed now to quote those which I personally know, in the order in which I believe them to have been executed:—

A small altarpiece in the Gallery at Munich, Cabinets, Nos. 48, 49, 54. The Adoration of the Kings, the centre picture, has decidedly the impress of the master; the wings, John the Baptist and St. Christopher, show, in their lengthy proportions and hard outlines, more the style of Rogier. Much of their original character, however, has been sacrificed by cleaning and over-paintings with glazing colours.

The Crucifixion, a large altar picture in the first room of the *Palais de Justice* at Paris. On the right of the cross is the Virgin fainting, supported by a woman, and with another woman, John the Baptist, and St. Louis; on the left, John the Evangelist, St. Denys, and Charlemagne. The building of the old Louvre and the Tour de Nesle, seen in the landscape, show that the painter executed this picture in Paris. The somewhat feeble drawing of the feet, and even of the hands, assigns this work to his early time. The heads, however, are masterly, and some of them of intense feeling.[2]

A small Diptych, with a rich composition of the Crucifixion on one side, and the donor, Jeanne de France,

---

[1] Margaret of Austria possessed a small altarpiece, the centre of which was by Rogier, and the wings by Memling. See 'Inventaire des Tableaux, &c., belonging to this princess, by Count de Laborde, p. 24.
[2] See further my article in 'Kunstblatt,' 1847, p. 186.

LARGE ALTARPIECE by Hans Memlinc of the LAST JUDGMENT At Dantzig

daughter of John, 2nd Duke of Bourbon, with her patron saint St. John the Baptist, and the Virgin and Child in the sky, on the other. A picture of miniature-like delicacy. In possession of the Rev. John Fuller Russell, Greenhithe, Kent.[1]

The wings of a smaller altarpiece, with the portraits of the founders, man and wife, and their patron saint. Formerly in Miss Rogers's collection, now belonging to Vernon Smith, Esq.; of great truth, very harmonious and warm tone, and admirable execution of the landscapes.

The Last Judgment, in the church of Our Lady at Dantzic; a large altar-picture.[2] The composition of this work, given in the annexed woodcut, is far richer and better arranged than that of the before-mentioned pictures of the same subject by Rogier, though his influence is still very perceptible. In the centre, on a large and brilliant rainbow, which touches the horizon, sits the Saviour, with the severe expression of the judge. A red sword is suspended on the left, a lily-branch on the right of his head; a golden ball (painted) hangs in the air as His footstool, and reflects the nearest objects. He is clothed in a red mantle fastened on the breast, and falling over the lap in beautiful folds. Above him hover four angels with the instruments of the Passion, and below him are three others with the trumpets of the Last Judgment. At his right kneels the Virgin, with an expression of mercy and maternal intercession; on the left is John the Baptist, and on both sides are ranged the Apostles—fine figures, with heads of great excellence, though of different degrees of beauty. In the lower half of the picture stands St. Michael, clad in golden armour, so bright as to reflect in the most complete manner all the surrounding objects. This figure is slender, but colossal as compared with the rest, and he seems to be bending earnestly forward; a splendid purple mantle extends from his shoulders to the ground, and he has large wings composed of glittering peacock's feathers. He holds the balance of justice in

---

[1] 'Galleries and Cabinets of Great Britain,' p. 285.
[2] First rightly attributed to him by Professor Hotho.

which the souls of men are weighed; the scale with the good rests on the earth, but that with the souls which are found wanting quickly mounts into the air: a demon stands ready to receive the Damned, and towards this scale St. Michael directs the end of a black staff with a rich handle, which he holds in his right hand. Around is a plain, out of which, as well as in the depth of the landscape background, the dead are rising from their graves; on one side are the Blessed in the act of ascending to heaven, on the other the Damned. Close behind the archangel, an angel and a demon are contending for a soul. Inexpressible anguish, grief, and despair bordering on madness, are depicted in the various groups of the Damned of every age and sex, who are crowded together on the left of St. Michael. Grotesque figures of demons, some of them decked out with coloured butterfly wings, are mixed up with the lost souls, and are driving them with demoniac glee into the abyss. On the right all is holy peace, and the countenances of the Blessed already express a foretaste of approaching bliss. The left wing represents Hell; between steep and craggy rocks flames are raging, and sparks and smoke burst forth, while the Damned are hurled downwards in frantic terror, and are tormented in various ways. Here a pair of lovers, fastened together with fine cords, are suspended between the teeth of a bat-winged fiend; there another stands on the throat of a falling woman, whilst with his hooked fork he drags a priest after him. Some ape-like demons are pulling down the lost souls by the hair, whilst others bear their prey upon their backs and torment them with firebrands. The variety of attitude and the boldness of the foreshortening are masterly—the gradations of tone given to the one prevailing expression of sorrow and despair are surprisingly varied. In the right side-picture is a splendid Gothic portal, adorned with columns, and through its open gates the Blessed are passing in. Subjects from the Old and New Testament in bas-relief embellish the façade and ceiling of the high-arched vestibule, whilst angels of great beauty clothed in rich vestments stand on the balustrades and on the two balconies of the building, singing, playing, and strewing flowers. Clouds surround the building on both sides. As the Blessed draw near, they are received and guided by angels, who clothe them in splendid garments. Peter, with the keys of Heaven, stands at the gate, and beckons to the elect. His figure is majestic. A host of priests have already ascended the steps. Here too we find the same variety of countenances, all apparently copied from nature, and the same truth which we have noticed in representing grief and despair, but here the predominant expression is that of humble astonishment and tranquil joy. The execution of detail, the depth and variety of expression in the heads, the force of colouring, and the modelling and rendering of every portion, are admirable. Judging from the numbers 67 on a tombstone, it is probable that this picture was painted in 1467. This is not only the most important by Memling that has descended to us, but one of the chefs-d'œuvre of the whole school.

King David and Bathsheba, in the Gallery at Stuttgart. The figure of Bathsheba is remarkable as the only one life-sized and undraped by Memling. The drawing and modelling are very successful for the period.

A small altarpiece in St. John's Hospital at Bruges, No. 16 : the centre represents a Pietà; the inner sides of the wings, the donor, Adrian Reims, a brother of the Order, and his patron saint, St. Adrian, with St. Barbara ; and the outer, SS. Helena and Mary Egyptiaca. The proportions are still too long, the heads very tender and of deep feeling. This has unfortunately lost something of its power and colour by cleaning.

A small altarpiece, also in St. John's Hospital, No. 3 : the Adoration in the centre, with the portrait of the founder, a brother of the Order ; the wings containing the Nativity and the Presentation in the Temple ; the outer sides John the Baptist and St. Veronica. This is the only instance where, besides the date 1479, the name of the painter occurs in full. The arrangement of the composition shows the influence of the often-quoted picture by Rogier van der Weyden in the Gallery at Munich. The heads are more delicate and sweet, but less earnest and grand—the execution freer, but less solid. This gem has also partially, but very seriously, suffered by cleaning.

The Annunciation, inscribed 1482, in possession of Prince Radzivil, at Berlin. A picture of very original conception and marvellous delicacy. Also injured in parts.

The Virgin and Child, with angel and donor, in the Vienna Gallery; there called Hugo van der Goes.

A large altarpiece, in the collection of the Academy at Bruges, No. 9; the centre containing St. Christopher, with SS. Egidius and Benedict at his side; on the inside of the wings, St. William, with the donor and his sons, and St. Barbara, with the donor's wife and her daughter; on the outside, in chiaroscuro, John the Baptist and St. George. Inscribed with the date 1484. All the heads very true to nature. In that of St. Christopher the moment of spiritual enlightenment is admirably expressed. The infant Christ is the feeblest figure. Of the saints, SS. Egidius, Benedict, and Barbara are refined in heads, and of mild expression, but St. John the Baptist is the most successful. Here the original excellent modelling is still in good preservation.

A small altarpiece, at Chiswick, seat of the Duke of Devonshire. The Virgin and Child, with the donors, Lord and Lady Clifford, with their children, adoring, and their patron saints Agnes and Barbara. On the wings, SS. John the Baptist and Evangelist. This picture, which is mentioned by Horace Walpole as by Jan van Eyck, is in every respect one of the finest works of the master.

St. Christopher, at Holker Hall, Lancashire, seat of the Duke of Devonshire. Very like the same saint on the wing-picture at Munich, but incomparably better rendered, and in excellent preservation. Erroneously called Albert Durer.

Portrait of an aged Canon of the Order of St. Norbert, in the Museum at Antwerp, No. 35. In the expression of simple and intense devotion this admirably-executed picture makes an impression on the mind as of an historical work.

Portrait of a member of the family of Croy, also in the Antwerp Museum, No. 36. Of uncommon truth and masterly rendering, in a somewhat cool tone.

Small altarpiece, in the collection of Rev. Mr. Heath, vicar of Enfield. The dead Christ bewailed by the Virgin, St. John, and the Magdalen. On the wings, St. James the Major and St. Christopher. The body of the Christ is very meagre; the expression of sorrow in those around fine and intense, and the colour very clear and powerful.[1]

The Marriage of St. Catherine, in St. John's Hospital.[2] The Virgin is placed in the centre, on a seat under a porch, with tapestry hanging down behind it: two angels hold a crown, with much grace, over her head; beside her kneels St. Catherine, her head one of the finest by Memling, on whose finger the beautiful infant Christ places a ring of betrothal; behind her is a charming figure of an angel playing on the organ; and further back St. John the Baptist, with a lamb at his side. On the other side kneels St. Barbara, reading; behind her another angel holds a book to the Virgin; and still deeper in the picture is St. John the Evangelist, whose figure is of great beauty, and of a mild and thoughtful character. Through the arcades of the porch we look out, at each side of the throne, on a rich landscape, in which are represented scenes from the lives of the two St. Johns. The panel on the right side contains the Beheading of the Baptist, and at a distance a building, with a glimpse into the landsape, in which are again introduced events from the life of the saint. On the left is St. John the Evangelist, on the island of Patmos, about to write in a book, and looking upwards, where the vision of the Apocalypse appears to him—the Lord, on a throne, in a glory of dazzling light, encompassed with a rainbow. In a larger circle are the host of the Elders, with a solemn character of countenance, in white garments, and with harps in their hands; opposite to them, among flames and mystic forms,

[1] 'Cabinets and Galleries of Great Britain,' p. 313, &c.
[2] Inscription and date, 1479, are apocryphal. See article by me in ' Kunstblatt' of 1854, p. 178.

is the four-headed beast. Below all is a landscape, in which men are fleeing, and seeking to conceal themselves among the rocks, whilst the four horsemen, in the swiftness of their might, are bursting on them. Finally, the sea, with its deep green crystal waves, reflects the entire subject, the rainbow, the glow of the sky, the mystic figures, and the forms on the shore, and thus unites these various objects into one great whole. On the outside of the wings are four saints, two male and two female, and kneeling before them are men and women in religious vestments. The whole forms a work strikingly poetical, and most impressive in character; it is highly finished, both in drawing and in its treatment as a picture, and is, with exception of the outer sides, which are over-cleaned and badly retouched, in tolerable preservation. This picture approaches very near to that in the Academy at Bruges; the better drawing, namely, of the feet, shows that it was painted somewhat later, probably in 1486.

A votive picture, somewhat larger than the centre compartment of the last-mentioned work, is in possession of Count Duchâtel of Paris. The head of the Virgin, who is enthroned in the centre with the Child, agrees closely with that of the last we have described. On the right are the men and youths, under the protection of John the Baptist; on the left the women and maidens, under that of another male saint; both parties in considerable numbers, and kneeling. It is greatly to be regretted that the flesh-parts of the Virgin, the Child, and of all the female figures in this fine picture, have become pale through over-cleaning. The work itself has great affinity with that of the Marriage of St. Catherine. The architecture of the background is of masterly treatment. This is one of the many pictures of this school which had made its way to Spain. It was there purchased by the same General Armagnac who possessed the small altarpiece by Rogier van der Weyden the elder, as described.

The Marriage of St. Catherine, in the Strasburg Gallery, there called Lucas van Leyden.

Of about the same time may be the Virgin and Child

THE RELIQUARY OF ST. URSULA.
By Hans Memling. In the Chapel of St. John's Hospital at Bruges

adored by Nevenhoven, the donor of the picture, dated 1487, in St. John's Hospital. The Virgin is of portrait-like character; the portrait itself of the utmost animation. The forms are decided, the colouring not so luminous as usual.

Portrait of a man with joined hands, dated 1487, in the Uffizi.

The Virgin and Child, in the collection of H. R. H. the Prince Consort at Kensington. This agrees so entirely with the last described picture that it must have been painted in the same year.

Portrait of a man with an open book in his hands, called St. Benedict, in the Uffizi.

A small picture, in the possession of the sculptor and medal die-sinker, M. Gatteau, at Paris, represents the Virgin seated with the Child in a cheerful hilly landscape, and placing the ring on the finger of St. Catherine, who closely resembles the same saint in the picture at Bruges. Next her are SS. Agnes and Cecilia, opposite SS. Ursula, Margaret, and Lucy. In the sky are three angels playing the flute. This picture is a marvel of beauty in the small heads, of great tenderness, feeling, delicacy of execution, and clearness of golden tone; and also in the rarest preservation.

To the same time belongs a small picture in the gallery of the Uffizi, the Virgin and Child, and two angels playing. This is very lovely in the heads, and of great glow of colour.

In St. John's Hospital is also the celebrated Reliquary of St. Ursula, see woodcut, a shrine about four feet in length; its style and form are those of rich Gothic church architecture, such as we often find adopted for the larger depositories of relics. The whole exterior of this casket is adorned with miniatures in oil by Memling. On each side of the cover are three medallions—a large one in the centre, and two smaller at the sides. The latter contain angels playing on musical instruments; in the centre, on one side, is a Coronation of the Virgin; on the other, the Glorification of St. Ursula and her companions, with two figures of Bishops. On the gable-end, in front, are the Virgin and

Child, before whom two sisters of the hospital are kneeling. At the other end is St. Ursula, with the arrow, the instrument of her martyrdom, and the virgins, who seek protection under her outspread mantle. On the longer sides of the Reliquary itself, in six rather large compartments, enclosed in Gothic arcades, is painted the history of St. Ursula. According to the legend, this saint was the daughter of an English king, who, with an innumerable train of companions, her pious lover, and an escort of knights, set out, by the command of God, on a pilgrimage to Rome. On their journey home they suffered martyrdom at Cologne. The subjects of each picture separately are—1. The landing at Cologne, in the beginning of the journey; Ursula, clothed in princely purple, and her hair braided with pearls, steps from the boat; whilst a virgin at her side carries a casket of jewels. With pious humility she bends kindly to the virgins who receive her. The view of Cologne is taken from the place, so that the principal buildings are easily recognised. 2. The landing at Basle. The princess, with part of her followers, has landed, and goes towards the old city. Two more ships approach the landing-place. In the background we see the Alps: here then the virgin host have already set out on their land journey. 3. The arrival in Rome. Pope Cyriacus receives the princess, who is followed from the mountains by her train. Youthful knights, with Conan, the lover of St. Ursula, at their head, accompany them. The church is thrown open, and in it some are in the act of receiving baptism, whilst others are at confession. 4. The second arrival at Basle. In the background are the gates of the city, from which the princess and her companions are advancing to the river. In the foreground the embarkation has already begun. In a large boat sit the pope between two cardinals, and St. Ursula between two virgins, engaged in devout discourse. 5. Commencement of the martyrdom. The camp of the Emperor Maximin, the enemy of the Christians, is seen on the banks of the Rhine; two ships are just putting in. Wild hordes, with clubs, swords, and bows, surround the boat: the youths on the

DEATH OF ST. URSULA.

One of the Paintings by Memling on the Reliquary of St. Ursula at Bruges.

banks fall beneath the weapons of the foe. A portion of the virgins in the ships, singing holy songs, await the shower of arrows with tranquil resignation; whilst others, as well as their priestly companions, are already stricken. 6. The death of St. Ursula, see woodcut: she and two virgins are in the tent of the emperor; a soldier has already aimed his arrow at her; she awaits death with cheerful submission to the will of God; some of the bystanders look on with interest, others with savage indifference. These little pictures are among the very best productions of the Flemish school. The drawing in these small figures is much more beautiful than in the larger examples by the same master: there is nothing in them meagre, stiff, or angular; the movements are free; the execution and tone of colour, with all its softness, very powerful; the expression in the single heads, of the highest excellence.

The six pictures on the cover are not so fine, and evidently executed by another hand.

Finally, a similar picture (see frontispiece) of a long form, now at Munich, and formerly in the Boisserée collection, deserves especial notice. It represents the principal events of the life of Christ and the Virgin (the seven joys and the seven sorrows of the Virgin); not in separate compartments, but as one great whole, united in a landscape, with an endless number of subordinate events: a whole world of life, and joy, and sorrow—all executed with wonderful grace and beauty.

A picture of similar size and refinement of art, representing all the scenes of the Passion from Palm Sunday to the recognition of Christ by the Disciples at Emmaus, in a number of separate groups, is in the Royal Gallery at Turin. It is probably the same which, according to Vasari, was founded by the Portinari family in the church of S. Maria Nuova, and afterwards came into the possession of Cosmo I., Duke of Tuscany.

A large altarpiece, with double wings, in the cathedral at Lubeck. On the outer sides of the first pair of wings is the Annunciation in chiaroscuro. The two figures are of slender and elevated character, the heads of great sweetness and refinement, and the draperies of excellent taste and very careful modelling. On the inner sides of these wings are SS. Blaise and Egidius, and, on the outsides of the next pair of wings, John the Baptist and St. Jerome. These four figures are among the finest specimens of the master's art. The inner sides of the last-mentioned wings are connected in subject with the centre picture. The right wing contains scenes from the life of Christ, from the Passion in the Garden to the Bearing of the Cross, which proceed from the background and terminate in the foreground. The centre picture shows the Crucifixion, including the two thieves—a composition of 35 figures. This is the most important representation of the subject which this school offers, full of original motives, and of admirable carrying out. On the left wing is the Entombment in the foreground, and in the middle distance and background the subsequent events, terminating with the Ascension. The date, 1491, on this picture, is the latest known on any picture by Memling, and shows him in his greatest perfection.[1]

I cannot say to what period the travelling altarpiece of Charles V., at Madrid, may be assigned, as I have never seen it. Passavant mentions it as a particularly fine work. The centre represents the Adoration of the Kings, the wings the Nativity and the Presentation in the Temple. The figures are about one-third life size.[2]

It is not surprising that an oil-painter who excelled in works on so small a scale should have been also an excellent miniature-painter. This is proved by the miniatures in the well-known Breviary bequeathed by Cardinal Grimani to the Library of St. Mark's at Venice. This relic, which is the richest and most beautiful specimen of early Netherlandish miniature-painting, was executed, I am convinced, for Mary of Burgundy, daughter of Charles the Bold.[3]

ROGIER VAN DER WEYDEN THE YOUNGER was the son and

---

[1] See article by me in the 'Kunstblatt' of 1846, No. 28.
[2] See Passavant's 'Christliche Kunst in Spanien,' p. 130. Cavalcaselle considers some portions of this altarpiece to be too feeble for Memling, and attributes them to a scholar: 'Early Flemish Painters,' p. 269.
[3] See article by me in the 'Kunstblatt' of 1847, No. 49.

scholar of the elder Rogier.[1] But beyond this we know nothing more than that he earned much by his art, was very benevolent, and that he died in Brussels in 1529, at a great age, of the so-called English sweating sickness.[2] He adhered throughout to the style of his father, to whom, in his earlier works, he approaches very near. Later, however, his proportions are not so long, his forms fuller, and his drawing more delicate. This applies especially to his hands and feet. On the other hand, he has little feeling for beauty, and, while his motives are occasionally the reverse of beautiful, his heads are frequently of a portrait-like and tasteless character. In general, he shows greater softness of outline, his flesh-tones are lighter and more broken, his lights of a cooler red, his shadows clearer, and his treatment, finally, broader. He appears especially to have devoted himself to the representation of the sufferings of Christ, and to the sorrow of the Virgin and the Disciples; almost every picture that is with any probability assigned to him belonging to this class of subject. His mode of conception must have been very congenial to the religious feeling of his period, for old copies of his works abound.

His principal work is one originally executed for the church of our Lady " Darbuyten," at Louvain, now in the Sacristy of S. Lorenzo of the Escurial—a Descent from the Cross, consisting of ten life-sized figures.[3] The Virgin has fainted at the right of the body of Christ, which is supported by Nicodemus and Joseph of Arimathea, and is upheld herself by one of the Maries and by St. John. At the feet of Christ, in passionate but ungraceful gestures, is the Magdalen. Behind the group of the Virgin is

---

[1] Sandrart distinctly says this ('Teutsche Academie,' p. 66) in his notice on oil-painting.
[2] Van Mander, plate 129 b, f. Because Van Mander in some respects confounds him with his father, Wauters, and Cavalcaselle after him, deny his existence. With these opinions I cannot agree. See my reasons in 'Kunstblatt' of 1847, p. 170, &c. Passavant also (see above-mentioned work, p. 134, &c.), and Hotho, are of my opinion.
[3] As I have not seen this picture myself, I adopt Passavant's description (see as before). I was, however, at one time inclined to agree with Wauters, who assigns this to the father (see p. 171), an opinion shared by Cavalcaselle (p. 185, &c.), who thinks that the specimen in the Gallery at Madrid is the original.

another woman weeping and covering her face with a cloth. The animation and highly-wrought pathos, the careful drawing of every portion, and especially of the Saviour's body, and that of the hands, have at all times rendered this picture the object of great admiration. Two of the cotemporary repetitions of the picture are also by the painter; one in the Madrid Gallery, No. 1046,[1] the other, dated 1488, in the Berlin Museum, No. 534.

Of the other works in Spain attributed by Passavant to him,[2] I only cite a small Crucifixion in the Gallery at Madrid, No. 466, with the false monogram of Albert Durer.

The Descent from the Cross, a small altarpiece, with wings, in the Liverpool Institution, No. 42,[3] is of the earlier time of the master, still hard in outline, but of great pathos.

Another Descent from the Cross, in the collection of the Prince Consort at Kensington, No. 36. The great warmth of colour, and the stricter carrying out, are again proofs of his early time.

An Ecce Homo, and a Mater Dolorosa, both at Kensington; half-length figures; the Virgin of elevated and intense feeling.[4]

An Ecce Homo, in the collection of Mr. Green, of Hadley, near Barnet, very like the foregoing.

An Entombment, in the collection of Sir Culling Eardley, at Belvedere, near Erith, of his earlier time. Of great energy of feeling and colour.[5]

A Descent from the Cross, in the Royal Gallery at Naples; a very rich and beautiful composition, purchased about twenty years ago.

The head of a Woman weeping, in the Gallery at Brussels, of much truth and depth of expression.

---

[1] 'Christliche Kunst in Spanien,' p. 134.
[2] Ibid. p. 137.
[3] 'Treasures of Art,' &c., vol. iii. p. 235.
[4] 'Treasures,' &c., vol. iv. p. 226, &c.
[5] Ibid. p. 278.

CHAPTER III.

THE VAN EYCK SCHOOL, UP TO THE PERIOD OF ITS TERMINATION.

1490—1530.

AT the period we now enter upon, very various tendencies come to view. In some instances the severer forms of the immediate scholars of Jan van Eyck are continued. A remarkable example of this is afforded by GOSWIN VAN DER WEYDEN, a descendant of Rogier van der Weyden the elder,[1] born 1465, who, according to the Book of the Guild of Painters at Antwerp, belonged to that body from 1503 to 1530,[2] and is chronicled as having painted an altarpiece for the church of Tongerloo,[3] representing the death of the Virgin, now in the Gallery of Brussels, No. 593. The heads are but little attractive, but some of them good in expression, and the flesh-tones are somewhat heavy and grey, which may be also said of the general effect, with exception of the transparent landscape. The rendering of the detail—namely, of the rich garments—is, in care and mastery, still worthy of the early school. Unfortunately, the upper part of the picture has suffered. The portraits of the donor, the abbot Arnold Streyter, and of other members of his family, on the wings, are meritorious. Judging from this picture, it is evident that another in the same gallery, No. 397, representing the same subject, is by the same hand, as well as several others of less importance. A third, also of the same subject, in the collec-

[1] See further in article by me, 'Kunstblatt,' 1847, p. 171.
[2] 'Catalogue of the Museum of Antwerp,' 1857, p. 30.
[3] A Latin inscription on the picture, given by Van Hasselt in his 'Recherches sur Trois Peintres Flamands,' Anvers, 1849, informs us that Goswin van der Weyden, at the age of seventy, as seen by his portrait in the picture, executed this work for Arnold Streyter, abbot of the church of Tongerloo, in imitation of the art of his ancester Rogier, known by the name of Apelles, in the year of our Lord 1535.

tion of the Prince Consort at Kensington, may, in my opinion, be adjudged to the same master.

Like Rogier van der Weyden the elder, Hans Memling also exercised in his time an influence on many painters, whose great and often successful aim it was to give worthy expression to the religious feeling of the day. They are characterised by the usually pleasing, and sometimes beautiful though monotonous, forms of their female heads, and by a character of art which, united with a sentiment of pathos, is generally more delicate and tender than energetic. The general tone of colour becomes brighter and cooler in the flesh-tones, and tending to violet; aërial perspective is somewhat more studied, and the execution is softer, though still minute in detail, especially in the rendering of landscape backgrounds, on which more stress is laid. The masters most worthy of note in this direction are the following:—

LIEVEN DE WITTE[1] and GERHART, both of Ghent, who, together with Memling, executed the miniatures in the Grimani Breviary at Venice. But, although there is every evidence that two painters of remarkable skill, though of obviously more modern character, united with him in this work, yet there is not the slightest help given to us in deciding which pictures are by Lievin and which by Gerhart. Judging, however, from the Adoration of the Kings in this Breviary, the best hand of the two may be considered the author of a number of very excellent oil pictures.[2] In these he shows himself to be an artist of fine feeling for pleasing character, truth of form, grace of movement, and with a tenderness of execution which in his earlier pictures is rendered in a brownish tone, and in his later by cooler tints. In the drawing of the nude he is, with the exception of the well-drawn hands, weak.

[1] See 'Anonimo,' by Morelli, p. 77, who calls him Lievin d'Anversa. I agree, however, with Passavant ('Kunstblatt,' 1841, p. 39), who considers him identical with the Lievin de Witte from Ghent, mentioned by Van Mander.

[2] Passavant's assumption that the author of these works is Lievin de Witte ('Kunstblatt,' 1841, p. 39) does not rest on sufficient critical evidence.

Among the works to which we allude is an important altarpiece in the Gallery at Rouen, the Virgin enthroned with the Child, surrounded with several female saints, and four angels of great beauty playing on musical instruments. In front are the admirable portraits of the founder, and of several women. Of great warmth and power of tone, and very careful execution.

The Descent from the Cross, formerly under the name of Mabuse in the collection of the King of Holland, now in that of Mr. Dingwall, London.

The Baptism of Christ, in the Academy at Bruges, No. 10, erroneously entitled Memling. On the inner sides of the wings are the Founder and his Family, with two patron saints; on the outer sides a woman kneeling with her daughter, in adoration. The elevated character of the heads and the highly developed landscape render this picture very attractive. Unfortunately, it is in parts much over-cleaned.

The Crucifixion, in the Berlin Museum, No. 573, hitherto erroneously called Mabuse. The expression of sorrow in the women is true and earnest, and the rich landscape of delicate cool tones, and of unusual aërial perspective.

The Adoration of the Kings, in the Gallery at Munich, First Room, No. 45, there wrongly ascribed to Jan van Eyck. A beautiful picture, unfortunately disfigured with partial retouches.

The same subject, only smaller, and corresponding in the simplified composition with that in the Grimani Breviary. The pendant to it, a Pietà. Both of the greatest tenderness of heads, and of delicate cool tones. Both also in the possession of Mr. Green, of Hadley, near Barnet.[1]

The Root of Jesse. Below, St. Anna enthroned, with two angels playing on musical instruments. At her feet the Virgin and Child. On one side the Founder with St. Anthony; on the other his wife with King David. Above them rises the genealogical tree upon a gold ground. Very

[1] 'Treasures of Art,' &c., vol. ii. p. 459.

delicate and refined in heads and general feeling, and painted in a cool, silvery tone. In the collection of Sir Culling Eardley.[1]

A totally different aspect of this master is seen in two pictures in the collection of the Academy at Bruges,[2] Nos. 20 and 21; the one representing King Cambyses condemning the corrupt Judge; the other, the culprit undergoing the punishment. Both were formerly in the Town Hall at Bruges. The first of the two is dated 1498. On a close comparison with the Baptism of Christ above mentioned, the same character of heads, landscape, and of touch, is seen. The far more powerful tone of colour may be attributed to the fact of these pictures not having been over-cleaned. The truth and detail with which the punishment is rendered shows the realistic feeling of the age in a very degenerate form.

JAN MOSTAERT, born at Haarlem 1474; died in the same place in 1555 or 56. In style of feeling and in development of landscape this painter shows a close affinity to the preceding master. Besides treating subjects of a religious order with an elevation and purity of feeling remarkable at so late a period, he was also, according to the evidence of Van Mander, a very popular portrait-painter. The only authenticated pictures also by him are two portraits, distinguished by warmth and clearness of tone, and a certain softness in the careful treatment, which are in the Museum at Antwerp.[3] Another picture by him, in the same gallery, No. 69, represents the Virgin and Child, surrounded by four angels, three prophets, and two sibyls —the latter with scrolls, on which are inscribed their prophecies regarding the Incarnation The features are pleasing, though generally portrait-like. As the most

---

[1] 'Galleries and Cabinets,' &c., p. 279, &c.

[2] In the catalogue of that collection, of 1845, these pictures are attributed to Anton Claeyssens, who died only in 1613.

[3] Judging from the armorial bearings upon them, these two portraits were erroneously taken for those of Jacqueline of Bavaria, died 1436; and of her husband, F. van Borselen, died 1470.

important work, in my opinion, by the master, I may mention a Virgin—represented as the Mater Dolorosa—in the church of Notre Dame at Bruges.¹ Of the pictures by him in England, I will only instance the Entombment, belonging to the Rev. Mr. Heath, at Enfield.²

JAN GOSSAERT, called JAN VAN MABUSE, from his native town of Maubeuge, where he was born probably about the year 1470. This painter, up to the period of his departure for Italy, which may be with probability assigned to the year 1513, belongs to the style of the later Van Eyck school. Till then he was unquestionably one of the first painters of the school, displaying great knowledge of composition, able drawing, warm colouring, an unusual mastery in the management of the brush, and a solidity in the carrying out of every portion such as few of his cotemporaries attained. His only deficiency consists sometimes in a certain coldness of religious feeling. His principal picture belonging to this period, and one inscribed with his name, is an Adoration of the Kings, at Castle Howard, the seat of the Earl of Carlisle; a rich composition, of considerable size, and admirable preservation.³ Next to this may be placed a picture representing the legend of the Count of Toulouse who journeyed as a pilgrim to Jerusalem. The event is represented with the utmost truth.⁴ Now in the possession of Sir John Nelthorpe, at his seat, Scawby, Lincolnshire. Finally, two pictures in the Antwerp Museum—the Virgin lamenting, with St. John, and other women, and the righteous judges, a group of horsemen; and, finally, the children of Henry VII. at Hampton Court—are worthy of notice.

Towards the end of the 15th century, in consequence of the transfer of commerce from Bruges to Antwerp, this latter city long became the centre of art, and especially of

¹ See notice on other works by this master in my article in the 'Kunstblatt' of 1847, No. 55.
² 'Treasures,' &c., vol. iv. p. 313. In the same work I have also given an account of other pictures by this master.
³ 'Treasures,' &c., vol. iii. p. 320, &c.
⁴ 'Galleries and Cabinets,' &c., p. 507.

Netherlandish painting. Here it is that we find QUENTIN MESSYS, or, more rightly, MASSYS, the greatest Belgian painter of his time. He was born probably in 1460, of a family of painters long resident in Antwerp; and died in 1530 or 31. Before becoming a painter he followed the trade of a blacksmith. He distinguishes, popularly speaking, the close of the last and the beginning of the next period. A number of pictures, representing sacred subjects, exhibit, with little feeling for real beauty of forms, such delicacy of features, beauty and earnestness of feeling, tenderness and clearness of colouring, and skilfulness of careful finish, as worthily recall the religious feeling of the middle ages, though at the very termination of them. In his draperies also we observe a tenderly broken tone, of the utmost charm, peculiar to himself. At the same time, in the subordinate figures introduced into sacred subjects, such as the executioners, &c., he takes pleasure in rendering coarse and tasteless caricatures. In subjects also taken from common life, such as money-changers, occasionally a loving couple, or a frightful old woman, he uses his brush with evident zest, and with great success. The pictures of his later time are also in this respect distinguished from those of most other Netherlandish painters, inasmuch as his figures are three-quarter life size, or full life size. His most important work is an altarpiece, painted originally for the Joiners' Guild as an ornament of their chapel in the Cathedral,[1] but now in the Museum of Antwerp, No. 50, which he undertook in the year 1508. The centre represents the Body of Christ after the descent from the Cross, mourned over by his friends and the holy women: the Virgin, sunk in the deepest grief, is supported by John; two venerable old men, Joseph of Arimathea and Nicodemus, sustain the head and the upper part of the body, whilst the holy women anoint the

---

[1] See Sir Joshua Reynolds's Journey in Flanders, Work, vol. ii. p. 288, who says, "There are heads in this picture not exceeded by Raphael, and indeed not unlike his manner of painting portraits: hard and minutely finished. The head of Herod, and that of a fat man, near the Christ, are excellent."

wounds of the Saviour. The figures are nearly the size of life, and so arranged that each appears distinct and significant. On the right wing, the head of John the Baptist is placed on the table of Herod, whilst musicians —absurd and disagreeable figures—play on an elevated platform. On the left wing is John the Evangelist in the caldron of boiling oil, and the executioners, who, with brutal jests, stir up the fire whilst the spectators are disputing. This picture is highly finished in execution, full of reality, and profound in the development of individual character. In the mourning figures of the centre division a fine pathetic feeling is expressed in all its various degrees.

Other pictures by him, of some importance, are an altarpiece in St. Peter's, at Louvain (in a side chapel of the choir), which represents the Virgin with the Child, and the holy personages of her family; on the side wings are scenes from the life of her parents.

A picture in the Berlin Museum, in which the Virgin is seated on a throne, kissing the infant Christ. In front, on a small table, are articles of food, well painted, No. 561. This already indicates a reference to earthly wants, which, like the more animated movement of the whole picture, would have been opposed to the feelings of the older masters; but the workmanship of the throne, particularly the agate pillars, and their embossed capitals of gold, is executed entirely in the serious style of earlier art.

Among his most original and attractive pictures are the half-length figures of Christ and the Virgin. These must have been very popular in his own time, for he has left several repetitions of them. Two heads, of this class, of marvellous delicacy of feeling, colouring, and expression, are in the Museum at Antwerp, Nos. 42 and 43. Two others, of equal beauty, only that the Christ is somewhat heavier in tone, have passed from the collection of the King of Holland into the National Gallery. Considering the rarity of his pictures representing this class of religious subjects, I may cite a Virgin and Child of his earlier period, in the hands of the Rev. Mr. Russell, Greenhithe, Kent; a Mater Dolorosa, belonging to the Rev. Mr. Heath, Enfield; and a Virgin and Child adored by SS. Catherine and Margaret, a picture of the rarest delicacy, in the possession of Alexander Barker, Esq., and erroneously designated as an Albert Durer.[1]

The most celebrated of his subject-pictures is that known by the name of the Two Misers, at Windsor Castle, of which a woodcut is subjoined. But I am not disposed to consider this example, or others I know of the same composition, as the originals, but rather as repetitions, and chiefly by his son Jan Massys.[2] A genuine and signed picture of this class is that of a Changer of Money weighing gold, of the utmost delicacy, in the Louvre, No. 279.[3]

CORNELIS ENGELBRECHTSEN, born at Leyden 1468; died 1533. His only authenticated work is an altarpiece in the Town Hall at Leyden: the centre picture representing the Crucifixion; the wings, the Sacrifice of Abraham, and the Brazen Serpent, in their well-known symbolic meaning; and the Predella, the Restoration of the race of Adam by the Atonement of Christ. In this picture the master departs much from the painters preceding him. The heads of his women, of a longish oval form, and with straight, pointed noses, have a pleasing but monotonous type. The flesh-tones are of a warm-brown colour, but heavy, the outlines hard, the effects crude, and the drawing moderate.

In Bruges the style of religious expression in art was preserved in the early Netherlandish form even up to the end of the 16th century, though with greatly inferior feeling and skill, by various masters. The most consider-

---

[1] Regarding other and chiefly earlier works, see my notice in the 'Kunstblatt' of 1847, p. 202.

[2] A close examination in the Manchester Exhibition, in 1857, convinced me of this fact.

[3] I have become convinced of the genuineness of this picture, in contradiction to my formerly-expressed opinion, 'Künstler und Kunstwerke in Paris,' p. 544.

THE MISERS.
A Painting by Quentin Massys at Windsor Castle.

able painter of this class is PETER CLARISSENS, by whom is a large work, dated 1608, representing the Virgin and Child, the Almighty with angels, and the founder, in the Pottery Hospital at Bruges.

A totally different course was taken by HIERONYMUS AGNEN, commonly called HIERONYMUS BOSCH, from his native place Herzogenbusch; died 1518. He distorted the fantastic element which already existed in the school into a form of the ghostly and demoniacal, in which he showed great talent, and became the founder of a tendency which, as we shall see, was followed by other painters. A Last Judgment by him is in the Museum at Berlin, No. 563; a Temptation of St. Anthony, in the Antwerp Museum, No. 41. He adopted the early technical process, and his execution was sharp and careful.

LUC JACOBEZ, called LUCAS VAN LEYDEN, born 1494; died 1533. Scholar of Engelbrechtsen, an artist of multifarious powers and very early development. He painted admirably, drew, and engraved. He followed that realistic tendency in the treatment of sacred subjects which Hubert van Eyck had so grandly tracked, and lowered it greatly from its previous elevation. His heads, for instance, are generally of very ugly character. At the same time his form of art found sympathy in the feeling of the period; and by the skill with which it was expressed, especially in his engravings, attracted a number of followers. In scenes from common life he is frequently full of truth and delicate observation of nature, showing occasionally a coarse humour. Pictures by him are very rare. One of the most important, at least in size, though not a pleasing specimen, is a Last Judgment, in the Town House at Leyden. The old arrangement is adopted in this picture: in the centre is the Judgment itself, and on the wings Heaven and Hell; the composition is strikingly poor and scattered; the expression of heavenly joy singularly flat and weak: in the figures of those risen from the dead there is little more than a careful study of the nude. It is only in a few instances, and those chiefly in the representation of Hell, that the figures or heads have any striking expression. On the contrary, two figures of St. Peter and St. Paul, on the outside of the wings, have great dignity, both in attitude and drapery. A small and interesting picture, a company of men and women at a cardtable, see woodcut, is in the possession of the Earl of Pembroke, at Wilton House ; the outline is spirited, but rather sharp. A beautiful and finely-painted work, of the year 1522, forms part of the Munich Gallery, Cabinets, No. 151. The composition consists of the Virgin and Child, with Mary Magdalen, and a man praying at their side. Both the style and the activity of this artist are far better estimated by his numerous engravings, of which Bartsch cites no fewer than 174,[1] some of which show considerable power. The following are some of the most remarkable : Esther and Ahasuerus, No. 31; the Adoration of the Kings, No. 37; Christ shown to the People, No. 71; the Crucifixion, No. 74; the Return of the Prodigal Son, No. 78; the Dance of the Magdalen, see woodcut, No. 122; and the Milkmaid, No. 158. The "Eulenspiegel," No. 159, is more celebrated for its great rarity than for its artistic merits. The Temptation of St. Anthony, No. 117, see woodcut, is remarkable as the work of a boy of fifteen.

JOACHIM PATINIER, or more properly DE PATINIR, of Dinant. He became member of the guild of painters at Antwerp in 1515, and is supposed to have been born in 1490, and to have died in 1545. In his earlier time he painted historical pictures in the taste of the later Van Eyck school; in his later time in that of Lucas van Leyden. By his habit of rendering his figures very small in proportion to his landscape background, he became the founder of landscape painting, as a separate study, in the Netherlands. His earlier pictures are marked by a warm tone; his later pictures are cool. His earlier landscapes exhibit a fantastic form of conception, are overladen with details, and are hard and crude, and of very defective perspective; in

---

[1] 'Le Peintre Graveur,' vol. vii. p. 331.

A CARD PARTY
By Lucas van Leyden   At Wilton House

1. "DANCE OF THE MAGDALEN" From an engraving by Lucas van Leyden in the British Museum. [p. 145, No. 2

From an Engraving by Lucas van Leyden
in the British Museum

his later works a more truthful rendering of accessories predominates, and more feeling for general effect.

As an example of his earlier style as historical painter, I may mention the Virgin with the Seven Sorrows, holding the stiff and meagre body of the Saviour on her lap, in the Museum at Brussels. His Flight into Egypt, in the Museum at Antwerp, No. 75, and his Crucifixion, executed at a later time, in the collection of the Prince Consort at Kensington, exhibit him more as a landscape painter.

HERRI DE BLES—born 1480, at Bouvignes; died, probably 1550, at Liege—showed a similar tendency in art. Upon the whole, the forms of his art are more modern, and his colouring cooler. In his earlier period, however, he is more nearly related to Patinier in colour; in his later time he becomes long in his proportions, mannered in motives, and dark and cold in colouring. The circumstance of his adopting an owl for his monogram procured him the name of *Civetta* in Italy. A male portrait, with landscape background, in the Museum at Berlin, No. 624, is of his earlier time. A Crucifixion, in the collection of the Prince Consort at Kensington, is a particularly good work of his middle period. An Adoration of the Kings, signed with his name, in the Munich Gallery, Cabinets, No. 91, belongs to his latest productions.

All these masters, from Quentin Massys downward, belong, it is true, in colouring and technical characteristics, and also partially in mode of conception, to the later branches of the Van Eyck school: at the same time in many respects they form the transition to the masters of the following epoch.

CHAPTER IV.

THE GERMAN SCHOOL, IN ITS TRANSITION FROM THE STYLE OF THE PRECEDING PERIOD TO THE REALISTIC TENDENCY.

1420—1460.

WHILE Art in the Netherlands had been carried, by means of the brothers Van Eyck, to so high a development of the realistic tendency, the Germans in all essentials had continued to adhere to the style of the former period, only admitting the influence of their neighbours as far as it served to impart greater perfection to their own modes of expression. The same noble type of head, and feeling of spiritual purity, which distinguished their conceptions of the Virgin, and of many of the saints, was retained, and fuller and more natural forms superadded. In some heads, however, a more portrait-like and often-repeated physiognomy was introduced, and one which a thick and large nose rendered by no means beautiful. The proportions of the human figure, which before this epoch were too long, became truer to nature, the separate forms fuller and more correct, and the motives freer. The rendering also of the quality of the draperies—such as gold brocades, velvets, &c.—was introduced; but, on the other hand, the sharp and angular breaks only occasionally admitted. Weapons, crowns, and such articles became more individual in character. Neither in colouring nor execution, it is true, was the same power, and truth, and modelling, or the same rendering of minute detail, aimed at as by the Van Eycks; at the same time their colouring, which shows much feeling for harmony, became more vigorous, their modelling more powerful, and their execution softer than in the preceding period. Least of all did they copy the Netherlandish painters in the close delineation of the backgrounds, but contented themselves with a general indication, retaining the gold ground principally for the sky.

Back of
Foldout
Not Imaged

At this time the school of Cologne distinguished itself before every other in Germany, and attained, in the person of STEPHAN LOTHENER, of Constance, called MEISTER STEPHAN, whose later prime dates from 1442 to 1451 (the year of his death), its highest form of originality. Although there is no proof of his having been a scholar of Meister Wilhelm, yet it is obvious that he formed himself from him. This appears especially in his small Madonna, with the hedge of roses, in the Museum at Cologne, which, in accordance with M. Hotho,[1] I consider the earliest work we know by him. Here much of the form of art and style of feeling belonging to Meister Wilhelm is seen, only combined with greater animation and truth of nature. Next in date to this I place a colossal Virgin and Child, which has been recently discovered and which is now in the collection of the Archbishop of Cologne. This picture shows a rare union of grandeur and mildness of expression. But the most authentic, and at the same time the principal, work of the master is the well-known picture[2] which was originally painted for the chapel of the Hôtel de Ville, but has been for many years in a chapel of the choir of Cologne Cathedral. It consists, as the accompanying woodcut shows, of a centre-piece with wings, on which last, when closed, is seen the Annunciation. In the inside, on the centre picture, is the Adoration of the Kings—the Virgin is seated on a throne, in a dark-blue mantle lined with ermine; at her side are the two elder kings kneeling; the younger one and the attendants stand around. On the

[1] 'Malerschule Hubert's van Eyck,' vol. i. p. 398.
[2] That the statement in Albert Durer's Journal of his having paid two silver pennies for the unlocking of the picture refers to this cathedral picture may be now accepted as certain. In addition to this, M. Merlo (see 'Die Meister der Altcölnischen Schule,' Cöln, 1852) has recently discovered in old registers, of the years 1442 and 1448, the name of a painter, *Stephan Lothener*, of Constance, who owned a house in Cologne; also, in the protocols of the Council-chamber, it appears that the same was twice chosen by his guild as councillor, and that he died in 1451, the last year of his office. It being thus proved that this Stephan Lothener was a painter of great consideration in his time, I quite agree with that profound art-critic, M. Sotzmann (see 'Deutsches Kunstblatt,' 1853, No. 6), that he was identical with the Meister Stephan mentioned by Albert Durer, and therefore the painter of the cathedral picture.

side panels are the patrons of the city—on the right St. Gereon, in his armour of gold and surcoat of blue velvet, surrounded by his men-at-arms; on the left St. Ursula, with her escort and her host of virgins.

This picture is remarkable for its solemnity and simple dignity of composition, for the depth and force of tone, and the beauty and harmony of its colour, which, in spite of the usual disadvantages of tempera, here approaches in splendour the effects of Venetian oil-painting. The arrangement of the figures is grand and simple, and the execution of the rich details finished with the greatest care. A feeling of ideal grace and beauty is breathed over the whole work, and is just as conspicuous in the loveliness of the Virgin with the divine Child as in the serene dignity of the kings who worship, and the youthful fulness of form and tenderness of expression in the holy virgins and the knights who accompany them.

Judging from the strong influence of the Van Eyck school seen in this work—from the individuality of many of the heads, the rendering of the materials of the draperies, and the sharp and angular breaks of the folds in the Annunciation—it may be considered to have belonged to the latest and maturest time of the master. This is corroborated by a work in the Darmstadt Museum—the Presentation in the Temple, bearing date 1447—which, although nearly related to the cathedral picture, is less developed in form of art. England also possesses at least one specimen of this rare master, of his somewhat earlier time, representing SS. Catherine, Matthew, and John the Evangelist, in the collection of the Prince Consort at Kensington, No. 22.

Among the number of pictures executed in part under the direction of Meister Stephan, and partly under his influence, and which are now distributed principally in the galleries of Cologne and Munich, and in the chapel of St. Maurice at Nuremberg, the compartments of a former altar-picture belonging to the Abbey of Heisterbach, near Bonn, are particularly remarkable. The single figures of saints in the Munich Gallery, Cabinets, Nos. 1 and 2, approach nearest in character to Meister Wilhelm; the Annunciation, Visitation, Nativity, and the Adoration of the Kings, Cabinets, Nos. 3, 6, 7, 8, show, on the other hand, in the rounder forms of the heads and in other respects, the prevailing influence of Meister Stephan. The same may be said of two pictures in the Berlin Museum—the Adoration of the Cross and of the Kings, Nos. 1205 and 1206.

Very characteristic of the course taken by the Cologne school of painters at this time is the altar-picture, the centre-piece of which is the Last Judgment, in the Museum at Cologne.[1] Although the character of Meister Stephan is still somewhat retained in the ideal figures of Christ, the Virgin, John the Baptist, &c., yet the early refinement of religious feeling is wanting in them, and also in the otherwise admirably-rendered saints on the wings, in the Munich Gallery, Cabinets, Nos. 10 and 14. At the same time, in the figures of those risen from the grave, and especially in those of the condemned, as well as in the accessories, a decidedly realistic feeling prevails. Side by side with the most surprising freedom of motives and truth of expression, are seen disgusting exaggerations and great coarseness of form, expression, and colour. According to the costume worn by the excellently-portrayed founder, the execution of the picture may be assigned to about 1450-60. How long, in some instances, the early tendency was still retained is shown by a Crucifixion, dated 1458, in the Museum at Cologne, and also by a Virgin and Child with two saints, and the numerous family of the founder, dated 1474, in the church of St. Andrew in the same city.

Next in succession to Cologne, the town of Nuremberg, judging from the few specimens preserved, seems to have done most in the way of painting at this period, although not a single name of a master has descended to us. I pro-

[1] I agree with M. Hotho, 'Malerschule Hubert's van Eyck,' vol. i. p. 413, in not attributing this work to Stephan Lothener, as others have done.

ceed to mention a few of the most notable pictures. On a pier in the nave of the church of St. Sebaldus is a Crucifixion with the Virgin and St. John; on the inner sides of the wings SS. Barbara and Catherine; on the outer sides Christ on the Mount of Olives, and the portrait of the founder; and on a pair of stationary wings St. Erasmus and another Bishop.

An altarpiece, formerly on the high altar in the church of the Chartreuse, now in the church of our Lady. The centre contains the Crucifixion, the Annunciation, and the Resurrection of Christ; the wings the Nativity and the Apostle Peter. This may be a somewhat later work by the same hand.[1] It shows many features taken from nature, and careful modelling. The master also, who painted an obituary picture—the Nativity—dated 1430, dedicated to the memory of Frau Waldburg Prünsterin, in the church of our Lady at Nuremberg, deserves notice.

An altarpiece, dedicated to St. Theocarus, in the church of St. Lawrence, containing the Transfiguration, the Miraculous Draught of Fishes, and four events from the life of the Saint. Though still essentially adhering to the forms of the former epoch, this picture shows a respectable stage of advancement.

Finally, a Virgin and Child in the Sacristy of the church of St. Laurence, dedicated to Margaretta Imhof (died 1449) and her son, is remarkable for the elevation of conception in the head of the Virgin, for the far advanced individuality of the portraits, and for good modelling in a transparent tone.

It is evident also that in Suabia, at this period, there was a successful effort to combine a more natural treatment of detail with the ecclesiastical forms of conception belonging to the former epoch. This appears especially in an altar-picture, dedicated to the Magdalen, at Tiefenbronn, executed in 1431 by LUCAS MOSER. The wings contain events from the legends of the Magdalen, and also

---

[1] Hotho, vol. i. p. 478, &c.

from those of Martha and Lazarus; the predella represents Christ, and the five wise and five foolish Virgins. The modelling in a warm colour of the pleasing heads is very careful, and hands and feet are of striking truth of nature.[1]

As regards the neighbouring territory of Alsatia, a similar stage of painting is shown by a Bible with miniatures, completed in 1428, and now in the Royal Library at Munich. The portrait of a Bishop, for whom it was executed, is already very individual. One JOHANN FREYBECHK, from the convent of Konigsbrück, in Alsatia, mentions himself at the close of the MS. as its author; whether he took part in the pictures it contains would be difficult to say.[2]

A large Missal, executed in the years 1447-8, for the Emperor Frederick III., and now in the Imperial Library at Vienna, No. 1767, gives the same evidence as regards the art of painting in Austria.[3]

CHAPTER V.

THE GERMAN SCHOOLS WHICH ADOPTED THE REALISTIC TENDENCY OF THE VAN EYCKS.

1460—1500.

IN consequence of the visits of German painters to the studio of Rogier van der Weyden the elder, at Brussels, a fact which has become accidentally known in the persons of Martin Schongauer and Frederick Herlen, the whole style of the Van Eycks, including their oil painting, was, from the year 1460, introduced into the different schools of Germany, under the form practised by Rogier. At the

[1] Hotho, vol. i. p. 460, &c.
[2] See article by me in 'Kunstblatt' of 1850, p. 323.
[3] Ibid., p. 324.

same time the character peculiar to the Germans asserted itself very decidedly here. Upon the whole, as regards ecclesiastical art, they display a far greater richness of invention, and also a higher conception of the distribution of figures in space, conformable to the laws of style. In the heads of sacred personages the loftier and more ideal beauty of the former period is frequently retained. On the other hand, where spiritual degradation is intended to be represented, they degenerate into far ruder and more unpleasing caricature than the Netherlanders, and also into greater meagreness of limb, especially of the hands. As to the draperies, the angular snapt folds, first seen in Jan van Eyck's pictures, found many followers, and were even further carried out in the same style. In the following respects also they may be considered inferior to the Netherlandish masters. In feeling for grace of movement, their motives having something angular and awkward; in feeling for colour, their colouring being sometimes cruder, sometimes duller and heavier; also in feeling for chiaroscuro and in the rich details of their backgrounds; that conception of a picture as a whole, as regards the effect of light, which Jan van Eyck possessed, not having been aimed at by the Germans until very late. Thus we find either the gold grounds long retained, or the indication of space merely rendered in the homeliest and most general manner. In management of the touch, also, their inferiority is manifest; the outlines remain harder, and the execution of detail by no means so developed. Altogether, painting may be considered to have been in so far, in many instances, a more mechanical art in Germany, from the fact that even great masters, according to the commission given them, sometimes took little or no part in the execution of their works, assigning it to their more or less gifted scholars. This explains the surprising inequality in the merit of pictures signed even with the name of a master, or showing other marks of authenticity.

Together with the general comparison which I have entered into here, the particular differences between the various schools of Germany and those of the Netherlands must also be taken into account.

THE SCHOOL OF COLOGNE AND THE LOWER RHINE.

In point of power of colouring and solidity of technical execution, the masters of this part of Germany approach very nearly to the Van Eyck school, though possessing slight peculiarities of their own.

In Cologne we are met by an anonymous painter, who, according to inscriptions on his pictures, flourished from 1463 to 1480, and who, from one of his chefs-d'œuvre, once in possession of M. Lyversberg of Cologne,[1] representing the Passion in eight compartments, has received the name of the Master of the Lyversberg Passion.[2] It is true that most of the compositions are arbitrary in arrangement, the effect of colour hard, and the figures of the guards of repelling coarseness; but, on the other hand, the head of Christ is dignified, and there is an elevated pathos in many of the other heads. Another altarpiece by the same hand, in the church of Linz on the Rhine, dated 1462, containing scenes from the life of the Virgin, the Passion, and the portrait of the founder, the Canon Tilmann Jael, shows a more advanced stage of art. In some of the pictures, for instance in the Coronation of the Virgin, a more successful general effect is apparent; the Virgin herself also is of a lofty character of physiognomy. In another large altarpiece, at Sinzig on the Rhine, with the Crucifixion as centre piece, he again appears to more advantage. But his best work, as respects composition, beauty and originality of motives, and animated and truthful heads of striking expression, is a Descent from the Cross, dated 1480, in the Museum of Cologne. (The wings

[1] Now the property of Mr. Baumeister, at Cologne.
[2] According to the arbitrary designation given by the Messrs. Boisserée to the works of this master in the Gallery at Munich, and in the chapel of St. Maurice at Nuremberg, they still continue to bear the name of Israel van Meekenen.

are a later addition.) Of his numerous specimens in the Munich Gallery, an altarpiece with wings, on which are the Apostles and John the Baptist, Cabinets, Nos. 18, 21, 22, and the Marriage and Coronation of the Virgin, and Joachim and Anna at the Golden Gate, Nos. 20, 31, 32, is the most remarkable. On the last-mentioned number appears the animated portrait of the founder of the whole series, an ecclesiastic of the name of Johann de Mechlinn. Another and also good picture belonging to this series is in the collection of the Prince Consort at Kensington, No. 23. The master we have been describing had a large number of followers, but one and all so far inferior and more mechanical, that it is not necessary to instance a single example of the many pictures by them in the Cologne Museum and elsewhere. They show a decided degeneration of the school to the close of the 15th century.

Another master of very notable merit is the painter of the picture on the high altar of the church at Calcar; the chief subject of which is the Death of the Virgin.

In the adjacent district of Westphalia a style of art was developed, which, in many respects, succeeded in combining the ideal feeling of the last epoch with the more realistic tendency which succeeded it. The most remarkable specimens of this kind are the relics of a large altarpiece in the former monastery of Liesborn, near Münster, dated 1465, which were long in the possession of M. Krüger at Minden, and have been for some years in the National Gallery. They consist principally of the half-length figures of six saints, and of the subjects of the Annunciation and Presentation. The heads are attractive for the purity of religious feeling and the expression of peace which pervade them, with which the clear and cheerful colouring is in unison. As regards truth of nature in the rendering of parts, however, they bear no comparison with the cotemporary Netherlandish painters. The pictures of a Soest master, who has signed his name as "Jarenus" on a Pietà in the collection of the Earl of

Pembroke at Wilton House, show the fusion of the
qualities of both schools to less advantage. The centre
picture of a large altarpiece by this master, in the Berlin
Museum, No. 1222, representing several scenes from the
Passion, is especially overladen and confused. The most
successful in composition, colour, and execution, are four
pictures belonging to one wing of this altarpiece, No.
1233, viz. the Annunciation, the Nativity, the Presentation, and the Adoration of the Kings. At a later period
the school of Westphalia takes a lower place than the
other schools of Germany; as examples of which I may
mention a large altar-picture by the brothers VICTOR and
HEINRICH DÜNWEGGE, in the parish church of Dortmund,
the centre of which contains the Crucifixion, and the inner
sides of the wings the Adoration of the Kings, the Virgin
and Child, and the Mother of Zebedee's children, with her
sons, and other relatives of the Virgin; a subject which
is called in Germany "a Holy Kith-and-Kin picture."
Although the picture is known to have been painted in
1523, it shows in its gold background, its hard and crude
colouring, and in the style of treatment, quite the form of
art belonging to the 15th century. At the same time
many of the heads are very animated, and of warm and
vigorous colour. A Crucifixion nearly related to the
above-mentioned pictures, only with a landscape background, is in the Berlin Museum, No. 1194.

A similar absence of participation in the progress of the
period is betrayed, as regards Lower Saxony, by the painter
JOHANN RAPHON VON EIMBECK, by whose hand is an altarpiece, dated 1508, in the choir of Halberstadt Cathedral.
The centre represents the Crucifixion—a rather over-
crowded composition—the wings, the Annunciation, Adoration of the Shepherds, of the Kings, and the Presentation.
The heads are lively and various in character, but at the
same time somewhat coarse; the colouring of the flesh
rather heavy and untrue, and cold in the lights.

In the department of the Middle Rhine, at Frank-
fort-on-the-Maine, we meet with the painter CONRAD FYOLL,

the notices of whom extend from 1461 to 1476.[1] He has something tender and mild in his heads, and a delicate, silvery, and, upon the whole, cool tone in his flesh. A large altarpiece in the Städel Institute at Frankfort is a principal picture by him. The centre contains the family of St. Anna, the wings the Birth and Death of the Virgin. A smaller altarpiece, with St. Anna and the Virgin and Child in the centre, No. 575, and SS. Barbara and Catherine and the Annunciation on the wings, No. 875 a, b, are in the Berlin Museum.

By far the greatest German painter of the 15th century was MARTIN SCHONGAUER, commonly called MARTIN SCHÖN, who flourished on the Upper Rhine. He derived his origin very probably from an artist family at Colmar,[2] where he at all events resided. Nothing certain is known regarding the date of his birth, though it probably occurred about 1420.[3] He visited the atélier of Rogier van der Weyden the elder, at Brussels,[4] and died at Colmar on the day of the Purification of the Virgin in 1488.[5] His pictures are exceedingly rare, and by no means suffice to show us the original qualities of this master in their full extent. Fortunately the deficiency is supplied by a number[6] of his engravings from compositions of his own, in which he appears as an artist of great powers of invention in the department of ecclesiastical art, both in the representation of single figures, and also frequently in that of very animated compositions. In this respect, as well as in his feeling for beauty and spirituality, in which he greatly refined and individualised the tendency of the former period, he

---

[1] See Passavant, 'Kunstblatt,' 1841, No. 101.

[2] See the communication of M. Hugot, keeper of the Records at Colmar, in the 'Kunstblatt' of 1841, p. 59. I doubt whether this painter took his origin from Ulm. See Passavant, 'Kunstblatt' of 1846, p. 107.

[3] This is rendered probable, according to Passavant (see same 'Kunstblatt'), by a portrait of the master in the collection of the Academy at Siena, inscribed, "Hipsch, Martin Schongauer, Maler 1453," and representing a man of about thirty-three years of age.

[4] See letter from Lambert Lombard, the painter, to Vasari, in Gaye's 'Carteggio,' vol. iii. p. 177.

[5] See Hugot, 'Kunstblatt,' 1841, p. 59.

[6] Bartsch (vol. vi. p. 103, &c.) instances ninety engravings.

THE ANNUNCIATION
From an Engraving by Martin Schongauer in the British Museum.

From an Engraving by Martin Schongauer
in the British Museum

page 131. No

ST. ANTHONY TORMENTED BY DEMONS
An Engraving by Martin Schongauer which Michael Angelo is said to have copied
From the British Museum.   page 131, No

excels his great master Rogier, and attained a European reputation. Among his most admirable engravings are the Death of the Virgin (Bartsch, No. 33); the Bearing of the Cross (No. 21); the Annunciation, see woodcut No. 1; those of the Passion (Nos. 9-20), of which see woodcut No. 2, of Christ appearing to the Magdalen; the Wise and Foolish Virgins (Nos. 77-86). Fantastic subjects he treats very rarely, though with great energy, as in his plate of the Temptation of St. Anthony (Bartsch, No. 47), see woodcut, of which Vasari testifies that Michael Angelo made a pen copy in his youth. Occasionally this great master exhibits a sound vein of humour in scenes from common life; as, for instance, in his Donkey Driver (Bartsch, No. 89). He is powerful in drawing, although his limbs, and especially his hands, are meagre. The principal and admirable motives of his drapery are more or less disturbed by the sharp and angular breaks. His pictures show a warm, powerful, and transparent colour. His execution, in the outlines, however, is more draughtsman-like than that of Rogier, and fails in the truth and fusion which distinguished his. Nor did Martin Schongauer lay so much stress on the making out of the background, occasionally even he resorts to a gold ground. Of the number of pictures attributed to him in various public and private galleries, the majority are by other painters after his engravings. The following alone I am inclined to consider genuine:—

The Death of the Virgin, a small picture, from the Gallery of the King of Holland, afterwards in the collection of M. de Beaucousin at Paris, and now in the National Gallery. I believe this to be the earliest work we know by him. It is of the rarest beauty, but at the same time displays, in conception, glow of colour, and exactitude of execution, something of the elder Rogier van der Weyden; belonging therefore to a time when the influence of that master was still fresh upon him. Martin Schongauer's peculiar type of head is, however, already very distinctly visible in those of the Virgin, and of the Almighty, who appears in the sky.

But his most important picture, and the one which, by comparison with his engravings, is the best authenticated, is that of the Virgin in the enclosure of roses in St. Martin's church at Colmar. The Virgin—fully the size of life—is seated on a grass-bank, with the Child on her lap; her features are noble and pure in expression, and her red drapery has a very luminous effect. The two angels suspending the crown over her head are very graceful; the hedge of roses, with the birds nestling in it, completes the cheerful naïve impression of the picture; the flesh-tones are clear and warm, and the painting of great finish.

Next to this we may place two wings from the monastery of St. Anthony at Isenheim, now in the Civic Library at Colmar; the inner sides containing the Child adored by the Virgin, and St. Anthony the Hermit, with the donor; the outer, the Annunciation. The ideal and slightly longing expression shows an affinity to Perugino; the Virgin in both the pictures has finely arched eyelids, and features of unwontedly regular beauty. The Child, on the other hand, which is of masterly modelling, and obviously painted closely from nature, exhibits a very forcible realistic feeling. The colouring is warm, and, in the dignifiedly conceived St. Anthony, of great depth. The treatment is somewhat broad, and, in the rendering of the outlines, a more draughtsmanlike hand is distinctly seen.

Slighter works, but of spirited character, are the Descent from the Cross, and the Entombment, part of a series of pictures in the same place; the other twelve of which were executed partly by a tolerably skilful artist, and partly by one of a more mechanical character.

A good though not important work is the youthful David with the head of Goliah, returning surrounded by warriors, and greeted with music by the maidens. In the Munich Gallery, Cabinets, No. 145.

One small but certain work by this rare master, the Virgin with the Child in a landscape, is in England, in the collection of the Prince Consort at Kensington, No. 30.¹

Another picture, representing Pilate asking the Jews whether he shall deliver to them Christ or Barabbas, in the collection of Mr. Green, of Hadley, near Barnet, agrees in so many respects with Martin Schön's engraving, that, in spite of the feebleness of the colour, I am inclined to consider it his work.²

FREDERICK HERLEN is a master who acted very decidedly upon the character of Suabian art. A cotemporary record of the year 1467, which states that, owing to his knowledge of the Netherlandish practice, he was admitted gratuitously to the privileges of a burgher in the town of Nördlingen,³ and the striking imitation of well-known works by Rogier van der Weyden the elder in his pictures, leave no doubt of his having learned his art from that master. His real significance seems, indeed, to have consisted in his thus importing the art of the Van Eyck school into Upper Germany, for he neither displays any particular originality of his own, nor does he attain to the feeling and conscientious execution of his model. Suffice it, therefore, to mention a few of his chief works: as, for instance, the separately-placed wings of an altar in the church at Nördlingen, dated 1462,⁴ representing the Annunciation, the Visitation, the Adoration of the Kings and of the Shepherds, the Presentation in the Temple, the Circumcision, the Flight into Egypt, and the youthful Christ teaching in the Temple. The wings of the high altar in the church at Rothenburg on the Tauber, chiefly the same subjects, but less delicately painted.⁵ Pilate showing Christ to the People, dated 1468, in the church at Nördlingen;⁶ and finally, in the same church, the Virgin enthroned with the Child, with the kneeling figure of Herlen himself with four sons presented by St. Joseph, and his wife with five daughters presented by St. Mar-

[1] 'Galleries and Cabinets of England,' p. 225.
[2] 'Treasures of Art,' vol. ii. p. 459.
[3] 'Kunstwerke und Künstler in Deutschland,' vol. i. p. 325.
[4] Ibid., p. 347, &c.   [5] Ibid., p. 324, &c.   [6] Ibid., p. 353.

garet—doubtless the offering of the painter. This picture, which bears date 1488, shows that his art had become coarser in character. He died 1491.

The painters of the Suabian school retained in a higher degree than any other German school the style of art thus introduced by Frederick Herlen. This is evidenced by their realistic conception in its nobler form, by their feeling for warm colouring of flesh, by a harmonious carrying out of other colours, by their soft and fusing, more than draughtsmanlike use of the brush. Nor in their drapery did they fall into such numerous, arbitrary, and sharp breaks as are shown in the productions of the other provinces of Germany. On the other hand, they may be distinguished from their Netherlandish models in many instances by a greater feeling for spirituality and beauty in their sacred personages, by a cooler scale of colour—a cool brown-red and a full green being favourite hues in their drapery—and, finally, by a less close rendering of detail. At the same time two chief divisions may be distinguished within the Suabian school; the one, which is the richest as to number of painters, had its seat at Augsburg, and early developed a decidedly realistic tendency; the other, belonging to Ulm, showed a purer and tenderer feeling for religion, and more sense of beauty.

In Augsburg the family of HOLBEIN for several generations especially come before us. The earliest of the family, HANS HOLBEIN THE GRANDFATHER, is known by a picture of the Virgin and Child seated upon a grass bank, signed " Hans Holbein, C. A. (Civis Augustanus), 1459." The development of the realistic tendency which this picture already exhibits is very striking. The heads have a thoroughly portrait-like look, and the body of the Child is decidedly and very carefully painted from nature. The modelling is very precise. Only in the folds of the drapery are seen the softer forms of the earlier period. On the other hand, the landscape is already well understood; and three birds—a bullfinch, a goldfinch, and a chaffinch, are given with great truth of nature.¹ The picture was originally painted for the Fugger family for St. Anne's church at Augsburg, and is now at Mergenthau, the former summer residence of the Jesuits near the city, the property of M. Samm. Another picture by the same, signed with his name, and dated 1499, representing the Coronation of the Virgin in the centre, and the Nativity, and the Beheading of St. Dorothea, at the sides, is in the Royal Gallery at Augsburg—the best place where the masters of this school can be studied. Strange to say, though so much later in time, it shows an earlier style of art and less study of nature than the other picture, though otherwise of considerable artistic value.²

His son, HANS HOLBEIN THE FATHER, was born probably about 1460, and died in 1518. He is the chief representative of the decided realistic style in this school, which, in point of truth of feeling and warmth and transparency of colour, he carried to a high degree of mastery. Sometimes, too, we find an expression of peculiar dignity, and, in his female heads particularly, a pleasing grace united with surprising softness and finish in the technical execution. At the same time, the fantastic element already mentioned in the works of Martin Schongauer is here visible in a still higher degree, and an inclination to violent and exaggerated character in the figures, especially of the adversaries of the faith, which occur in his numerous pictures of the sufferings of the saints. Frequently among these adversaries there appears a pale figure, with a sharp, pinched, Italian physiognomy, in a green hunting-suit, and a cock's feather in his hat. His principal work is a large picture, executed in 1504, with scenes from the legendary life of St. Paul, and above, Christ crowned with thorns, in the Augsburg Gallery. The painter has introduced himself and his two sons, Ambrose and a little boy of about six years old, afterwards the far-famed master, Hans

[1] 'Deutsches Kunstblatt' of 1854, p. 192.
[2] See further in my 'Kunstwerke und Künstler in Deutschland,' vol. ii. p. 16, &c.

Holbein. No other picture exhibits this master so truly in his force and his feebleness.[1] Next to it in value are eight pictures painted in 1502, now in the Munich Gallery,—four from the life of the Virgin, Nos. 6, 9, 14, 19, and four from the Passion, Nos. 5, 8, 15, 20. Many other pictures by him are found in the chapel of St. Maurice at Nuremberg, in the Städel Institute at Frankfort, and in the Basle Museum. Two excellent chiaroscuro panels, representing saints, and bearing the name of the painter, are also in the Gallery at Prague.

SIGISMUND HOLBEIN, brother of the preceding, was also an excellent painter.[2] This is seen by a small picture in the Landauer Brüderhaus at Nuremberg, the Virgin and Child, which bears his name.

After the family of Holbein, that of Burgkmair plays the most important part in the art of Augsburg. THOMAS BURGKMAIR, mentioned in public documents in the year 1489, may be considered first. Though possessing a certain ability and energy, he is inferior to the Holbeins. His figures are short, his flesh-tones of a heavy brown, his outlines hard. In the Augsburg Cathedral are two pictures, presented in 1480, on the columns of the choir: one is Christ conversing with St. Ulric, the other the Virgin with St. Elizabeth of Thüringen, and the wife of the donor, the Burgomaster Walther. The Gallery at Augsburg also contains a large picture with the Martyrdom of St. Stephen, with St. Lawrence, and scenes from the Passion.[3]

The chief representative of the other branch of the Suabian school, which flourished in Ulm, is BARTHOLOMEW ZEITBLOM, born probably about the middle of the 15th century, and, according to known notices of him, living still in 1517. In technical qualities he appears to have formed

---

[1] See 'Kunstwerke und Künstler in Deutschland,' vol. ii. p. 19, &c., and Passavant, in the 'Kunstblatt' of 1846, p. 183.

[2] 'Kunstwerke und Künstler in Deutschland,' vol. i. p. 217.

[3] See Passavant, 'Kunstblatt' of 1846, p. 186, and my last-quoted work, vol. ii. p. 33, &c.

himself from Frederick Herlen, and also to have partially imitated him in composition. But in the elevated and spiritual tendency of his art, as well as in the style of his flesh painting, it is obvious that Martin Schongauer exercised no small influence over him. Though inferior to him in sense of beauty, he has a power of attraction in the simplicity, purity, and earnestness of his religious feeling, which few possess. In this respect he may be called the most German of all German painters. In some instances he even rises to the sublime. At the same time his limbs are still, for the most part, meagre and inflexible, and a favourite type of head is too often repeated; this, however, is rendered with so much care, and with such warm, transparent, and, in his later pictures, refined colouring, as to rival the works of Quentin Massys. Finally, his broad drapery, devoid of the sharp and angular character, has a peculiar and harmonious combination of colour.

Among his early works are two wings of an altar from the monastery of Roggenburg near Ulm, in the collection of M. Abel of Ludwigsburg,[1] containing figures of the Virgin, the Magdalen, SS. Helena and John. The wings of an altar-chest, with carved-work in the centre, dated 1488, show already a more original development. They were formerly in the village of Hausen near Ulm, and are now in the possession of Professor Hassler at Ulm: they represent SS. Nicholas and Francis, and Christ on the Mount of Olives. The master, however, appears in the highest form of his art in the wings of a large altarpiece painted for the parish church of Eschach in 1496, now in M. Abel's collection; the inner sides containing the Annunciation and the Presentation in the Temple; the outer, in figures somewhat larger than life, both the SS. John. These last, in point of dignity, tenderness of feeling, and delicately balanced harmony of the warm and clear colouring, are among the most important works which the German school, taken altogether, produced at this time. 'Two angels holding a sudarium, of uncommon

[1] This collection was recently purchased by the Wirtemberg government.

grandeur of character, formed once a portion of the predella of the same altarpiece. This is now in the Berlin Museum, No. 606 A. To this, his maturest time, belong also the wings, executed 1497, of an altarpiece, at the church of Heerberg, a small place in Suabia, representing scenes from the life of the Virgin; and, finally, eight pictures on two wings, of similar subjects, in the castle of Sigmaringen. A head also of St. Anna, in the Berlin Museum, No. 561 B, of delicate feeling and warm and clear colouring, shows this master in his full excellence.

The Franconian school, of which Nuremberg, as in the former epoch, constituted the centre, received with the oil painting of the Netherlands also the realistic modes of conception proper to that country. In many of their compositions also the influence of Rogier van der Weyden the Elder is perceptible. As compared with the Suabian school, however, this school remained more true to the traditional treatment of ecclesiastical subjects; its compositions are also more conformable to style. At the same time the draughtsmanlike character prevails infinitely more here, the outlines not being, as in Suabia, lost and fused in the forms. Separate colours are more lively, but far less harmonious in relation to each other, so that Franconian pictures have generally a gaudy look. The motives also are more angular, the drapery sharper and more arbitrary in the breaks; and if the heads of many a saintly personage show that an attempt at ideal beauty has been preserved from the former period, the vulgarity and coarseness of the caricatured heads, especially of the soldiers, are much more objectionable than in the Suabian school.

Belonging to the beginning of this epoch are the pictures on the wings of the altar, executed 1453, in the chapel of the noble family of Löffelholz, in the church of St. Sebaldus at Nuremberg. The inner sides contain events from the legends of the Emperor Henry II. and his consort Kunigunda, the outer the Adoration of the three Kings

[1] 'Kunstwerke und Künstler in Deutschland,' vol. i. p. 217.

and St. George killing the Dragon. On the inner side of the predella are Christ and Saints, on the outer the portraits of the numerous family of Löffelholz. The motives in some cases are very successful, and in those heads which have not been painted over may be seen a thorough study, good, warm colouring, and conscientious technical execution.

The chief master of this period was MICHAEL WOHLGEMUTH, born 1434, died 1519. All his pictures show great power and clearness of colouring: otherwise there are few painters so unequal in merit. This arises not only from the circumstance that, being sought far and near to execute large altar-chests, in which the charge of colouring the figures or reliefs in wood was also included, he left much to the workmanship of rude assistants, but also because he himself devoted his own powers very capriciously to the task. The following are some of his principal works:— Four pictures representing scenes from the Passion, of somewhat coarse character, belonging to his earlier time, originally in the church of the Holy Trinity at Hof, in Bavaria, now in the Munich Gallery, Nos. 22, 27, 34, and 39. The large altarpiece at Zwickau, executed 1479, is an improvement on the last-mentioned in some of the panels, especially in the four of the life of the Virgin.[1] He is seen, however, to most advantage in single figures of saints, life-size, portions of an altarpiece, painted in 1487 for the Augustin church, now in the chapel of St. Maurice, at Nuremberg, Nos. 45, 53, 74, and 80.[2] Of the altarpiece in the church at Schwabach, not far from Nuremberg, painted from 1506 to 1508, only the stately figures of John the Baptist and St. Martin are probably by the master's hand.[3] His best work I am inclined to consider the paintings on an altarpiece in the church of Heilsbronn, also in the same part of Franconia. They represent scenes from the life of Christ, the Mass of Pope Gregory, and the portraits of the donor, the Markgraf Frederick IV., and his family. The heads of the sacred

---

[1] 'Kunstwerke und Künstler in Deutschland,' vol. i. p. 56.
[2] Ibid., vol. i. pp. 184, 190.   [3] Ibid., p. 294.

personages are here of higher and more varied character, and the portraits more living than usual.[1] In England I only met with one notable picture by Wohlgemuth, formerly in the Campe collection at Nuremberg, now in that of the Rev. J. Fuller Russell. It represents in a rich composition the Bearing of the Cross, and belongs to his most careful works. The same may be said of two pictures in the Liverpool Institution, representing Pilate washing his hands, and the Descent from the Cross. This master also made the designs for a series of woodcuts in the now rare chronicle of Nuremberg by Schedel, a copy of which is also in Mr. Russell's possession.

In Nuremberg and other towns in Franconia may be seen many a picture, obviously of the school of Wohlgemuth, though collectively falling short of his excellence in art. They serve to show that, with the exception of the great Albert Durer, he attracted no other scholar of any repute.

The cotemporary artists of Bavaria are still less interesting. By one of them, GABRIEL MÄHSELKIRCHER of Munich, who flourished about 1470, are two pictures of very large dimensions in the Gallery of Schleissheim, representing Christ bearing the Cross, and the Crucifixion, which are marked with a sort of wild barbarism and fantastic extravagance. In the same collection is a large and rude Crucifixion by ULRICH FÜTERER of Landshut, about 1480, painted to imitate sculpture in compartments of Gothic architecture.

Nor are the pictures by HANS VON OLENDORF, at Schleissheim, of a higher character. They exhibit no feeling, the drawing is feeble, and the colour very hard.

[1] 'Kunstwerke und Künstler in Deutschland,' p. 307, &c. The large picture attributed to him in the Gallery at Vienna differs, to my view, both in conception and technical qualities, too much from all his authenticated works, to be by his hand.

CHAPTER VI.

THE GERMAN SCHOOLS FROM 1500 TO 1550.

DURING this period the realistic tendency adopted in Germany attained, by means of a greater command of the materials and qualities of art, partly founded on the improved sciences of proportion and perspective, to a higher truthfulness of representation. A number of spirited inventions, embodying scenes not only of a religious character, but taken also from allegory and from common life, thus found expression. In the abundance of these inventions, in the feeling for style with which they were composed, and in mastery of drawing, the German artists decidedly surpassed their Netherlandish cotemporaries, such as Quentin Massys, Lucas van Leyden, &c. On the other hand, as regards colour, they are found, with few exceptions, to be in arrear of the Netherlands; in their treatment, also, the draughtsmanlike feeling prevails in the indication of the outline, and in the frequently hatched shadows, which give a certain hardness peculiar to their pictures. Nor do they stand quite on an equality with the painters of the Netherlands in management of detail, though gold grounds, with few exceptions, had been abolished, and landscape backgrounds, frequently of great finish, introduced. Indeed we find them, in some cases, painting landscape for its own sake. Still more do the Germans fall short of the excellence of cotemporary Italian masters. But while admitting that their inferiority in those qualities—ideality of conception, simplification and beauty of forms, and grace of movement—which give the highest charm to the works of a Leonardo, a Raphael, and a Correggio, is partly owing to a difference in their innate feeling for art, partly to the less favourable conditions of beauty in man, nature, and climate, yet the fact itself, that German painters did not, even in the mode of art peculiar to themselves, arrive at that perfectly harmonious development of every quality,—form, colour, and chiaroscuro,—which distinguishes the Italian, must be sought for in various other causes. The taste for the fantastic in art peculiar to the middle ages, though it engendered clever and spirited works, was still unfavourable to the cultivation of pure beauty. This taste, which the Italians had long thrown off, found, even in this period, favour with the Germans: scenes from the Apocalypse, Dances of Death, &c., being among their favourite subjects for art. On the other hand, the pictorial treatment of antique literature, a world so suggestive of beautiful forms, was so little comprehended by the German mind, that they only sought to express it through the medium of those fantastic forms, with very childish and even tasteless results. We must also remember that that average education of the various classes of society, of princes, nobles, burghers, which the fine arts require for their protection, stood on a far lower footing in Germany than in that then favoured land which, from the beginning of the 15th century, had taken the lead of all others. In Italy, consequently, the favour with which works of art were regarded, was far more widely extended, and entailed a far higher standard of merit. This again gave rise to a more elevated personal position on the part of the artist, which, in Italy, was not only one of more consideration, but, owing to its pecuniary rewards, of incomparably greater independence. In this latter respect Germany was so deficient that the genius even of an Albert Durer and Holbein was miserably cramped and hindered in development by the poverty and littleness of surrounding circumstances. It is known that of all the German princes no one but the Elector Frederic the Wise ever gave Albert Durer a commission for pictures,[1] while a writing, addressed by the great painter to the magistracy of Nuremberg, tells us that his native city never gave him employment even to the value of 500 florins.[2] At the same time his pictures were so meanly paid, that for the means of subsistence, as he says himself,

---

[1] 'Reliquien von Albrecht Dürer, von Campe,' Nürnberg, 1818, p. 59.
[2] Same work, pp. 34 and 37.

he was compelled to devote himself to engraving.¹ How far more such a man as Albert Durer would have been appreciated in Italy and in the Netherlands is further. evidenced in the above-mentioned writing, where he states that he was offered 200 ducats a-year in Venice, and 300 Philipsgulden in Antwerp, if he would settle in either of those cities. And Holbein fared still worse: there is no evidence whatever that any German prince ever troubled himself at all about the great painter; while in the city of Basle his art was so little cared for, that necessity compelled him to go to England,² where a genius fitted for the highest undertakings of historical painting was limited to the sphere of portraiture. The crowning impediments, finally, which hindered the progress of German art, and also perverted it from its true aim, were the Reformation, which narrowed the sphere of ecclesiastical works, and the pernicious imitation of the great Italian masters which ensued.

THE FRANCONIAN SCHOOL.

The head of this school, at this period, was the celebrated ALBERT DURER.³ In him the style of art already existing attained its most original and highest perfection. He became the representative of German art of this period. His spirit was rich and inexhaustible: not content with painting and the other arts of design, he exerted his powers in the kindred studies of sculpture and architecture; he was gifted with a power of conception which traced Nature through all her finest shades, and with a lively sense, as well for the solemn and the sublime, as for simple grace and tenderness; above all, he had an earnest and truthful

---

[1] 'Reliquien von Albrecht Dürer, von Campe,' Nürnberg, 1818, p. 49.
[2] "Hic frigent artes. Petit Angliam ut corradat aliquot Angelatus," says Erasmus of Rotterdam, in a letter he gave Holbein in Basle to his friend Petrus Egydius in Antwerp, in 1526.
[3] There are several special works on Durer. The oldest is by H. C. Arend, 'Das Gedächtniss der Ehren Albrecht Dürer's,' Gosslar, 1728. Later ones are: Weisse, 'A. Dürer und sein Zeitalter,' Leipzig, 1819; 'Reliquien von A. Dürer,' Nürnberg, 1828. J. Heller, 'Das Leben und die Werke A. Dürer's,' Leipzig, 1831.

feeling in art, united with a capacity for the severest study, such as is shown in the composition of his various theoretical works.[1] These qualities were sufficient to place him by the side of the greatest artists whom the world has ever seen. But he again was unable wholly to renounce the general tendency to the fantastic—a tendency which essentially obstructed the pure development of his power as an artist. It must be admitted that in his hands this principle gave birth to single productions of such beauty and importance as we rarely meet with elsewhere; calling into life works which may truly be called "Poems," and of which the mysterious subjects excite the liveliest interest. Albert Durer's drawing is full of life and character; he fails, however, in feeling for beauty, and his nude is vulgar and sometimes even ugly in character: his drapery, too, is frequently cut up into those sharp forms which were the fashion of his day, but by no means favourable to the development of the figure. In ideal drapery his folds are almost always cast in large and beautiful masses; but even here, in the breaks and angles, he cannot wholly discard that singular mannerism which confuses the eye, and disturbs the noble impression of the principal forms. His colouring is unequal: sometimes very brilliant, but generally wanting in truth and transparency; while the hard outlines show rather the hand of a great draughtsman. Even in the expression and form of the countenance, Durer follows a certain form, which cannot be called the normal type of ideal beauty, nor, in some instances, even a faithful copy of common life after the manner of his predecessors, but can only be explained from his prevailing tendency towards what is singular. When, however, in spite of all this, the greater number of his works make a deep impression on the mind and feelings of the spectator, it is a strong proof of the peculiar greatness of his abilities as an artist.

The consideration of the single works of this master, to

---

[1] 'Underweysung der messung mit dem zirckel und richtscheyt,' &c., 1525; 'Etliche underricht zu befestigung der Stett, Schlosz, und Flecken,' 1527; 'Vier bücher von menschlicher Proportion,' 1528. There are different editions and translations of all the above, of a later date.

which we now pass, will explain more clearly the observations just made, and the chronological arrangement of these works will afford an opportunity for some interesting notices of his progress as an artist. I shall especially consider his pictures (so far at least as they have come under my own observation), since it is only in them that the full extent of his unwearied powers can be recognized. The most important of his numerous woodcuts and engravings must also be noticed with a particular reference to their dates when known.

Albert Durer was born in the year 1471, at Nuremberg, and died in that city in 1528. His father was a goldsmith. He learned the mechanical part of painting from Michael Wohlgemuth, and travelled as an apprentice in the years 1490-1494. In the latter year he established himself in Nuremberg. Little is known with certainty of his youthful works.

The earliest portrait by Albert Durer known to me is that of his father, Albrecht Dürer the goldsmith, dated 1497. In the year 1644 this picture, which is engraved by Hollar, was in the collection of the Earl of Arundel; it is now in that of the Duke of Northumberland, at Sion House. It is of most animated conception; the execution light but spirited, and of a draughtsmanlike character; the colouring warm, and truly harmonious.[1]

The same portrait, bearing the same date (1497), but differing in many respects, and with the following inscription—

"Das malt ich nach meines Vaters gestalt,
Da er war siebenzig Jahr alt,"—

is now in the Munich Gallery, Cabinets, No. 128. It is closely allied to the former in conception and treatment, and is also of great excellence, though of less force of colour.

Again, the same portrait, bearing date 1498, is in the gallery of the Uffizj at Florence. This one is yellower in

[1] 'Galleries and Cabinets of Art,' &c., p. 267. A very good school copy of this picture is in the Städel Institute, Frankfort.

the flesh-tones, and with a greenish background; also of more body than the two preceding. It was presented, with the next-mentioned portrait, its companion, by the city of Nuremberg to Charles I. of England; at the sale of whose gallery, both pictures were purchased for the Grand Duke of Tuscany.

The next picture by the master known to us is his own portrait, of the year 1498, in the Florentine collection of artists' portraits painted by themselves, in the Uffizj; the arrangement of the picture is well known—the artist, a half-length figure, stands at a window, the hands resting on the window-sill. He is arrayed in a peculiar holiday dress—a shirt neatly plaited and cut low in the neck, a white jerkin striped with black, a pointed cap, and a brown mantle over the left shoulder, the hair falling in carefully arranged curls. The painting, with some sharpness in the drawing, has a breadth and softness, especially in the lights, which we rarely find at a later period; the shadows of the carnation have a light bronze tint. The expression of the countenance is honest and homely, with a certain naïve self-complacency, which is indeed tolerably manifest in the letters written by him to Pirckheimer about eight years later.

In the same year, 1498, appeared his woodcuts illustrating the Book of Revelations, and which we should perhaps regard as proofs of his activity in the years immediately preceding. Here the artist already exhibits a great and peculiar excellence, though, as might be expected from the subject, the fantastic element forms the groundwork of the whole. These mystical subjects are conceived in a singularly poetic spirit: the marvellous and the monstrous meet us in living bodily forms. Some of them exhibit a power of representation to the eye, and a grandeur of conception, the more surprising, since the shapeless exuberance of the scriptural visions might easily have led the artist astray, as has indeed frequently happened in the case of others who have attempted these subjects. How powerful is that second plate, in which He with eyes of flaming

ALBERT DÜRER.
ainted by himself. In the Collection of Artists' Portraits at Florence

fire, the seven stars in his right hand, and a two-edged sword in his mouth, sits enthroned among the seven golden candlesticks, with St. John kneeling in adoration before him! In the fourth plate, how mighty is the descent upon the earth of the four riders, with scales, bows, swords, and other weapons of death! In the eighth, how the four angels of the Euphrates dash to the ground with their swords the mighty and the proud of the earth, whilst over them ride the awful company of horsemen on the lion-headed horses, spitting forth fire! But it would occupy too much time to enter upon all the details of these remarkable works. We now return to his pictures.

Several of Albert Durer's pictures of the year 1500 are known to us. The first and most important is his own portrait in the Munich Gallery, Cabinets, No. 124, which represents him in front, with his hand laid on the fur trimming of his robe. There is a considerable difference between this and the Florence portrait, although the artist is here but two years older—a difference from which we may infer that a remarkable crisis had taken place in the development of his mind. In the Florence picture he is a good-natured harmless youth, see woodcut: in that at Munich he has suddenly ripened into manhood; his features have become full and powerful, they have gained the expression of a formed character; the forehead and eyes give evidence of an earnest and deep-thinking spirit. The technical treatment, too, which contributes so much to give a peculiar stamp to his later works, is here fully matured, particularly the thin glazing in the shadows of the carnations, which lends to the picture we speak of an almost glassy transparency. The modelling is excellent, although still somewhat severe, and although considerable restorations are perceptible. The hair falls on both shoulders in beautiful profusion, and is very finely painted; the hand which holds the fur of the upper garment over the breast is still stiff in the drawing, and, what is in striking contrast to the painting of the face, the colour is thickly laid on.

Of the same year is a Hercules attacking the Harpies, painted in distemper; a fine, powerfully-drawn figure, but much injured. In the collection of the Landauer Brüderhaus at Nuremberg.

In the gallery of the Belvedere, in Vienna, is a Virgin nursing the Infant, of the year 1503. It contains little more than the heads of both figures. Though lightly and very pleasingly painted, it is uninteresting in expression, and seems nothing more than the portrait of the sturdy wife of some burgher.

But the engraving of the same date, of the coat of arms with the Death's head, is far more interesting. The two supporters—the smiling woman with the braided tresses and fantastic crown, and the wild man who grasps her, and turns, as if to kiss her—have a peculiar and fantastic charm about them. The engraving, too, of Adam and Eve, of the year 1504, ranks among the best of the master's works.

The finest picture of the year 1504 is an Adoration of the Kings; originally painted for Frederick the Wise, Elector of Saxony, subsequently presented by the Elector Christian II. to the Emperor Rudolph II., and finally, on the occasion of an exchange of pictures, transferred from Vienna to Florence, where it now hangs in the Tribune of the Uffizj. The heads are of thoroughly realistic treatment; the Virgin a portrait from some model of no attractive character; the second king the portrait of the painter himself. The landscape background exactly resembles that in the well-known engraving of St. Eustace, the period of which is thus pretty nearly defined. It is carefully painted in a fine body of colour.

To about the same time we may assign the fine portrait of a man with broad-brimmed hat and an order round his neck, now in the collection of the Duke of Rutland at Belvoir Castle.

In the year 1506 Albert Durer made a journey into Upper Italy, and remained a considerable time at Venice. Of his occupations in this city the letters written to his friend Wilibald Pirckheimer, which have come down to us, give many interesting particulars. He there executed for the German Company a picture which brought him great fame, and by its brilliant colouring silenced the assertion of his envious adversaries, "that he was a good engraver, but knew not how to deal with colours." In the centre of the landscape is the Virgin, seated, with the Child, and crowned by two angels; on her right is a Pope with priests, kneeling; on her left the Emperor Maximilian I. with knights; various members of the German Company are also kneeling: all are being crowned with garlands of roses by the Virgin, the Child, St. Dominick—who stands behind the Virgin—and by angels. The painter and his friend Pirckheimer are seen standing in the background on the right; the painter holds a tablet, with the inscription " Exegit quinque mestri spatio, Albertus Durer Germanus, MDVI," and his monogram. This picture, which is one of his largest and finest, was purchased of the church at a high price by the Emperor Rudolph II. for his gallery at Prague, where it remained until sold in 1782, with other objects from the same collection, by the Emperor Joseph II. It then became the property of the Præmonstratensian monastery of Strahow at Prague, where it still exists, though in very injured condition and greatly over-painted. In the Museum at Lyons may be seen a copy, with various important alterations, which was executed towards the close of the 16th century, and which there passes for the original.[1]

In the Gallery of the Belvedere, at Vienna, is a portrait, of the year 1507, of a young man, with a high colour. It is wonderfully beautiful, true to life, and finely painted, so as to equal the painter's best works in portraiture; but it is unfortunately not in as good preservation as we could wish. This picture allows us to judge of the excellence of another painted in the same year, and which afterwards passed from the possession of the Council of Nuremberg into the gallery of the Emperor Rudolph II. It represents, on two different panels, Adam

---

[1] A good lithograph, executed with the pen by Bademann, taken from the original, was published in Prague in 1835. For further description of this important picture, see an article by me in the 'Kunstblatt' of 1854, p. 200, &c.

and Eve, life-size, at the moment of the Fall. On that containing Eve is the inscription, "Albertus Durer Alemanus faciebat post Virginis partum, 1507," with the monogram. The head of Eve is very delicately formed for the painter, the drawing good, the outlines animated, and the modelling careful. These panels are now in the Madrid Gallery.[1] Another example of the same subject, of great beauty, and proceeding undoubtedly from the studio of Albert Durer, is in the Pitti Palace. A third, also called an original picture, in the Mayence Gallery, is, on the other hand, an early copy.

With these productions begins the zenith of this master's fame, in which a great number of distinguished works follow one another within a short period. Of these we first notice a picture of 1508, in the Belvedere Gallery at Vienna, painted for Duke Frederick of Saxony, and which afterwards adorned the gallery of the Emperor Rudolph II. It represents the Martyrdom of the Ten Thousand Saints. In the centre of the picture stand the master and his friend Pirckheimer as spectators, both in black dresses. Albert Durer has a mantle thrown over the shoulder in the Italian fashion, and stands in a firm attitude. He folds his hands, and holds a small flag, on which is inscribed, "Iste faciebat anno domini 1508 Albertus Durer Alemanus." There are a multitude of single groups around, exhibiting every species of martyrdom, but there is a want of general connection of the whole. The scenes in the background, where the Christians are led naked up the rocks, and are precipitated down from the top, appear to me particularly excellent. The whole is very minute and miniature-like; the colouring is beautifully brilliant, and it is painted (the accessories particularly) with extraordinary care. There is also much that is good in the drawing of single parts, but the conception wants real dignity, power, and individuality. It is only here and there that pain is well expressed; for instance, in the last but one of the nude figures who are led up the mountain,

---

[1] Passavant's 'Christliche Kunst in Spanien,' p. 142.

and who totters along, weary to the death, with a deep wound in the head. The background forms an excellent but fanciful landscape of rocks and trees. In the Schleissheim Gallery there is a repetition of this picture—no doubt an old copy.

In the following year Albert Durer painted the celebrated Assumption of the Virgin for Jacob Heller of Frankfort, a picture which he executed with the most persevering diligence, and the centre-piece without any assistance. Here again the painter himself stands in the centre, leaning upon a tablet inscribed with his name, and with the date. There are numerous ancient testimonies to the excellence of this work. In the beginning of the seventeenth century it was brought to Munich, and there perished in the fire at the palace.

Two excellent woodcuts may also be mentioned as examples of his activity in 1510. The first is the beautiful plate which represents a Penitent kneeling before the altar and scourging himself on his naked back, and the second that in which Death seizes upon an armed warrior.

In 1511 he published three large series of woodcuts, some of which, as shown by their dates, had been executed in the two preceding years. These were the greater and the lesser Passion, and the Life of the Virgin. They are some of the best of Albert Durer's works which have descended to us; in them we find, almost more than in any others, intimations of a lively feeling for beauty and simple dignity, whilst the fantastic features of his style and the homeliness of his conception are less offensively prominent. We can take but a rapid glance at a few of this rich series.

The Great Passion.—The title-page represents Christ sitting naked on a stone, with the crown of thorns, whilst one of the soldiers thrusts into his hand the reed. The form of Christ is most noble, full, and beautiful; the soldier, in the costume of the middle ages, is fierce and scornful, but also a finely formed and well-developed figure. The Saviour is wringing his hands, while he turns his majestic head, full of divine compassion, towards the spectator—for, as a frontispiece, this representation has here a symbolical meaning: it is not the mockery of Christ, as an event of history, but the lasting reproach cast upon the Saviour by sinners; hence the wounds on the hands and feet are already marked. The Bearing of the Cross is a composition with numerous figures thickly grouped, yet conveying the most perfect view of the subject, and the clearest development of the action. In the centre the Saviour sinks on his knee under the weight of the cross; on the right the executioner, in whose figure there is an ostentatious display of muscular power, drags him up by the rope; on the left is St. Veronica kneeling, with the handkerchief in her hands, while Christ turns to her with an expression of tender love. Behind him is another executioner, who with savage haste appears to throw Jesus forward among stones and thistles; whilst Simon of Cyrene, a benevolent old man, is in the act of taking the weight of the cross from his shoulders. Further back, on one side, are the centurion and soldiers, and on the other the Virgin and the friends of Jesus: behind them the Thieves are being led through the city-gate. The composition bears a similarity, not to be mistaken, to Raphael's picture, Lo Spasimo di Sicilia; and though in this latter work we acknowledge the hand of a more matured artist, yet, in single parts, the comparison is certainly favourable to the older German composition. The figure of Christ, particularly, is more important, more dignified, and more decidedly the central point of interest in the action. Christ's Descent into Hell displays the wildest fancy in the figures of the demons, perfect majesty in that of the Redeemer, and excellent drawing of the nude in the figures of those released. The Body of Christ taken down from the Cross, and mourned over by his followers, is a composition which may unhesitatingly be placed by the side of the most profound works of the great Italian masters. The most perfect grouping is made consistent with the greatest simplicity of design; and, however indifferently the engraver has executed his part, the varied expression of the single figures, and the peculiar grace of the lines and movements, cannot be concealed. When we look at such works we easily comprehend why the later Italians valued Albert Durer's compositions so highly, and how it was that a translation of them, as it were, into Italian was so much desired.

The Lesser Passion.—Of this series the most beautiful compositions are—Christ taking leave of his Mother; distinguished by the dignity and beauty of the drapery. Christ washing the Feet of his Disciples; remarkable for the excellent and simple arrangement of a large number of figures in a small space, whilst the principal group in the foreground is beautiful and full of feeling. Christ praying on the Mount of Olives,—which is extremely simple, and, with the highest dignity and beauty, full of the most profound and tender feeling. Christ appearing to his Mother in her chamber, and to Mary Magdalen as the gardener, after his resurrection, are both, the latter particularly, compositions of peculiar grace and simple beauty.

The Life of the Virgin.—The leading character of the last-mentioned works is grand and tragic; that of this series is graceful and pleasing. In these we are introduced into the more tender relations of family life, where the master shows a refinement of amiable feeling in which he has few equals. It appears almost superfluous to enter into the details of a work so well known, but we shall briefly notice a few compositions of particular beauty. The Golden Gate—Joachim and Anna support one another, after their mournful separation, with the expectation of a joyful futurity; the former is a mild-looking, aged man—Anna full of womanly softness and resignation. In the background the steward and other servants of Joachim, who had come to welcome their lord, are engaged in talking over the event. The Birth of the Virgin—a composition of the most attractive *naïveté*. The scene is the lying-in chamber of a Nuremberg house, with a numerous company of women and maidens, offering an interesting comparison with Florentine life, in similar scenes, by Ghirlandajo and others. The Circumcision:—this subject, frequently so disagreeable, and bordering, even in the hands of great masters, on the absurd,—here offers a pleasing representation of a characteristic national custom. Numerous as are the figures in this composition, nothing is superfluous: each seems necessarily and individually interested in the action; and the whole is formed into simple and natural groups. The Flight into Egypt:—in contrast to the Circumcision the space is here skilfully filled up with few figures; the pleasant aspect of a thick and fruitful wood, through which the Holy Family are journeying, adds to the charm of this attractive subject. The Repose in Egypt:—a courtyard, with a dwelling built into the ruins of an ancient palace; the Virgin, with a spindle, sits beside the cradle; beautiful angels worship at her side; Joseph is employed in carpenter's work, with a number of little angels, who, in merry sport, assist him in his labour. This is a scene of the most graceful repose and undisturbed serenity. The Death of the Virgin:—the perfect composition, simple division of the principal groups, fine forms, and deep feeling, combine to place this design very high amongst the works of Albert Durer. It has frequently been copied in colours by his followers; and, in many galleries, pictures of this kind bear his name.

There are also other woodcuts by the master inscribed with the date 1511, such as the well-known and grand composition of the Trinity, several Holy Families, &c.

Between the years 1507 and 1513, but principally in 1512, was executed the large series of small engravings which contain a third representation of the Passion. Among these are many of much merit, the more interesting from the delicate execution of the master's own hand being visible throughout. In order not to weary the reader, I shall refrain from going into the details of single plates.

To this fruitful time, 1511, belongs also one of his most celebrated pictures, the Adoration of the Trinity, see woodcut. It was painted for the chapel of the Landauer Brüderhaus, in Nuremberg, whence, like many of his works, it was removed to Prague, where it was presented to the Emperor Rodolph II.; at present it

ADORATION OF THE TRINITY.
Painted by Albert Durer   Now in the Belvedere at Vienna

is in the Belvedere at Vienna. Above, in the centre of the picture, are seen the First Person, who holds the Saviour in his arms, while the Holy Spirit is seen above; some angels spread out the priestly mantle of the Almighty, whilst others hover near with the instruments of Christ's passion. On the left hand, a little lower down, is a choir of females with the Virgin at their head; on the right are the male saints with St. John the Baptist. Below all these kneel a host of the blessed, of all ranks and nations, extending over the whole of this part of the picture. Underneath the whole is a beautiful landscape, and in a corner of the picture the artist himself, richly clothed in a fur mantle, with a tablet next him, with the words "Albertus Durer Noricus faciebat anno a Virginis partu, 1511." The execution here also is masterly and of exceeding delicacy, but again with the same glazing of the colours. The cast of the drapery is in general grand; the figures in the Trinity are dignified, and not without beauty. In other parts the picture is deficient in loftiness of conception, and a few only of the other heads—that of David, for instance—can be called beautiful. In the greater number, even in the figures of the saints, we again find a feeling of common life, bordering on caricature. It may be assumed beyond doubt that he held in particular esteem those pictures into which he introduced his own portrait.

In the Belvedere is a picture of the following year, 1512, the Virgin holding the naked Child in her arms. She has a veil over her head, and blue drapery. Her face is of the form usual with Albert Durer, but of a soft and maidenly character; the Child is beautiful—the countenance particularly so. It is painted with exceeding delicacy of finish, but, unfortunately, with grayish shadows in the flesh.

A series of his pictures, to which there is no precise date, may be mentioned here, since the greater number of them must belong to the middle period of the artist's career:—

A Mater Dolorosa, in the Munich Gallery, Cabinets,

No. 153, standing with folded hands, is beautiful, simple, and dignified.

An altarpiece, with wings, in the Munich Gallery, painted at the request of the Baumgartner family, for St. Catherine's church at Nuremberg, was brought to Munich in the year 1612 by the Elector Maximilian I. The subject of the middle picture is the Nativity; the Child is in the centre, surrounded by five little angels, whilst the Virgin and Joseph kneel at the side. As a whole, the picture is clever, but it wants depth and fine feeling. ' The wings contain portraits of the two donors, under the form of St. George and St. Eustace, represented as knights in steel armour and red surcoats. One is a highly interesting figure, though rather fantastic in attitude; his countenance has much character, is well developed, and expresses at once decision and resignation. The thin figure who stands beside his horse reminds us of the knight in the engraving —dated 1513—of "The Knight, Death, and the Devil," and the defile and castle from that design are also repeated in the background; we may therefore infer that the picture was executed about the same time. · The man on the second wing is stouter and less poetic. The painting of both is peculiarly free.

The Body of our Lord taken down from the Cross and mourned by his followers, is in the chapel of St. Maurice at Nuremberg. It was originally ordered by the family of Holzschuher for the church of St. Sebaldus; it then came into the possession of the Peller family, and at a later period into the Boisserée Gallery. The composition consists of numerous figures, beautifully arranged, particularly the dead body, the drawing of which, though stiff, is of a fine character. There is no great depth of expression in the heads; the background is a rich mountain-landscape. This picture was probably executed between 1515 and 1518.[1] A repetition, which is in the original place in St. Sebaldus, is undoubtedly an old, but not worthless copy;

---

[1] 'Künstler und Kunstwerke in Deutschland,' vol. i. p. 186.

THE KNIGHT, DEATH, AND THE DEVIL
An Engraving by Albert Durer

MELANCHOLY.
Engraving by Albert Durer

the colouring, particularly in the body of Christ, is, however, much drier.

The portraits of the Emperors Charlemagne and Sigismund, in the castle at Nuremberg, are two powerful and dignified figures, executed in Albert Durer's forcible outline and free painting.[1]

A portrait, in distemper, of Jacob Fuggers, in the Munich Gallery, is a clever picture, No. 51.

Some engravings, which our historical survey now leads us to notice, are more interesting than the greater part of the pictures just described.

The first of these is the celebrated plate of The Knight, Death, and the Devil, inscribed with the date 1513 (see woodcut). I believe that I do not exaggerate when I particularize this print as the most important work which the fantastic spirit of German Art has ever produced. The invention may be ascribed unreservedly to the imagination of the master. We see a solitary Knight riding through a dark glen; two demons rise up before him, the most fearful which the human breast can conceive—the personification of thoughts at which the cheek grows pale—the horrible figure of Death on the lame horse, and the bewildering apparition of the Devil. But the Knight, prepared for combat wherever resistance can avail, with a countenance on which Time has imprinted his furrows, and to which care and self-denial have imparted an expression of deep and unconquerable determination, looks steadily forward on the path which he has chosen, and allows these creations of a delusive dream to sink again into their visionary kingdom. The masterly execution of the engraving is well known.

Several excellent plates were also executed by Albert Durer in the year 1514. Of these we may first name his "Melancholy." In the seated figure of this grand winged woman, absorbed in thought, see woodcut, he has expressed, in a highly original and intellectual manner, the insufficiency of the human reason, either to explore the secrets of life, fortune, and science, or to unravel those of the past. Symbolical allusions of various kinds lie around, in the shape

[1] 'Künstler und Kunstwerke in Deutschland,' vol. i. p. 201, &c.

of the sphere, the book, the crystal polygon, the crucible, the bell, the hour-glass, &c., with many implements of human activity, such as the plane, the hammer, and the rule. The intention of the plate is greatly enhanced by the grandly melancholy character of the landscape background.

A perfect contrast to the Melancholy is to be found in its cotemporary print of St. Jerome in his study. There, too, we see the figure of a man sunk in deep thought, and a chamber filled with various apparatus. The whole is arranged with the most ingenious fancy, but pervaded by a serenity and grace which keep aloof all the dreams and visionary forms created by the imagination, and bring before us the simple reality of homely life in its most pleasing form. Gerard Dow, the most feeling of the Dutch genre-painters, has produced nothing so pleasing and touching as this print, which, even in the most trifling accessories, bears the impress of a lofty and gentle nature.

After the year 1520 Albert Durer engraved various plates of Madonnas and Apostles, among which occur additional examples of dignity and fine feeling.

The largest woodcut executed by this master is inscribed with the year 1515. It is the Triumphal Arch of the Emperor Maximilian: a strange work, with an endless variety of historical representations, portraits, and fanciful ornaments. In spite, however, of the immense amount of details, the effect of the whole is very stately. To the architectural parts the artist has given the most grotesque and fantastic forms, yet they are often composed with singular ingenuity and skill: this applies particularly to the principal columns, which are arranged in pairs; their composition is remarkable throughout for its strict consistency and its reference to the office assigned to them; they have not the weight of a continuous entablature to support, but in reality each pair only sustains isolated niches, which contain statues. The ornaments, taken singly, are very tasteful, and drawn with much force and spirit; the series of portraits—which represent the predecessors and ancestors of the Emperor, from Julius Cæsar and the Merovingian Clodovic, with all

BORDER FROM THE PRAYERBOOK OF MAXIMILIAN
Drawn by Albert Durer.   In the Royal Library, Munich

BORDER FROM THE PRAYERBOOK OF MAXIMILIAN.
Drawn by Albert Durer. In the Royal Library, Munich.

his kindred—is very remarkable for the extraordinary variety and character of the heads, which the artist, having no existing originals to work from, was obliged himself to invent. The historical representations relate to the most brilliant events of the Emperor's life, but in them we trace the hand of the imperial historiographer who arranged, rather than that of the artist who executed them. Very few of these compositions are remarkable for the qualities which we look for in works of art, yet there are parts, particularly where the action consists of few figures, which are very striking. The whole work proves in a brilliant manner the singular versatility of this master's powers.

In the year 1515 Albert Durer executed also the celebrated borders for the Prayer-book of the Emperor Maximilian, see woodcuts, now in the Royal Library at Munich. In these spirited pen-and-ink drawings the fancy of the artist revels in perfect liberty, sometimes serious and dignified, sometimes gracefully playful, sometimes humorous and gay. Here his task was not to represent a given subject of particular depth of meaning, but merely to fill up tastefully an allotted space: and if he does not always seem to keep in mind the full meaning of the text which he has adorned with his arabesques, still the play of fancy is neither whimsical nor extravagant, the humour never degenerates into vulgarity, as is often the case in this kind of ornament; and the combined effect makes so pleasing an impression on the spectator, that criticism is content to be silent.

Two of his pictures in the Florentine Gallery of the Uffizj, which represent the Apostles Philip and James, bear the date of 1516. They were gifts from the Emperor Ferdinand III., in the middle of the seventeenth century, to the Duke of Tuscany. Both are painted in tempera, and powerfully modelled; the character is forcible and energetic.

Of the same year is the portrait of his master, Wohlgemuth, in the Munich Gallery, Cabinets, No. 130, a strangely sharp and bony countenance. It is of masterly painting, in a draughtsmanlike style.

The fantastic composition, consisting of four woodcuts of a pillar on which a Satyr is seated, was executed in 1517.

In 1518 occurs the charming woodcut of the Virgin as Queen of Heaven, surrounded by Angels.

A Lucretia, the size of life, in the Munich Gallery, was taken from some very unattractive original in Nuremberg. It is, however, of masterly modelling in all parts, and worthy of Leonardo da Vinci.

In the year 1519 Albert Durer executed a portrait of the Emperor Maximilian; a half-length, with a pomegranate, the imperial symbol, in the left hand. It is in the Gallery of the Belvedere in Vienna. The conception is fine, and the execution, in a warm tone, very careful. A good original repetition was in the collection of the late Lord Northwick at Thirlestain Hall.[1]

In the year 1520-21 he undertook a journey to the Netherlands. His journal is still preserved, and tells us of the great honours with which he was received there by the native artists. He appears at this time as a man conscious of his long and ardent labours, and anxious to derive from those labours only such advantages as every honourable man must wish to enjoy. This journey, however, it appears, must have exercised an important influence on his tendency in art, and perhaps opened his eyes to the peculiarity of his manner. There are at least changes in the feeling and treatment visible in his later works, and Melancthon tells us, from the painter's own confession, that the beauty of nature had not unfolded itself to him until a late period; that he had then only learned that simplicity is the greatest charm of art; that he sighed over the motley pictures of his early days, and mourned that he could no longer hope to emulate the great prototype—Nature.[2]

---

[1] 'Treasures of Art, &c.' vol. iii. p. 210.

[2] Memini virum excellentem ingenio et virtute Albertum Durerum pictorem dicere, se juvenem floridas et maxime varias picturas amâsse, seque admiratorem suorum operum valde lætatum esse, contemplatem hanc varietatem in suâ aliquâ picturâ. Postea se senem cœpisse intueri Naturam, et illius nativam faciem intueri conatum esse, eamque simplicitatem tunc intellexisse summum artis decus esse. Quam cum non prorsus adsequi posset, dicebat se jam non esse admiratorem operum suorum ut olim, sed sæpe gemere intuentem suas tabulas, et cogitantem de infirmitate sua. Etc. (Epistolæ Ph. Melanch-

Durer's Woodcut of the "CAR OF MAXIMILIAN," in the British Museum

page 101

From Albert Dürer's Woodcut of the CAR of MAXIMILIAN in the British Museum

In the Gallery of the Belvedere, in Vienna, is a singular picture by Albert Durer, of the year 1520, which differs in a striking manner from the rest of his works. In execution and conception it bears a likeness, not to be mistaken, to the works of the artists of the Low Countries of that period, particularly to those of Quentin Massys. It was probably executed whilst he was on the journey, under the influence of the new objects around him. The subject is the Virgin, a half-length figure in a fur mantle; the Child, naked, with a string of amber round his neck, is on her lap; on the green table before her lies a cut lemon. The head of the Virgin is particularly soft and mild; the Child is not remarkably beautiful.

In 1522 he published the series of woodcuts which form the Triumphal Car of the Emperor Maximilian, see woodcuts. The allegory is rather poor, and the elaborate ornaments of the car are whimsical and even tasteless; on the other hand, the allegorical female figures, despite the disagreeable crumpled appearance of the drapery, display motives of extraordinary beauty, such as might have proceeded from the graceful simplicity of Raphael. This circumstance also must not be overlooked with reference to the change in the tendency of Albert Durer's feeling in his later time.

The two half-length pictures of SS. Joseph and Joachim, and Simeon and Lazarus, in the Munich Gallery, Cabinets, 123, 127, are of the year 1523. They formed the side-wings of an altarpiece. The colouring is beautiful, the expression dignified, but they are not essentially different from his earlier works.

Scarce as are the genuine pictures by Albert Durer in England, I may observe that a Nativity by him, under the erroneous name of Herri de Bles—a small but fine picture—is in the collection of the Marquis of Exeter at Burleigh House.

During this period he engraved on copper those remarkable portraits of his celebrated cotemporaries—Cardinal Albert of Brandenburg, the Elector Frederick the

thonis, etc., Ep. 47, p. 42 E. apud Epist. D. Erasmi Roter. et Ph. Melanch. Londini, 1642, fol.)

Wise, Pirckheimer, Melancthon, Erasmus of Rotterdam, and others—which are distinguished by the most spirited conception of life, as well as by an execution of wonderful delicacy. This was the time at which religious discord had burst over Germany, and when Nuremberg especially was severely visited by it: consequently the desire for religious works of art may naturally have decreased. It is probable, however, that Albert Durer, whose mind had imbibed the new doctrine with the deepest devotion, may have laboured with more satisfaction in the province of every-day life than in many of the subjects which art had previously treated. We are indebted, at any rate, to these circumstances for a series of most admirable works, which without them would probably never have been called into existence.

Three excellent portraits in oil exist, of the year 1526. One in the Gallery of the Belvedere, at Vienna, represents a citizen of Nuremberg, John Kleeberger: it is a pale manly head, with large black eyes, altogether of a peculiar beauty; the nose only is rather small; the shadows are unfortunately of a strong gray tone. The second is in the possession of the Holzschuher family in Nuremberg, and represents one of their ancestors, Jerome Holzschuher, painted at the age of fifty-seven. The expression of this head is very fine and dignified; the eyes are brilliant, and, notwithstanding the white hair, the face appears to possess the vigour of youth. Strictly speaking, this picture is painted in the master's thin glazed manner, but it is extraordinarily well executed. It combines the most perfect modelling with the freest handling of the colours, and is certainly the most beautiful of all this master's portraits, since it plainly shows how well he could seize Nature in her happiest moments, and represent her with irresistible power. The third portrait is that of Jacob Muffel, Burgomaster of Nuremberg, now in the collection of Count Schönborn at Pommersfelden near Bamberg. It is truthfully conceived, and of masterly modelling, but somewhat heavy and gray in colour.

The same year, 1526, was also distinguished by the two

THE APOSTLES MARK AND PAUL
By Albert Durer   In the Munich Gallery

pictures, corresponding with each other, of the four Apostles, John and Peter, Mark and Paul, see woodcut; the figures are the size of life. This, which is the master's grandest work, and the last of importance executed by him, is now in the Munich Gallery. We know with certainty that it was presented by Albert Durer himself to the council of his native city in remembrance of his career as an artist, and at the same time as conveying to his fellow-citizens an earnest and lasting exhortation suited to that stormy period. In the year 1627, however, the pictures were allowed to pass into the hands of the Elector Maximilian I. of Bavaria. The inscriptions selected by the painter himself might have given offence to a Catholic prince, and were therefore cut off and joined to the copies by John Fischer, which were intended to indemnify the city of Nuremberg for the loss of the originals. These copies are still in the collection of the Laudauer Brüderhaus at Nuremberg.

These pictures are the fruit of the deepest thought which then stirred the mind of Albert Durer, and are executed with overpowering force. Finished as they are, they form the first complete work of art produced by Protestantism. As the inscription, taken from the Gospels and Epistles of the Apostles, contains pressing warnings not to swerve from the word of God, nor to believe in the doctrines of false prophets, so the figures themselves represent the steadfast and faithful guardians of that holy Scripture which they bear in their hands. There is also an old tradition, handed down from the master's own times,[1] that these figures represent the four temperaments. This notion is confirmed by the pictures themselves; and though, at first sight, it may appear to rest on a mere accidental combination, it serves, in truth, to carry out more completely the artist's thought, and gives to the figures greater individuality. It shows how every quality of the human mind may be called into the service of the Divine Word. Thus, in the first picture, we see

[1] Neudörffer, 'Nachrichten von den vornehmsten Künstlern Nürnbergs, Nürnb. 1828,' in the notices on Durer.

the whole force of the mind absorbed in contemplation, and we are taught that true watchfulness in behalf of the Scripture must begin by devotion to its study. St. John stands in front, the open book in his hand; his high forehead and his whole countenance bear the impress of earnest and deep thought. This is the melancholic temperament, which does not shrink from the most profound inquiry. Behind him St. Peter bends over the book, and gazes earnestly at its contents; a hoary head, full of meditative repose. This figure represents the phlegmatic temperament, which reviews its own thoughts in tranquil reflection. The second picture shows the outward operation of the conviction thus attained and its relation to daily life. St. Mark, in the background, is the man of sanguine temperament; he looks boldly round, and appears to speak to his hearers with animation, earnestly urging them to share those advantages which he has himself derived from the holy Scriptures. St. Paul, on the contrary, in the foreground, holds the book and sword in his hands; he looks angrily and severely over his shoulder, ready to defend the Word, and to annihilate the blasphemer with the sword of God's power. He is the representative of the choleric temperament. Then what masterly finish there is in the execution! such as is only suited to a subject of such sublime meaning. What dignity and sublimity pervade these heads of varied character! What simplicity and majesty in the lines of the drapery! What sublime and statue-like repose in their movements! Here we no longer find any disturbing element: there are no small angular breaks in the folds, no arbitrary or fantastic features in the countenance, or even in the fall of the hair. The colouring, too, is perfect: true to nature in its power and warmth. There is scarcely any trace of the bright glazing, or of those sharply-defined forms, but everywhere a free, pure impasto. Well might the artist now close his eyes. He had in this picture attained the summit of art: here he stands side by side with the greatest masters known in history.

Albert Durer died in 1528. I know of no important

work of a later date than that just described. His portrait, in a woodcut of the year 1527, represents him earnest and serious in demeanour, as would naturally follow from his advancing age and the pressure of eventful times. His head is no longer adorned with those richly-flowing locks, on which, in his earlier days, he had set so high a value, as we learn from his pictures and from jests still recorded of him. That excellence to which he had raised German art in his last master-work passed away with him, and centuries saw no sign of its revival.[1]

A large number of pictures in galleries and private collections throughout Europe bearing the name of Albert Durer are here purposely omitted, owing to the number of painters, often of no mean technical merit, but of no power of invention, who executed pictures from the engravings and woodcuts of this great master, which are systematically given out for his original works. No man has had so many pictures erroneously assigned to him as Albert Durer.

His scholars and followers imbibed, as was often the case in other schools, the external characteristics of his manner, particularly the peculiar motives of his drawing, without in general catching the profound spirit of their master. But even among them the fantastic principle of art, in particular instances, was carried out with wonderful success. Most of these artists, like himself, are known both as painters and engravers, and many of their designs exist also in woodcuts.

One of the most pleasing of Albert Durer's scholars is HANS VON KULMBACH, whose name was HANS WAGNER, died 1540, and who came to him from the school of Jacob Walch. Upon the whole, he adheres faithfully to the style of Albert Durer; but, while far below him in power

---

[1] Among the drawings in the collection of the Archduke Charles of Austria there is a study of drapery for the figure of St. Paul, executed so early as 1523. This and three other finely-draped figures in the same collection, and of the same year, are beautifully rendered. Hence it is evident that, directly after the journey to the Netherlands, Albert Durer endeavoured to lay aside his capricious style in the cast of his drapery, and was eager to adopt one more grand and noble, and grounded upon the study of Nature.

of conception, he surpasses him in taste and pure feeling for nature. He is also more equal in warmth and harmony of colour.

Among his numerous pictures preserved in Nuremberg are two remarkable panels in the chapel of St. Maurice—wing-pictures, with figures of saints—one of which, No. 57, especially, is very clever. In St. Sebaldus, also, there is a very remarkable large picture. In consists of three panels: in the centre one is the Virgin enthroned with the Child, and angels bearing musical instruments; SS. Catherine and Barbara stand beside them; other saints, and the kneeling figure of the donor, Lawrence Tucher, are on the side pictures. It is in every respect the masterpiece of this painter.[1] In the Munich Gallery, Nos. 16, 21, 43, 58, there are pictures by Hans von Kulmbach of beautiful and brilliant effect, with very excellent single parts. In the Städel Institute at Frankfort there is a good altarpiece by the same master; and in the monastery of Heilsbronn, between Anspach and Nuremberg, there are some pleasing figures of saints by his hand.

HEINRICH ALDEGREVER, born at Soest 1502, died 1562, is, as a painter, a less important master. Pictures by him are very rare, but he was a very clever engraver. A Last Judgment in the Berlin Gallery deserves notice. The upper group, of Christ with the Virgin and John the Baptist, is very peculiar; their draperies are agitated by the storm of the Last Day. The angels with the trumpets, and the fantastic figures of the demons among the Damned, are of merit. The host of naked figures of the dead who have risen are certainly very drily painted, yet there is something striking in their solemn measured movements. The saints in the foreground also are dignified figures. The portraits of the donors are full of life. A clever portrait of a youth is in the Lichtenstein Gallery at Vienna; another, of an elderly man, in the Museum at Berlin.

Numerous pictures by HANS SCHÄUFFELIN, died 1540, are

---

[1] Notwithstanding Sandrart's assertion that he possessed Durer's design for the picture, I find the composition so different from him, that I believe the whole belongs to Kulmbach. Compare Kunst und Künstler in Deutschland, vol. i. p. 231.

dispersed in various places. He was a clever and dexterous artist, who imitated the manner of his master, and, in his best pictures, successfully. But he is very unequal, and many of his works are very slight productions. Among his paintings preserved in Nuremberg, a St. Bridget, in the chapel of St. Maurice, appeared to me to deserve most notice : it is prettily and neatly painted, and has some pretension to grandeur of style. There is also, in the castle, the subject of Christ mocked, of the year 1517, an animated picture of very large size, in tempera, and unfortunately injured in parts. A small picture with numerous figures, also at Nuremberg, representing the History of Judith, reminds us, in some respects, of Schäuffelin's more gifted fellow-pupil, Altdorfer. The same composition, painted in tempera upon the wall, is in the Town-hall at Nordlingen, Schäuffelin's native town, and the chief theatre of his pictorial activity. His finest work is an altarpiece in the principal church, which he executed in 1521, for Nicholas Ziegler, the Vice-Chancellor of Charles V. The centre—a Pietà—is, in point of feeling, sense of beauty, clearness of golden tone, and conscientious carrying out, one of the finest pictures of the German school of this period. The saints also, on the wings, are dignified figures, and the St. Barbara of remarkable beauty. Four other pictures by him in the same church may be also classed among his best works.[1] The clever designs for the woodcuts in the Teuerdank[2] are by his hand as well.

BARTHEL BEHAM, born at Nuremberg 1496, died 1540. His earlier works are quite in the manner of Albert Durer. As a rule, his figures are coarsely realistic, broad, and slight in execution, and of lively but somewhat crude colouring. Pictures by him in this style include—a Christ bearing the Cross, in the chapel of St. Maurice; Christ on the Mount of Olives, and several single saints, in the Berlin Gallery. He afterwards went to Italy, and attempted, though with

[1] See further in 'Kunst und Künstler in Deutschland,' vol. i. pp. 349 and 355.
[2] This is the title of a long German poem by Melchior Pfinzing, which celebrates in an allegorical form the adventures of the Emperor Maximilian I. It appeared in Nuremberg in 1517.

little success, to adopt the transalpine style of art. Specimens of this class are the Miracle of a Woman raised from the Dead by the True Cross, of the year 1530, with several animated heads; and Marcus Curtius leaping into the Gulf, of the year 1540, with gaudy and overladen antique architecture,—both in the Munich Gallery, Nos. 2 and 98. A number of portraits of Bavarian princes and princesses, in the gallery at Schleissheim, show that, though somewhat crude in general keeping, he was an admirable portrait artist. He is more important, however, as an engraver. His portraits of the Emperor Charles V., and his brother the Emperor Ferdinand I., are well known for their fine conception and masterly treatment.

HANS SEBALD BEHAM, a nephew of the foregoing, born at Nuremberg in 1500, had the advantage first of his uncle's instructions in painting and engraving, and then of Albert Durer's. In 1540 the unsteadiness of his life compelled him to leave Nuremberg, when he migrated to Frankfort, where he died towards the year 1550. He possessed singular powers of invention, generally exercised on secular, and often on coarsely humorous subjects, occasionally also on those of a vulgar and indecorous class. At the same time he was not deficient in feeling for beauty and grace, and was an excellent draughtsman. Of his oil pictures one only is known, now in the Louvre, executed 1534, in the form of a table, for Albrecht, Archbishop of Mayence. It represents, in small but spirited figures, scenes from the life of David, and is carefully painted in a warm and clear tone.[1] Five miniatures, executed in a prayer-book for the same ecclesiastic, in 1531, now in the Royal Library at Aschaffenburg in ancient Franconia, are evidences of his skill in this line of art. But his most important artistic phase was that of engraving. He handled the graver with spirit and lightness; and several of his numerous plates—for instance, his Patience, Melancholy, St. Sebaldus, his History of the Prodigal Son, and his twelve engravings, with Dancers at a Peasant Wedding—are among the finest specimens of the master

[1] 'Kunst und Künstler in Paris,' p. 549.

on a small scale. His powers of invention are best seen in his designs for woodcuts. His triumphal entry of Charles V. into Munich, and his two processions of soldiers, are the cleverest examples art has preserved to us of the manners and customs of that time.

ALBERT ALTDORFER was born 1488 at Altdorf near Landshuth in Bavaria, and settled at Ratisbon, where he died 1538. He is one of the most important and original of all Albert Durer's scholars and imitators. He seized the fantastic tendency of the time with a poetic feeling at once rich and pleasing, and he developed it so as to attain a perfection in this sort of romantic painting, such as no other artist has ever reached. In general, he knows so well how to give to his representations the peculiar charm of the fabulous, and sets before the spectator what is marvellous in nature in such fulness, that we willingly give ourselves up to his magic influence, and, stopping short on the way to the highest perfection, we repose with pleasure among these graceful dreams. As a draughtsman he displayed no great force, and is frequently deficient in good taste; he is, however, an excellent colourist. In his later period he was strongly influenced by Italian art. Altdorfer's principal work is in the Munich Gallery, Cabinets, No. 169. "It represents the Victory of Alexander the Great over Darius; the costume is that of the artist's own day, as it would be treated in the chivalrous poems of the middle ages—man and horse are sheathed in plate and mail, with surcoats of gold or embroidery; the chanfrons upon the heads of the horses, the glittering lances and stirrups, and the variety of the weapons, form altogether a scene of indescribable splendour and richness. There is no blood or other disgusting object—no scattered limbs or distortions deform this picture;—only in the immediate foreground, if we examine very closely, we see under the feet of the charging hosts, and the hoofs of their war-horses, several lines of bodies lying closely together, as in a web, forming as it were a groundwork to this world of war and arms—of dazzling weapons and of still brighter fame and chivalry. It is, in truth, a

I

little world on a few square feet of canvas; the hosts of combatants, who advance on all sides against each other, are innumerable, and the view into the background appears interminable. In the distance is the ocean, with high rocks, and a rugged island between them; ships of war appear in the offing, and a whole fleet of vessels—on the left the moon is setting—on the right, the sun rising; both shining through the opening clouds—a clear and striking image of the events represented. The armies are arranged in rank and column, without the strange attitudes, contrasts, and distortions, generally exhibited in so-called battle-pieces. How indeed would this have been possible with such a vast multitude of figures? The whole is in the plain and severe, or it may be the stiff, manner of the old style. At the same time, the character and execution of these little figures is most masterly and profound. And what variety, what expression there is, not merely in the character of the single warriors and knights, but in the hosts themselves! Here crowds of black archers rush down, troop after troop, from the mountain with the rage of a foaming torrent; on the other side, high upon the rocks in the far distance, a scattered crowd of flying men are turning round in a defile. The point of the greatest interest stands out brilliantly from the centre of the whole,—Alexander and Darius, both in armour of burnished gold: Alexander, on Bucephalus, with his lance in rest, advances far before his men, and presses on the flying Darius, whose charioteer has already fallen on his white horses, and who looks back upon his conqueror with all the despair of a vanquished monarch."[1] It may moreover be remarked that the landscape rivals the works of the cotemporary Netherlanders, Patenier and others, or rather it surpasses them in truth and grandeur. A rocky mountain in the centre of the picture, with beautiful hanging woods, is particularly good; above is a castle and a path leading to it; at the foot of the mountain, a ruin illuminated by the setting sun. This ruin is painted with

---

[1] Werke von Friedrich Schlegel, Wien, 1828, vol. vi. p. 166.

so true a feeling for the beauties of Nature, that a power of such high order would of itself have qualified the artist for the most masterly productions. A fine landscape in the Landauer Brüderhaus at Nuremberg shows him to have been the creator of landscape-painting in Germany.

Another picture by this artist, in the Munich Gallery, Cabinets, No. 138, is inscribed with his monogram and the date 1526. It represents the history of Susanna. The garden with the bath, on the left, and a mass of varied architecture on the right, make up a rich and fanciful composition.

There is a good picture from the hand of this master in the chapel of St. Maurice at Nuremberg. It represents a man and two women occupied in drawing the body of St. Quirinus out of the water, and, in fact, forms a well-arranged *genre* scene. The thickly-covered banks of the river are another instance of his happy conception of nature. The light of the setting sun—a golden tint surrounded by a circle of clouds, melting away into shades of red—is full of imagination. A Crucifixion, by Altdorfer, at once pleasing and effective, is preserved in the Landauer Brüderhaus of the same city, No. 179. A chef-d'œuvre of the master is an altarpiece with wings, in the Augsburg Gallery, executed in 1517. The interior pictures represent the Crucifixion, the exterior the Annunciation. This latter subject exhibits capital figures, and fine features and expression.[1]

Another picture by him, a Nativity of the Virgin, shows him to be a skilful architectural painter as regards lines and aërial perspective. It is in the same gallery.[2]

Among the pictures by this master at Regensburg, an Adoration of the Shepherds in the collection of the Historical Society is remarkable for its dramatic character.[3]

I know of but one picture by him in England, of large size, in the collection of the Rev. J. Fuller Russell. It represents the Saviour taking leave of his Mother, and is

---

[1] 'Kunst und Künstler in Deutschland,' vol. ii. p. 38, &c.
[2] Ibid. p. 38, &c.   [3] Ibid. p. 123.

remarkable for its powerful colouring, and for the developed character of the landscape.[1]

The engravings by Altdorfer are not inferior to his paintings in invention and clever execution.

A master-work of such interest as Altdorfer's Battle of Alexander naturally produced many imitations. Thus, in the Munich Gallery, there is a picture by MARTIN FESELE, of about 1530, of which the subject is the siege of Rome under Porsenna. This composition possesses the same richness, and the figures are as fine and evince as much taste as those in Altdorfer's picture, but it is inferior to the latter work in poetic feeling.

GEORGE PENCZ, born at Nuremberg 1500, died at Breslau 1550. This painter was one of Albert Durer's most gifted scholars, combining excellent drawing, and clear, warm, and vigorous colouring, with a felicitious power of conception, and a decided feeling for beauty. Later in life he went to Italy, where he zealously studied the works of Raphael, without however degenerating into the tasteless and mistaken manner of most of the Netherlandish and German painters who attempted to Italianise their style. On the contrary, he never departed from his own original feeling, but only gave a higher character to the taste of his compositions and to his drawing. In the art of engraving, where he occupies the first place among Albert Durer's followers, he also attained such perfection under the guidance of Marc Antonio as closely to approach the great Italian in several plates. In the great rarity of his historical pictures, we can only judge from his engravings of the success with which he treated both sacred and profane history, allegory and mythology, scenes from common life, and the department of ornamentation. And a number of portraits still existing serve to show that for animation of conception, excellent drawing and modelling, and warm transparent colouring, he was one of the first German painters in this line.

An historical picture in his German manner is a St.

---

[1] See 'Treasures,' &c., vol. ii. p. 463, where the picture is erroneously attributed to Albert Durer.

Jerome, in the chapel of St. Maurice at Nuremberg, No. 76. It is a capital work—at the same time I am inclined to attribute the original invention, which has been repeated by several painters, to Quentin Massys.

An excellent picture, in his Italian manner, is Venus and Cupid, in the gallery at Munich, No. 95. It is graceful in motive, pure in form, and well modelled. The following are masterly portraits by him:—a young man, No. 585, and the painter Schwetzer and his wife, Nos. 582 and 587, in the Berlin Museum; General Sebaldus Schirmer, No. 77, in the Landauer Brüderhaus at Nuremberg; and Erasmus of Rotterdam, after Holbein, at Windsor Castle. Amongst the engravings by Pencz, a series of plates from the history of Tobit are remarkable for beautiful and tender feeling. They combine, very happily and simply, the German homeliness and naïveté of conception with that higher grace which may be considered as an inheritance from Raphael. What he also accomplished as an engraver in the way of portraits is proved by that of the Elector John Frederick the Generous, of Saxony. How entirely he had adopted the manner of Marc Antonio is seen in his large plate of the Taking of Carthage, from a drawing by Julio Romano, the only instance in which he did not work from his own compositions.

JACOB BINK, born at Cologne either 1490 or 1504. Judging from his engravings, he must have formed himself from Albert Durer; he also studied in Italy. Further than this we know nothing of his life, except that he was in the service of the king of Denmark as a portrait-painter previous to the year 1546; that he spent some time at Königsberg, at the court of Albrecht of Hohenzollern, Duke of Prussia, and was sent by that prince, in 1549, to the Netherlands, for the purpose of erecting a monument to the duke's late wife; that he entered regularly into his service in 1551, and died at Königsberg about the year 1560. It is singular that no historical picture by him is known; also of the portraits attributed to him, I have seen only the one in the gallery at Vienna. It is of energetic conception and delicate drawing, and of cool but harmonious colouring. In the *Garderobe* at Copenhagen are preserved, as I understand, portraits by him of Christian III. of Denmark, and of his queen Dorothea; in that of Königsberg, those of Duke Albrecht, of the duke's first wife, and of the Chancellor Fries, dated 1549. His engravings are very unequal in merit.[1] The best of them give evidence of a first-rate artist, who, like Pencz, succeeded in combining German feeling and treatment with the nobler forms and purer taste of the Italians, and who treated subjects of the most various kinds with no common excellence. The following are among his best plates: Christ with the Woman of Samaria (Bartsch, No. 12); the Virgin (No. 20); the portraits of Christian II. king of Denmark, and Elizabeth his queen (Nos. 91, 92); and the portrait of himself. He also frequently copied the works of other engravers.

The style of Albert Durer, as may be easily supposed, was also variously called into practice in the form of miniature-painting; in Nuremberg especially, by the numerous family of GLOCKENTHON, among whom GEORGE GLOCKENTHON the elder, born 1492, died 1553, and his son NICHOLAS, died 1560, were the most distinguished.[2] A missal and a prayer-book, with miniatures by the son, executed for Albrecht, Archbishop of Mayence, for the first of which the artist received five hundred florins, is in the Royal Library at Aschaffenburg. He appears there as an artist of first-rate technical attainments, but of feeble powers of invention and uncertain drawing.[3]

At this time there was also another painter, living in the northern part of Franconia, who occupied an independent position by the side of Albert Durer and his school. This was MATTHEW GRUNEWALD, born probably in Frankfort, and who established himself in Aschaffenburg, where he was employed chiefly by the Archbishop Albrecht of Mayence. Of the other circumstances of his life just nothing is known. At the same time it may be affirmed

---

[1] See Bartsch, 'Le Peintre Graveur,' vol. viii., p. 249, &c., for an account of this master, and of the engravings and woodcuts justly attributed to him.
[2] See Johann Neudörfer's ' Nachrichten alten Künstlern in Nürnberg-Campe,' p. 41, &c.
[3] 'Kunst und Künstler in Deutschland,' vol. ii. p. 382, &c.

with certainty that he died, at the earliest, towards the year 1530.[1] His works testify to his being, after Albert Durer and Holbein, the greatest German painter of this period. He takes a happy halfway position between the Franconian and the Suabian schools, and must have owed his artistic education to each. The feeling for style in the arrangement of his works, wherein he followed, though with a certain exercise of freedom, the old rules of symmetry—the dignity of his male characters, and the firmness of his drawing, show his affinity to the Franconian school: his greater feeling for beauty, especially in female figures— the fulness of his forms—the purer taste of his drapery, which is less broken up by sharp folds—his more careful modelling—frequently harmonious arrangement of colour, in which a dark violet, a deep crimson, and a luminous green prevail—and, finally, the better union of his outlines and forms—all these qualities exhibit the decided influence of the school of Suabia. The proportions of his figures are generally somewhat short—the flesh-tones of his men of a pale brown—those of his women and children of a pleasing reddish, clear colour. His most important and only positively authentic work is an altarpiece consisting of six panels, which he executed by commission for Albrecht, Archbishop of Mayence, for the church of SS. Maurice and Magdalen, at Halle on the Saale. After the introduction of the reformed doctrine at Halle this work was transferred to the conventual church of SS. Peter and Alexander at Aschaffenburg, and was next placed in the gallery of that town, whence it was transferred in 1836 to the gallery at Munich.[2] The centre picture, No. 69, represents the Conversion of St. Maurice by St. Erasmus—the latter being a portrait of the archbishop;—and the wings contain the figures of St. Lazarus, No. 68—the Magdalen, No. 63—St. Chrysostom, No. 75—and St. Valentinian. The last-named is still in the church at Aschaffenburg. The figures are colossal, drawn with great mastery, and of earnest, dig-

---

[1] See Passavant in 'Kunstblatt,' 1841, p. 430, &c.
[2] Merkel's MSS. of the Court Library at Aschaffenburg: Aschaffenburg, 1836, p. 11.

nified, and grandly individual character. Another chef-d'œuvre, also executed for the same potentate, is still in the place for which it was originally painted, the church of our Lady at Halle. The centre picture, however, representing the Virgin in glory, surrounded with angels, and adored by the donor, the inner sides with SS. Maurice and Alexander, and perhaps the outer sides of the centre picture with SS. Augustine and John the Evangelist, are the only parts by Grunewald. Among the other portions of this altarpiece, executed by his assistants, the most remarkable are the figures of SS. Magdalen, Ursula, Catherine, and Erasmus, probably by the hand of Lucas Cranach.[1] The subject of the Annunciation, also comprised in this work, and its weakest portion, bears date 1529, whence we may conclude that the master must have been in the zenith of his powers at this time. Also a so-called Rosary picture in the chapel of St. Anthony, in the Cathedral at Bamberg, is a first-rate work by the master. It represents, within a large wreath of roses, the Trinity adored by numerous saints, and below, the figures of Leo X. and Maximilian I., who were cotemporary with the picture. The same excellence is seen in the wings of an altarpiece at Heilsbronn in Franconia, and in two altarpieces in the church at Annaberg in Saxony.[2] England also possesses a fine work by his hand, in the collection of the Prince Consort at Kensington—an altarpiece, with the Virgin and Child in glory in the centre, adored by SS. Catherine and Barbara. The inner sides of the wings contain SS. Nicholas and George. The outer sides, with SS. James and Erasmus, show the hand of a scholar.

HANS GRIMMER.—Scholar of Matthew Grunewald. Existing pictures show him to have been a portrait-painter of lively conception, delicate drawing, clear colouring, and careful finish. This description is especially applicable to the portrait of a woman in the chapel of St. Maurice, No. 140. The companion to it, a man, No. 136, is inferior in colouring.

[1] See Passavant's essay in 'Kunstblatt,' 1846, No. 48. Also, my remarks on Förster's 'Geschichte der Malerei in Deutschland,' in the 'Deutsches Kunstblatt,' 1854, p. 202.
[2] 'Kunst und Künstler in Deutschland,' vol. i. pp. 46 and 306.

SAXON PAINTERS.

No original school can be traced in Saxony, or in the domain of the Elector of Brandenburg; but various Franconian artists exercised their art in these parts: a proof of this is seen in the works by Matthew Grunewald, above mentioned, executed for Halle. The figures of saints on the wings of the altar at Brandenburg, dated 1518—works exhibiting a first-rate master in the dignified character of the figures and elevated taste of the drapery—point also for their author to Grunewald. And even the master who, in the capacity of painter to Frederick the Wise, at Wittenberg, founded a kind of school in Saxony, namely LUCAS CRANACH,[1] not only owed his birth to Cranach,[2] a place in Northern Franconia, but his early works bear the character of Franconian art. Born in 1472, of a family of the name of SUNDER, he received his first instructions in art from his father, his later teaching probably from Matthew Grunewald; at all events, his whole style of art bears the impress of having been formed from the works of that master. If inferior to him in grandeur of conception, in feeling for style, in drawing (his weakest part), and in thoroughness of execution, he excels him in richness and variety of invention, in peculiar clearness of colour, and finally, though often degenerating into a mechanical and slight manner, in the lightness of his treatment. In some instances he attained to the expression of dignity, earnestness, and feeling, but generally his characteristics are a naïve and childlike cheerfulness, and a gentle and almost timid grace. A certain charm of animation, and a warm, blooming colouring, must be accepted in most of his works as substitutes for a strict understanding of form. In these respects his art partakes in a high degree of a national character; even his humour has something of the coarse popular wit of his time. The impression produced by his style of representation reminds one of the " Volksbücher " and

[1] 'Lucas Cranach des älteren Leben und Werke,' by Christian Schuchardt, 2 vols. Leipsic, Brockhaus, 1851.
[2] Ibid. vol. ii. p. 240-255.

"Volkslieder;" and, as in those, the tenderest flowers of art are found in the naïvest way in immediate juxta-position with all that is tasteless and even childish. Many of his church pictures have a very peculiar significance: in these he stands forth, properly speaking, as the painter of the Reformation. Intimate both with Luther and Melancthon, he seizes on the essential aim of their doctrine, viz. the insufficiency of good works, and the sole efficacy of faith in a Saviour, and endeavours to embody it in the form of art. As specimens of this kind may be mentioned a dying man, dated 1518, in the Town Museum of Leipsic; the Fall and the Redemption of man, dated 1529, in the Ducal Gallery of Gotha; a large altarpiece in the church of the town of Schneeberg in Saxony; and a picture in the Gallery of the Estates at Prague, also dated 1529. All these pictures, some of them accompanied with explanatory inscriptions, are at the same time excellent works by the master. Only in the picture at Schneeberg do we remark the assistance of pupils. Among his pictures of Scriptural subjects, that of the Woman taken in Adultery, in the Munich Gallery, No. 56, deserves particular mention. The heads of Christ and of the woman are admirable. Lucas Cranach is especially successful in affectionate and childlike subjects. This we see in his various pictures of Christ receiving little children, one of the finest of which is in the gallery of Thomas Baring, Esq., in London—another in the church of St. Wenceslaus at Naumburg. On occasions where he treats mythological subjects, the result, considered in that light, must be looked upon rather as a parody, yet even these appeal directly to the eye, like real portraits; and sometimes also by means of a certain grace and naïveté of motive. We may cite as an instance the Diana seated on a stag, in a small picture in the Museum at Berlin, No. 564, where she is represented with her less happily conceived brother Apollo. Occasionally, it is true, these works are disfigured by a too obvious aim at grace, and by means of a laboured and even violently distorted motive; as, for instance, in his subjects of Venus and Cupid, who is complaining to his mother of being stung by a bee—also in the Berlin Museum, Nos. 593, 1190, and 1203—where the position of the goddess's lower limbs illustrates what we have said. He treated this subject frequently. The Hercules and Omphale in the same gallery, No. 576, is very naïve. As specimens of his coarse humour may be quoted his old man caressing a girl, dated 1531, in the Estates Gallery at Prague, and the Fountain of Youth in the Berlin Museum, No. 593. This last is a picture of peculiar character; a large basin, surrounded by steps, and with a richly adorned fountain, forms the centre. On one side, where the country is stony and barren, a multitude of old women are dragged forward on horses, waggons, or carriages, and with much trouble are got into the water. On the other side of the fountain they appear as young maidens, splashing about and amusing themselves with all kinds of playful mischief; close by is a large pavilion, into which a herald courteously invites them to enter, and where they are arrayed in costly apparel. A feast is prepared in a smiling meadow, which seems to be followed by a dance; the gay crowd loses itself in a neighbouring grove. The men unfortunately have not become young, and retain their gray beards. This picture is of the year 1546, the seventy-fourth of Cranach's age.

His great excellence lies in purely realistic subjects, to which department his art properly belongs—such as his hunts of wild animals,[1] and his portraits. A small but first-rate picture of a stag-hunt is in the collection of Lord Taunton at Stoke. His portraits are so numerous that I can only particularise a few—for instance, the Elector Albrecht of Mayence, represented full length as St. Jerome, of the year 1527, in the Berlin Museum, No. 589, and that of the unfortunate Elector, John Frederick the Generous, No. 590. Also the portrait of the Elector John the Constant, in the Grand Ducal Gallery at Weimar, is one of his best male portraits. Turning to his female portraits, we may cite the pleasingly conceived and warm

[1] See lithographs from his border drawings in Albert Durer's Prayer-book in the Munich Library, by Strixner. Munich, 1818.

and luminously coloured head in the National Gallery, No. 291, as a good specimen. These qualities of colour, however, he only attained after 1515, probably after a meeting with some wandering painter from the Netherlands. On the other hand, his earliest known work, the fine Repose in Egypt, now in the Sciarra Colonna Palace at Rome, dated 1504; two pictures of SS. Jerome and Leopold, dated 1515, in the Belvedere Gallery at Vienna; and the portrait of the Burgomaster of Eisenach, in the Berlin Museum, No. 618 a, show a more broken but less clear brownish flesh-tone, in the manner of Matthew Grunewald. He may be said to have reached the zenith of his art towards the year 1530; for, besides the two above-mentioned pictures of that time, the two following, bearing the same date, may be reckoned among his finest productions, viz., Samson and Dalilah, in the Royal Gallery at Augsburg, and his Melancholy, from the Campe collection, now in the possession of Lord Lindsay. In the first of these Dalilah is seen seated in a beautiful garden, while Samson, attired as a stately knight, with rich golden greaves, and the jawbone of the ass in his hand, sleeps in her lap; she is cutting off his hair with a pair of bright scissors; the Philistines, well armed, creep stealthily through the wood; a rich and beautiful view opens itself at the side. Cranach retained his artistic powers unenfeebled till his death in 1553, as is evident from the centre picture of the altarpiece at Weimar, which I concur with Schuchart in considering his most important work (see woodcut). This also embodies, as above mentioned, the one great object of the Reformation, representing the Saviour on the cross, with St. John the Baptist directing the attention of Luther and Cranach—two admirable portraits—to the sacrifice by which alone Redemption was purchased. On the left is Christ again, triumphant over Satan, who is seen in the middle distance driving sinners into the gulf of fire. This painter also distinguished himself occasionally in the execution of miniatures; he was a skilful engraver, and also designed a series of drawings, including some of great excellence, for woodcutting; the subjects of

ALTARPIECE IN THE CHURCH AT WEIMAR: CONTAINING PORTRAITS OF LUTHER, MELANCTHON, AND THE PAINTER HIMSELF
By Lucas Cranach

several of these show that he took an energetic part in the struggle between Luther and the Papacy.[1]

Considered also in a personal light, Lucas Cranach is entitled to great respect. The Electors John the Constant and John Frederick the Generous, successors to Frederick the Wise, both retained him in their service. He even shared the five years' captivity of Frederick the Generous, after the battle of Mühlberg, in 1547, alleviating it by his art and his cheerful society. In Wittenberg he was held in such high esteem by the citizens as to be elected Burgomaster in 1537, and again in 1540. He voluntarily relinquished this dignity in 1544.

The long life of this painter, and the rapidity of his brush, which was such as to obtain him the title of "celerrimus pictor" on his grave-stone, will account for the very large number of pictures which he executed. Nevertheless, of the works bearing his name, many are the production of his son Lucas Cranach the younger—of whom I have more to say; also probably of another son, called Johann Lucas, who died at an early age in Italy.[2] A large remainder are by less skilful and often even by spiritless and mechanical journeymen painters. Among the pictures thus manufactured may be included a large number of small portraits of Luther, Melancthon, and of the Electors Frederick the Wise and John the Constant, which bear the date 1532. By allowing, however, his monogram to be inscribed on these works, Lucas Cranach himself contributed to lower his reputation with succeeding generations. Although Schuchart may be right in maintaining that an altarpiece in the church at Wittenberg, assigned to Lucas Cranach, was little if at all touched by his hand, but is only one of the better productions of his workshop,[3] yet the composition, which at all events proceeded from him, is too remarkable not to be mentioned here. The centre represents the Last Supper, and is peculiar in its arrange-

---

[1] 'Schuchart,' vol. ii. p. 240-255.
[2] See notice of this son, who died at Bologna, 1536, 'Schuchart,' vol. i. p. 96, &c.
[3] Ibid. vol. ii. p. 147, &c.

ment, for the disciples, with heads of varied character, are seated round a circular table. On the right wing is painted the sacrament of Baptism, administered by Melancthon in presence of an assistant and three sponsors. A group of richly dressed women, as spectators, stand in the foreground. A peculiar but pleasing tone of feeling pervades the whole. The left wing, representing Confession, is superior to the former picture. In the confessor we recognise the portrait of Bugenhagen, who, with severe dignity, absolves a kneeling penitent (a citizen), with the key in his right hand, whilst at the same time, with the one in his left, he motions back a warrior who has drawn near, with a haughty, rather than a repentant air, and whose hands are still fettered. On the predella is a fourth painting with smaller figures: in the centre is the image of Christ crucified; on one side a pulpit, from which Luther preaches, in front of a graceful and simple group of listening maidens, and women with children; and deeper in the picture is as fine a group of serious men and youths. This work is at once a representation of the most remarkable rite of the Protestant Church, and a memorial of the most honoured teachers of Holy Writ.[1]

LUCAS CRANACH THE YOUNGER, like his father, in his later years filled the office of Burgomaster of Wittenberg. He appears to have formed his style both on that of his father and of Albert Durer, as is evident from the different peculiarities in his works, which remind us sometimes of the one and sometimes of the other. He has, however, a soft grace and a sweetness peculiarly his own, which are particularly seen in his glowing, but, at times, somewhat too rosy colouring. He died in 1586, and was one of those who most steadily adhered to the true style of ancient art; whilst his cotemporaries, almost in a body, began to yield to the influence of foreign mannerism.

In the principal church at Wittenberg[2] are preserved several of this artist's pictures:—Christ and the two

[1] Schadow, Wittenberg's Denkmäler der Bildnerei, Baukunst, und Malerei Wittenberg, 1825.   [2] Ibid., p. 99.

thieves on the Cross, with the family of the donor kneeling at the foot, is an excellent work; a Nativity, in which the rafters of the stable are covered with a crowd of joyous little angels. The Conversion of Saul is unimportant. One singular subject bears again a distinct reference to the state of the Church in his time: it is the Vineyard of the Lord, one half of which is being destroyed by the assembled clergy of the Romish Church, whilst the heroes of the Reformation are employed in cultivating the other—a composition, it must be owned, in which the simple poetic feeling of the conception far surpasses the merit as a painting.

John the Baptist preaching. The saint has the features of Melancthon. This picture is in the Brunswick Gallery, and may be considered one of his best works. The same may be said of a Virgin giving a bunch of grapes to the Child who is standing before her, and which is hung by the name of the elder Cranach in the Munich Gallery, Cabinets, No. 1212. Of his later and somewhat slighter period is a Crucifixion in the Dresden Gallery, No. 1667. Two admirable portraits of the Electors Augustus and Maurice of Saxony are also in the same gallery, Nos. 1671 and 1672.

THE SUABIAN SCHOOL.

The chief master of the Augsburg school at this period was HANS BURGKMAIR, born 1473, died 1559, son of the Thomas Burgkmair of the preceding period. He was an artist of very varied powers of invention; for besides executing those subjects which the Church then dictated, he was also the first master of his time in the delineation of such knightly and courtly themes as the court of Maximilian I. had then introduced into Germany. This is especially seen in the miniatures of his Tournament books,[1] and in his designs for woodcuts[2] for those

[1] A Tournament book of this description is in the possession of his Highness the Prince of Hohenzollern Sigmaringen.
[2] See further concerning these works in Bartsch, 'Le Peintre Graveur,' vol. vii. p. 223, &c.

works executed for Maximilian—the Genealogy of that emperor, the Weisskunig, and the Triumph.[1] On the whole, he remains true to the characteristics of the Suabian school. His compositions are generally devoid of style, and his drawing, especially in his earlier time, is not correct. Although occasionally not wanting in feeling for dignity and beauty, the chief aim of his art was the representation of truth. His heads have therefore a portraitlike air; he is greatly wanting also in feeling for lines, and may even be pronounced to be often highly tasteless in his motives. On the other hand, he has a lively sense of colour; the tone of his flesh is generally warm and powerful, the colour of his draperies of great power and depth, and the modelling and execution of the detail, in his better works, of great carefulness. At the same time he is answerable for many works of a hard and mechanical character. This painter, with Altdorfer, was the first in Germany who worked out the detail of his landscape backgrounds in accordance with nature, though I am not aware that he painted landscapes, properly speaking, like Altdorfer. But in his long life two periods may be very clearly distinguished. In the first, which extends to about 1508, he adheres to the forms of art prevailing in Germany in the 15th century; the folds of his drapery are sharper than those of the elder Hans Holbein, and he frequently employs gold, both in drapery and in ornaments. Only in his architecture is the Italian taste indicated: in the second period it appears in the fuller rendering of forms, in the drapery, and in the more harmonious keeping. Nevertheless his German nature is never repudiated in essentials, and, in the woodcuts executed from his drawings, the influence of Albert Durer is distinctly traceable. His strong feeling for the realistic in art is occasionally seen too in his successful treatment of scenes from common life. Sandrart mentions fresco paintings by him, but none have descended to us. Of his

---

[1] These are the titles of works executed by command of the emperor to glorify his feats and his family.

numerous oil pictures still existing I can only mention
a portion. The following, in the Augsburg Gallery, are
the chefs-d'œuvre of his earlier time. A rich picture of
numerous subjects, dated 1501—among them Christ on the
Mount of Olives, and also, in a mandorla, St. Peter, the
Virgin and Child, and fourteen saints. The expression
of the Christ is very dignified; the form of the male
heads noble, that of the female heads refined, but rather
monotonous. The foreshortening of the mouth and eyes
is generally defective.[1] Another picture, with Christ and
the Virgin adored by numerous Saints, is of the same
year. A picture, with the Crucifixion in the centre, and
the Martyrdom of St. Ursula at the sides, is of the year
1504. The animation in this latter, and the contrast
between the ferocity of the heathen and the resignation
of the tender maiden, are very successful. Of about the
same time is a large picture of the same subject in the
Dresden Gallery, No. 1637.

Admirable specimens of his second period are the following. The Virgin seated under a tree, and giving a
bunch of grapes to the Child, dated 1510, in the chapel
of St. Maurice at Nuremberg. This little picture displays a degree of taste and delicacy of rendering such
as Burgkmair but seldom attained.[2] The Crucifixion,
in the Augsburg Gallery, of the year 1519;[3] also the
Adoration of the Kings, in the same gallery. This last,
in character of heads, delicacy of treatment in a cool
tone, and mastery of carrying out, is, to my knowledge,
the chef-d'œuvre of the second period. Considering the
rarity of this master's works in England, I may mention
an Adoration of the Shepherds, in his decidedly realistic
manner, and of great merit, in the collection of the Prince
Consort at Kensington, No. 40. A St. John in the Isle of
Patmos, in the Munich Gallery, No. 65, affords a specimen
of the great development he attained in landscape; the
inspiration of the head is also well expressed. A Mother

---

[1] See further concerning this and the following pictures in 'Künstler und Kunstwerke in Deutschland,' vol. ii. p. 28, &c.
[2] Ibid., vol. i. p. 197.   [3] Ibid., vol. ii. p. 32, &c.

with two Children, dated 1541, in the Landauer Brüderhaus, No. 94,[1] is characteristic of his naïveté and truth of treatment in subjects taken from common life. It is there attributed to Hans Olmdorf. Finally he appears as a mannered imitator of Italian art in a picture in the church of St. Anna at Augsburg—Christ delivering Souls from Purgatory, probably executed soon after 1533. As a portrait-painter he is seen to most advantage in the portrait of a Duke Frederick of Saxony, in the castle at Nuremberg, and there attributed to Hans von Culmbach. The picture is remarkable for a pure feeling for nature and delicate flesh-tones. The portraits of Duke William of Bavaria and his wife are harder in outline and heavier in flesh-tones. They are in the Munich Gallery, Cabinets, Nos. 136 and 150. Portraits of himself and his wife, dated 1528, in the Belvedere Gallery at Vienna, are far warmer and clearer in colour, and very animated in conception. The wife holds a mirror, in which they are both represented as death's heads, showing that the fantastic feeling of the middle ages was by no means extinct in the Suabian school at this time. How much it was characteristic of Burgkmair appears in various woodcuts from his designs, namely, in that of a young woman endeavouring to escape from Death, who is killing a young man; in the Seven Cardinal Virtues; the Seven Deadly Sins; and in the Three Good Men and Women, Christian, Jew, and Pagan.[2] He also executed an etching on iron.[3]

But the greatest artist whom Augsburg produced was HANS HOLBEIN THE YOUNGER, born there 1498.[4] In him the realistic tendency of the German school attained its noblest and highest development, and he may be unreservedly pronounced to be one of the greatest masters who laboured, generally speaking, in this department of art. A com-

---

[1] 'Künstler und Kunstwerke in Deutschland,' vol. i. p. 197.
[2] Bartsch, 'Le Peintre Graveur,' vol. vii. p. 215, &c.
[3] Ibid. p. 199.
[4] The chief works relating to Holbein are Ulrich Hegner's 'Hans Holbein der Jüngere,' Berlin, 1827, and Chrétien de Meckel's 'Œuvres de Jean Holbein, ou Recueil de Gravures d'après ses plus beaux Ouvrages,' Basle, 1780. Also, Horace Walpole's 'Anecdotes on Painting.'

parison with his elder cotemporary, Albert Durer, will best serve to place his pictorial merits in a clear light. As respects grandeur and depth of feeling, and richness of invention in the field of ecclesiastic art, as well as conformability to style in the arrangement of his subjects, he stands far below the great Nuremberg master. Although also affected by the fantastic element which prevailed in the middle ages, Holbein shows it in a very different way. While Albert Durer treated the subjects of the Apocalypse in the freer forms of his art, though with an adherence to the feeling of the middle ages, and in his Melancholy shows the solemn sense of the insufficiency and instability of all sublunary things, yet in his etching of the Knight with Death and the Devil he gives an expression of a human security and power which may be said to resist and morally to triumph over these assailants. Holbein, on the other hand, seized the mediæval subject of the Dance of Death; and availing himself of his improved means of representation in the expression of the deadliest irony and malignity, he shows us, under every form, from that of the pope down to the beggar, how helpless are the terrors of the human race in every encounter with its invincible foe. While Albert Durer's art thus exhibits a close affinity to the religious ideas of the middle ages, Holbein appears imbued with the sentiments of a more modern time, strictly consequent on which we find him decidedly excelling his great rival in closeness and delicacy of observation in the delineation of nature. A proof of this is afforded by the evidence of Erasmus of Rotterdam—himself gifted with a fine eye in matters of art—who says that, as regards the portraits made of him by both of these painters, that by Holbein was the most like.[1] In feeling for beauty of form also, in grace of movement, tasteful arrangement of drapery, in colouring, and above all in the art of painting, wherein he had derived from his father a modelling and fusing

---

[1] This is told by Van Mander, fol. 142 b. Also the well-known engraving of Erasmus, by Albert Durer, Bartsch, No. 107, shows a very different conception of his subject as compared with the various portraits of the same by Holbein.

manner, as opposed to that of a draughtsman, Holbein must be placed above Albert Durer. Uniting therefore with all these qualities admirable powers of drawing and composition, he may justly be considered, of all the German masters, the one most fitted by Nature to attain that supremacy of art in historical painting which the works of his great Italian cotemporaries—Raphael, Andrea del Sarto, and others—display. That he did not rival them in this respect must be ascribed to the circumstances of his life, which seldom allowed him to treat subjects of that class. In portrait-painting, to which his powers were especially devoted, he stands on a level with the greatest masters. His genius was precocious in development, and highly versatile in application. He was skilled in various styles of painting—in fresco, oil-colours, and tempera, and also in the execution of miniatures—being at the same time so subject to influences from other painters, that in the meagre notices we possess of his life it becomes exceedingly difficult to define the chronological succession of his works. So numerous are these that I must content myself with noticing such as are most characteristic of his various periods.

The pictures of his earliest time have somewhat heavy yellow-brown flesh-tones. One of the most remarkable of this class, in the Gallery of Augsburg,[1] is the St. Sebastian, known by documentary evidence to have been executed in 1515. The truth of the forms and action render this a marvellous production for a youth of seventeen. The heads are very individual, the rich landscape well carried out and of great transparency. The finest work, and probably one of the last works executed in Augsburg, are the wings of an altar, wrongly assigned to his father, in the Munich Gallery, Nos. 40 and 46, the one representing St. Elizabeth of Thuringen giving food to the poor, the other St. Barbara. These are both not only very true to nature, but also, and especially the St. Barbara, noble and slender figures of refined feeling. The year 1516 was probably the date of his removal to Basle, which continued the chief arena of his

---

[1] 'Künstler und Kunstwerke in Deutschland,' vol. ii. p. 24, &c.

labours until 1526. Various pictures with this first-mentioned date were decidedly executed in Basle. Of these the portrait of the Basle painter, Johann Horbster, now in the collection of Thomas Baring, Esq.,[1] shows most affinity in tone of colouring with the above-mentioned picture of St. Sebastian. The portraits of the burgomaster Jacob Meyer, surnamed "zum Hasen,"[2] and his wife, in the Basle Gallery, though also bearing date 1516, must have been executed later in the year. The conception is more refined; and the clearer and more reddishly-inclined brown flesh-tones which characterise his pictures up to 1526 begin already to be apparent. To the earlier period of his residence at Basle may be assigned a Last Supper, on cloth, in the Basle Museum. Although rather overladen in composition, yet the moment when Christ gives the sop to Judas is vividly conceived, and the heads of admirable character.

In 1517 Holbein decorated the house of the bailiff Jacob van Hartenstein at Lucerne with frescoes. The destruction of these is the more to be regretted from the variety of subjects which, according to an existing record, were there represented. In the interior he painted the proprietor's patron saints, scenes from the legends of the same, hunts, deeds of war, and a Fountain of Youth. On the outside, between the windows, feats of ancient heroes; below, a frieze of children playing with arms; above, another with a triumphal procession, after Mantegna; and higher still, events from Roman history. Probably only a year or two later he executed the wings of an altarpiece now in the cathedral at Freiburg, in the grand-dukedom of Baden—the one the Adoration of the Shepherds, treated as a night effect, and with the chief light proceeding from the Child, the effect of the light altogether given with extraordinary truth; the other the Adoration of the Kings, an excellent composition. A remarkable figure here is the companion of the Moorish king, who, as if dazzled, is looking up with his hand before his eyes at the stars. The

---

[1] Galleries and Cabinets of Art, p. 97.
[2] This appellation is necessarily given in order to distinguish him from other burgomasters of Basle of the same name.

heads show great truth of nature and every variety of character, from the beautiful to the boorish; the forms, and especially the hands, are delicately carried out. This picture is worthily followed by the portrait of Boniface Amerbach, a zealous patron of Holbein, now in Basle Gallery. In simple unpretending conception, and pure feeling for nature, this is one of the finest portraits by the master of this period. To about the year 1521 may be assigned various works in fresco which Holbein executed in the Town-house at Basle. Side by side with illustrations of the stern administration of justice, as seen in similar buildings in the Netherlands, were placed traits of republican virtue—the Blinding of the aged Zaleucus, the suicide of Charondas, and Curius Dentatus with the Sabine Envoys. The sole relics of these frescoes now preserved in the Basle Gallery are three heads of the envoys from the last-named subject, the spirited, energetic, and yet finely-tempered character of which shows the mastery Holbein had already obtained in history painting, and how high a place he would have won had more frequent opportunities been accorded him.

That he also treated subjects of ecclesiastical import, requiring the expression of deep pathos, with extraordinary success, is evident from his well-known representation of the Passion, in eight compartments, in the Basle Gallery. In colouring and treatment these strikingly recall the fine picture from the life of St. Paul by his father, in Augsburg. The Crucifixion and the Entombment (which latter reminds us, in the chief group, of Raphael's Entombment in the Borghese) are admirable in composition, feeling, and rendering; while the Christ on the Mount of Olives shows a beauty and depth of feeling scarcely inferior to that in Correggio's celebrated picture. It would appear incredible that these works should belong to this early period, were not the egregious false drawing and repelling caricatures and exaggerations—as, for instance, in the Flagellation and the Crucifixion—only to be accounted for by the earliness of their date. Other pictures of this period, showing the decided influence of Leonardo da Vinci, render it probable that Holbein may have made a hasty visit to Northern Italy at this time. In one of them—a Last Supper, in the Basle Gallery, No. 33, one portion of which is wanting—there is a symmetry of arrangement, an elevation of heads, especially in that of the Saviour, and a certain equality of treatment, which show the unmistakeable influence of Leonardo's Last Supper, at Milan. The head of Judas alone, a Jew of frightful vulgarity of character, betrays the realistic feeling of Holbein in all its force. In the other picture in the same gallery, No. 21, a Dead Christ, this tendency is seen in its utmost rudeness, combined with an attempt to model in the style peculiar to Leonardo. It is difficult to believe that this pale greenish form, with streaming blood, taken evidently from one who had died a violent death, and drawn with a mastery marvellous in an artist of twenty-three years of age, could have been really intended to represent a dead Christ. The inscription, however, "Jesus Nazarenus, Rex Jud: H. H. 1521," leaves no doubt.

One of the most admirable pictures, not only of this period but of the master, is the portrait of Erasmus, his patron, dated MDXXIII., one of the chief ornaments of Lord Radnor's rich gallery at Longford Castle.[1] One hardly knows which most to admire, the refined and animated conception, or the masterly carrying out of the minutest details which are united here. This is doubtless the portrait sent by Erasmus to his friend Sir Thomas More in 1525, in order to give him a proof of Holbein's powers, and to serve as a recommendation to the great master, who even then contemplated a visit to England. Sir Thomas replied, " Your painter, my dear Erasmus, is an admirable artist," and added the promise of giving Holbein his protection.[2] To the same year may be also assigned the admirable por-

[1] Galleries and Cabinets, &c., p. 356.
[2] Considering the interest attached to Holbein in England, I subjoin the entire passage from the letter in the original Latin : " Pictor tuus, Erasme carissime, mirus est artifex, sed vereor, ne non sensurus sit Angliam tam fœcundam ac fertilem, quam sperarat ; quanquam ne reperiat omnino sterilem, quoad per me fieri potest efficiam. Ex Aulâ Grenwici, 18 Dec. 1525."

trait of Erasmus in the Louvre, which represents him in profile. Also doubtless the stately portrait of George Frundsberg, Field Marshal to Charles V., in the Berlin Museum, No. 577.

Among the last works executed by the painter at Basle, before his first visit to England in the autumn of 1526, we may place the beautiful picture in the possession of Princess Charles of Hesse at Darmstadt. It represents the Virgin as Queen of Heaven, standing in a niche, with the Child in her arms, and with the family of the Burgomaster Jacob Meyer of Basle kneeling at her side. With the utmost life, and a truth to nature which brings these kneeling figures actually into our presence, there is combined, in a most exquisite degree, an expression of great earnestness, as if the mind were fixed on some lofty object. This is shown not merely by the introduction of divine beings into the circle of human sympathies, but particularly in the relation so skilfully indicated between the Holy Virgin and her worshippers, and in her manifest desire to communicate to those who are around her the sacred peace and tranquillity expressed in her own countenance and attitude, and implied in the infantine gestures of the Saviour. In this direct union of the divine with the human, and in their reciprocal harmony, there is involved a devout and earnest purity of feeling such as the arts among our fathers only were capable of representing. This picture was doubtless founded by the zealous Catholic donor for a Chapel of our Lady. The painting is fresh and marrowy, and the flesh-tones of a warm brown. From various little differences between this and the well-known Dresden picture, see woodcut, it is apparent that it was painted at an earlier period. It is easy also to understand that the patron, desiring to possess such excellent portraits of his own family, thus devoutly engaged, as the ornament of one of his rooms, was induced to give Holbein the commission to paint a repetition of the subject, which in the needy circumstances of the painter could only have been acceptable to him. I am therefore convinced that the Dresden picture owes its creation to some such circumstance. The altera-

THE BURGOMASTER MEYER'S VOTIVE PICTURE.
Painted by Hans Holbein, and now in the Gallery at Dresden   page 192

tions also which a comparison with the first picture exhibits are such as render it more suitable for that closer inspection which the walls of a room would permit. The head of the Virgin is lovelier and milder in form and expression; the treatment of less body, tenderer, and more inclined to detail. The same remarks apply more or less to most of the other portions. The head of the Burgomaster alone is rather hard and empty. The somewhat coarse and slightly-painted carpet may be the work of a scholar.

Two other pictures in the Basle Gallery, also executed in 1526, differ much in style of treatment from all foregone works of the master, showing, by the greater tenderness of the warm yellowish local tones, in the more abundant use of glazings, and increased softness of outline, so strong an influence from Netherlandish art, that even a connoisseur like Herr von Rumohr supposed them to be works by Bernard van Orley. The one, No. 34, represents a beautiful young girl in elegant attire, nominally the portrait of a member of the Offenburg family at Basle, with the inscription, "Lais Corinthiaca."[1] The other, No. 35, taken from the same model, but less attractive, represents Venus, with a somewhat ugly Cupid. Although the last only is dated 1526, yet the first corresponds with it too entirely in every respect to leave any doubt of its belonging to the same time. The remarkable style of these pictures may be best explained by the probability that Holbein, on occasion of a visit to Antwerp in September, had become acquainted with the manner of Quentin Massys, to which these works most approximate. The already-mentioned letter from Erasmus to his friend Egidius in Antwerp, dated the 29th August, states that, if Holbein desired to visit Quentin Massys, and if he (Egidius) should not have the time to conduct him, he would depute his "Famulus" to show him the house. Who will doubt therefore that one so eager as Holbein to appropriate every fresh means of improvement would profit by this opportunity? That he must have paid a somewhat lengthened visit to Antwerp is further

[1] For suppositions regarding this appellation, see Hegner, p. 162, &c.

K

proved by the animated and masterly portrait of his friend Egidius, also in Longford Castle, the whole style of which shows the probability of its having been painted during that stay.[1] In all probability, also, the master sent the two small pictures above named, as specimens of his success in the adoption of a new style, to his patron Amerbach at Basle, from whose collection they were derived.[2]

On his arrival in England Sir Thomas More received the painter in the most friendly manner into his own house, built by himself on the Thames, not far from London, retaining him there for some time without bringing him to the notice of King Henry VIII.[3] Various grounds for this proceeding are easy to conjecture. Sir Thomas may have wished, as was fair, that he and his family should first profit by the painter's genius; also to give Holbein the opportunity of becoming acquainted with the language and manners of the country before making his début on a larger theatre. It is certain, however, that even in the first year of his English residence he painted other individuals who were probably personal friends of the Chancellor. Among the works thus produced is the portrait of Sir Bryan Tuke, treasurer to his Majesty, which shows the closest affinity in style with his latest pictures in Basle, and of which two equally excellent examples exist. The one, which I saw in 1835 in the Methuen Collection in Corsham House,[4] is inscribed, "Brianus Tuke, Miles, anno ætates suæ LVII.," with the motto, "Droit et avant." An expression of slight melancholy is perceptible in the refined features, and corresponds with a passage from the Book of Job on a paper, "Numquid non paucitas dierum meorum finietur brevi?"—chap. x. ver. 20. He is dressed in black, with under sleeves of a delicate gold pattern. The feeling for nature conveyed by this portrait is refined, and of masterly rendering. As regards the not less successful example now in Munich, Cabinets, No. 143, the inscriptions on

[1] 'Galleries and Cabinets,' &c., p. 356.
[2] The Amerbach collection forms the principal part of the Basle Gallery.
[3] But not three years, as Van Mander reports.
[4] Many pictures from this collection having been sold, I know not whether the picture in question be still there.

the background are absent. The passage from Job, however, is there, with the addition of "Job cap: 10," and "10. HOLPAIN." A skeleton pointing to an almost spent hourglass gives the answer to the question. The portrait of Sir Henry Guildford at Hampton Court, which has unfortunately darkened, is also dated 1527, the first year of Holbein's stay in England. The next year (1528) constitutes another step in the artist's career. The admirable picture of Richard Southwell, Privy Councillor to Henry VIII., in the Uffizi at Florence, which, in addition to the year, bears date the " x July," may be concluded to be the earliest of the dated pictures of this year. In conception and colouring it closely follows that of Sir Bryan Tuke. Next in order probably succeeds that of William Warham, Archbishop of Canterbury, No. 207, in the Louvre. The treatment of this is somewhat broader. The portrait of Nicholas Kratzer, astronomer to Henry VIII., also dated 1527, and also in the Louvre, No. 206, shows a larger conception and greater simplicity of forms, but is of a deep and far less transparent brown colour. From these pictures it is evident that the entertainment described by Van Mander [1] as given by Sir Thomas More to Henry VIII. for the purpose of showing him Holbein's work, and of presenting the artist to him, could not have taken place later than the first half of the year 1528; for it was impossible that he could have painted all these individuals without the King's knowledge. The monarch on this occasion was so pleased, both with the pictures and the painter, that he immediately took him into his service. Holbein received a salary of 30l. (no inconsiderable sum for that period), and a lodging in the palace, his pictures being separately paid for besides.[2] Of the genuine portraits of Henry VIII. in England, that in Lord Yarborough's collection was probably executed during this earlier period.

The most important picture for extent and richness of representation which I know, by Holbein, in England —the so-called Ambassadors, in the collection of Lord

[1] Van Mander, folio 143 a.
[2] Walpole's 'Anecdotes,' vol. i. p. 110, 161.

Radnor at Longford Castle—belongs, in my opinion, to the following year 1529.¹ Of the two full-length, life-sized figures, standing side by side, the one in rich attire and with the order of St. Michael represents, as Lord Folkestone informed me, Sir Thomas Wyatt, one of the most learned and accomplished Englishmen of his time. The other figure has both the expression and simpler dress of a learned professor; and various mathematical instruments, a globe, and some wind-instruments, treated precisely like those in the portrait of Nicholas Kratzer, give further evidence of his particular calling. In the conception of the forms this picture is also closely related to the portrait of Kratzer, but it is clearer in the yellowish-brown flesh-tones, and very easy in motives. Another work belonging probably to this time is the energetically conceived and powerfully modelled portrait of Bishop Fisher, formerly in Lord Northwick's collection.²

The picture in Barbers' Hall, representing eighteen portraits of members of the Guild receiving a grant of privileges from Henry VIII., is one of the richest compositions by the master. Unfortunately it is placed in too unfavourable a light for any decided opinion: conjecturally, however, I am inclined to place it next in succession.³ In this year, and probably in August,⁴ Holbein paid a visit to Basle. On that occasion he doubtless painted the portraits of his wife and two children,⁵ now in the Basle Gallery. To all those who judge of a work of art, not by its subject, but by the amount of skill bestowed on it, this picture is an object of great admiration; but it is no less true that the cross-looking woman with red eyes, the plain little girl, and the half-starved boy baby are not attractive. The conception, however, is of such simple and unpretending truth, the full forms so masterly, the colouring, with rather grey shadows, so bright and clear, and the treatment so free and light, that,

---

¹ 'Treasures,' &c., vol. iii. p. 138 ; also 'Galleries and Cabinets,' &c., p. 359.
² 'Treasures,' vol. iii. p. 210.
³ Ibid., vol. ii. p. 328.   ⁴ Hegner's work, p. 234.
⁵ 'Kunstwerke und Künstler in Deutschland,' vol. ii. p. 277, &c.

with these before one, the unpleasing character of the individuals can be well endured, and also the capricious and unartistic arrangement of the picture. Unvarnished reality appears here in its full artistic excellence. It is probable that the portrait of Erasmus in the same gallery, No. 28, was also painted during this visit to Basle. In a letter from Erasmus to Sir Thomas More, dated September 25th, 1529, he expresses his great gratification at a representation of Sir Thomas and his whole family[1] which Holbein had brought with him. This must have been the clever pen sketch, now in the Basle Gallery, for the well-known, but, alas! vanished picture, now solely though well represented by an early, and in many respects excellent copy at Nostall Priory, the seat of the Wynn family, in Yorkshire.[2] This comprises ten full-length, life-sized figures, of easy arrangement, of extraordinary truth and animation of the heads, great freedom of motives, and of masterly rendering in every part. The year 1530 is inscribed on that example of finely carried out chiaroscuro and delicate modelling the portrait of Dr. Stokesby, Bishop of London, now in Windsor Castle. Also, judging from the whole style of art, it is probable that the masterly portrait of Henry VIII., at Windsor, was painted in this same year.

The year 1532 witnessed a new epoch in Holbein's art. The portrait of one Stallhof, a merchant, dated 1532, now in Windsor Castle, unites with an increasing delicacy of drawing his usual brownish local flesh-tone.[3] On the other hand, a portrait of George Gysen, a merchant, executed in London, but now in the Berlin Museum, No. 586, shows that, in the attempt to attain the utmost possible delicacy of modelling, the master abandoned his in that respect untractable brownish tone for one of a cool but very clear nature, to which he adhered in subsequent years. In close affinity with the last portrait is a delicate picture of a woman in a red dress with fur, and a veil, a rosary in her hand, in the Cassel Gallery, No. 50. The portraits executed in 1533 show greyer and heavier

---

[1] Hegner's work, p. 235.   [2] 'Treasures,' &c., vol. iii. p. 333, &c.
[3] Ibid., vol. ii. p. 431.

shadows and half-tones. To these belongs that of Geryck Tybis in the Belvedere Gallery at Vienna: he is standing behind a table, in the act of sealing a letter. On a paper is inscribed the date 1533, with the name and age of the individual. The same date is also attached to the beautiful portrait of a young man in black dress and cap in Windsor Castle.[1] Taking the resemblance to these two last-named works, and also to a male portrait in the Brunswick Gallery, No. 387, dated 1533, as our criterion, the following admirable portraits may belong to the same year:—that of Sir Henry Guildford, at Windsor;[2] of Thomas Morrett, goldsmith to Henry VIII., in the Dresden Gallery;[3] of the morose-looking John Chambers,[4] body physician to Henry VIII., in the Belvedere Gallery; and the portrait of a man, taken full front, in the Pitti Palace (Saloon of the Iliad). Finally, his finest female portrait I know of this period is that of Lady Vaux at Hampton Court.[5] A water-colour drawing of the favourite subject of the day—the Wheel of Fortune—at Chatsworth, spirited alike in invention and execution, is also dated 1533.[6]

In consequence of the appreciation Holbein met with in England, he came into greater favour also at Basle. A friendly missive from the magistracy of Basle, dated 2nd September, 1532, calls upon him to return to that city; and, as an inducement for him to remain there, promises him the yearly sum of thirty pieces of money. This communication only reached the artist in 1533, on the occasion of his accompanying King Henry to the celebrated meeting with Francis I., called the Field of the Cloth of Gold.[7] Considering the continual favour in which he was held by the English monarch, and the considerable profits which his pictures earned for him, it is not surprising that he should have returned to England as soon as possible. It is probable that the following years saw the execution of the only comprehensive work in which he found opportunity to

---

[1] 'Treasures,' &c., vol. ii. p. 431.   [2] Ibid.
[3] Engraved by Hollar, in the Arundel Collection.
[4] Also engraved by Hollar.   [5] 'Treasures,' vol. ii. p. 361.
[6] Ibid. vol. iii. p. 351.   [7] See Hegner, p. 242, &c.

Back of
Foldout
Not Imaged

THE TRIUMPH OF POVERTY

From a design by Holbein In the possession of Sir Charles Lawrence, PRA

display his powers of historical painting in England.¹ At the request of his countrymen, the Company of German Merchants in London, he executed two large pictures in tempera, called the Triumph of Riches and the Triumph of Poverty, see woodcuts, in the banqueting hall of the Easterlings, in the Steelyard. These pictures were of such excellence that Federigo Zucchero, according to the evidence of Van Mander,² placed them on the same level with works by Raphael, and himself took copies of them with the pen. Nor does Van Mander admire them less. Indeed, all admiration is fully justified by the masterly pen-drawing by Holbein,³ acquired within the last few years by the British Museum, in which he occupies a place in art between Mantegna and Raphael, and also by the fine drawings by Vostermann from both the Triumphs, now in Sir Charles Eastlake's possession. The composition is distributed in the space with much feeling for style, the motives are graceful and grand, and the coldness of allegory corrected by the fine individuality of the heads.

The Company of the German Merchants in London having been dissolved, these two pictures were, on the 22nd of January, 1616, presented by them to Prince Henry of Wales, a fact which is placed beyond doubt by the documentary researches of Dr. Lappenburg.⁴ This is the last *certain* record we have of them; for while it may be inferred with much probability that they passed at the death of that prince—two years later—into the possession of his brother Prince Charles, afterwards Charles I., yet, as they are not enumerated among the works of art belonging to that monarch which were sold by Cromwell, Dr. Lappenburg concludes they may have perished in the fire at Whitehall in 1697. But such evidence as we further

---

¹ I am inclined to attribute this undertaking to this period because the master here appears to have reached the summit of his art.
² Schilderbock, fol. 144 a.
³ 'Galleries and Cabinets,' &c., p. 36.
⁴ See Dr. Lappenburg's excellent work, 'Urkundliche Geschichte des Hansischen Stalhof zu London,' Hamburg, 1851, vol. i., 4to, p. 83. The usual assumption that these pictures were burnt in the banqueting-hall of the Easterlings in the Great Fire of London in 1666 is thus set aside.

possess is not in favour of this conclusion, for it is remarkable that in the well-known catalogue of Charles I.'s collection, by the keeper Van der Doort, which contains notices of several less important works by Holbein, and even of two miniatures by him,[1] these fine pictures are not mentioned at all.

After 1533 it is rare to find a dated picture by the master. He continued, however, to practise the last-described style of art in 1536, as proved by the portrait of Jane Seymour, queen of Henry VIII., in the Belvedere Gallery, where she appears in rich attire in which much gold is introduced. The local flesh-tone is here cold but very clear, the shadows decidedly grey, and the handwriting, so to say, of his brush of the utmost precision. Of about the same period may be the portrait of the king, a full-length, life-sized figure, in the stiff, full front position common to all his pictures, in the possession of Henry Danby Seymour, Esq., London.[2] The portraits by the master appertaining to 1539 give proof that, owing either to the remarks of others or to his own conviction, he adopted a tender reddish local tone for his flesh, in lieu of the cold tint which had before characterised him, retaining at the same time his grey shadows. The sight, perhaps, of his earlier warmly-coloured pictures in Basle may have worked this change, he having visited the city, though for only a short time,[3] in the September of 1538, in consequence of another flattering invitation from the magistracy.[4] A specimen of this alteration in style is afforded by the full-length, life-sized portrait, taken decidedly in 1539,[5] of

---

[1] See reprint of this catalogue at the end of 1st vol. of 'Treasures of Art,' &c., under the head of Holbein.
[2] 'Treasures,' &c., vol. ii. p. 241.
[3] This visit, and also the happiness Holbein enjoyed in England, may be gathered from the following passage in a letter from Gualter, then studying at Basle, to Antistes Bullinger at Zurich, in the middle of Sept. 1538:—" Venit nuper Basileam ex Anglia Joannes Holbein adeo felicem ejus regni statum prædicans, quod aliquot septimanis exactis rursum eo migraturus est."
[4] Hegner, p. 246, &c.
[5] This appears from a cotemporary notice of the 30th December, 1539, to the effect that Holbein received 10*l*. from the King for a journey to Upper Burgundy. Walpole's 'Anecdotes,' vol. i. p. 161.

Christina, widow of the Duke of Milan, a lady for whose hand the king sued after the death of Jane Seymour, at Arundel Castle, seat of the Duke of Norfolk.[1] The hands are especially finely drawn. This tender reddish tone is, however, seen in fuller development in the fine portrait of Anne of Cleves, fourth wife of Henry VIII., executed in 1540, and now in the Louvre, No. 211.[2] Admirable pictures in this style are also the portraits of King Edward VI. as a child, in Sion House,[3] in the gallery of Lord Yarborough in London,[4] and in the country house called Herrenhausen near Hanover: also of the same as a boy at Burleigh House:[5] and the portraits of Henry VIII., at Petworth,[6] and at Serlby; the latter dated 1543.[7]

About the year 1546 another and final change in the master's colouring took place, consisting of a light-yellowish local tone in the flesh, though retaining still the grey shadows. Portraits of this character are those of Henry VIII. at Windsor Castle, and of his son Edward VI. in the same place.[8] This period also includes the large picture of Edward VI., as king, in Bridewell Hospital. The bad state and high position of this, the most important work of Holbein's latest time, permit no opinion, properly speaking, upon it.[9]

Considered also as a miniature-painter, in which department Van Mander[10] reports him to have soon outstripped his master Lucas, whom he found at the court of Henry VIII., Holbein displayed rare excellence. I quote only the portraits of Henry and of Anne of Cleves in the collection of Colonel Meyrick. The portrait of the lady is termed by Walpole "the most exquisitely perfect of all Holbein's works."

---

[1] 'Treasures,' vol. iii, p. 29.
[2] 'Künstler und Kunstwerke,' Paris, p. 552. This picture was engraved by Hollar.
[3] 'Galleries and Cabinets,' &c., p. 269.   [4] Ibid, p. 69.
[5] 'Treasures,' vol. iii. p. 407.   [6] Ibid. p. 41.
[7] 'Galleries and Cabinets,' &c., p. 517.
[8] 'Treasures,' vol. ii. p. 31, &c.
[9] For further portraits by the master I must refer the reader to my 'Treasures of Art,' &c.
[10] Van Mander, fol. 140 b.

How early this master succeeded in rendering individual character only with such means as a draughtsman may command, may be seen in the portraits drawn with the silver point, and all executed in Augsburg, which were formerly in a sketch-book, and are now in the collection of engravings at Berlin. His further extraordinary achievements in this walk of art are sufficiently proved by the 89 portraits of persons attached to the court of Henry, and of other cotemporary individuals, in the royal collection at Windsor. In most of these red chalk and Indian ink are the sole materials employed, though sufficient to express a liveliness of conception, purity of feeling for nature, and a lightness and decision of touch such as have been never surpassed.[1] Many of these drawings have unfortunately suffered. I have described the most remarkable in my 'Treasures.'[2]

As regards Holbein's powers of invention, some idea of their fruitfulness may be obtained from various designs, and especially from the woodcuts and engravings taken from his drawings. Of these latter there is a large collection in the Basle Gallery.[3] A furious onslaught of Swiss native soldiers, No. 35, shows us with what energy and tremendous truth he rendered the momentary exhibition of passion. This is the most living and spirited picture of that old Swiss race which broke the power of Burgundy, and the force of whose weapons was long considered to be irresistible.

Among his biblical subjects a composition of Christ carrying his cross is remarkable for richness and beauty; also a Virgin and Child for elevation of feeling. A rich series of cartoons, executed with pen and Indian ink, for glass paintings, and of powerful effect, are very important in character, though not all equal in value. Seven similar cartoons, representing the Passion, drawn also in the master's earlier time, are in the collection of engravings

---

[1] Bartolozzi's plates in Chamberlain's well-known work are estimable, though giving but feeble representations of these qualities.
[2] 'Treasures,' vol. ii. p. 448, &c.
[3] 'Künstler und Kunstwerke in Deutschland,' vol. ii. p. 283 to 291.

in the British Museum.[1] The elevated taste with which he treated subjects from common life is shown by three drawings in the same Museum — a woman with three children, another in bed with six children, and Henry VIII. alone at table.[2] Of the engravings from his designs I may observe, as a specimen of the degree in which he was qualified to treat historical subjects, the visit of the Queen of Sheba to Solomon, engraved by Hollar.

But the greatest number of his compositions are seen in the woodcuts,[3] executed by highly skilful hands, and especially by Hans Lützelburger, and which, with few exceptions, belong to the period before his removal to England. The series of subjects called the Dance of Death comprise his most original and spirited inventions. These, with the exception of a few proof-sheets, were first published at Lyons in 41 plates, and in a subsequent edition, which also appeared at Lyons, in 1547, were increased by 12 additional plates. We have already alluded to the feeling which pervades these compositions. So much was Holbein in love with the subject, that he treated it afresh in another series of alphabetical woodcuts, and again in a drawing, of which many examples exist, for the handle of a dagger. Next in order the woodcuts for the Old Testament deserve mention. This work, which consists of 90 subjects, the first four of which are the large Dance of Death, was also published at Lyons in 1538. Some of the designs are most remarkable. The woodcuts for two other alphabets worthily succeed these last: one of the series contains a dance of peasants, the other of children. The rare woodcuts to Cranmer's Catechism are less important. Of the single woodcuts which bespeak the invention of Holbein I will only mention the portrait of Erasmus, with the terminal figure, and two dagger-sheaths.

[1] 'Treasures,' vol. i. p. 236.
[2] 'Galleries and Cabinets,' &c., p. 36, &c.
[3] In this view I concur with Herr Sotzmann in the 'Tübinger Kunstblatt,' 1836, Nos. 30 to 32; and with Herr Vischer in the same work, 1838, Nos. 50 to 54; 1843, Nos. 15 and 102; and 1846, No. 27. On the other hand, it is believed by some, at the head of whom is Rumohr, that he was himself a wood-engraver. Rumohr's ' H. Holbein in seinem Verhältnesse zum Deutschen Formschnitt,' Leipsic, 1836; and a reply to Sotzmann in the same work.

Finally, I may mention that Holbein executed a large number of designs for domestic furniture,—stoves, clocks, —and especially for weapons and goldsmith's work. These contain an abundance of original inventions, both as regards the forms of a developed Renaissance style and the figures introduced. Admirable specimens of this kind are in the engraving department of the British Museum, and also in the library.[1]

This great master died of the plague in London in the year 1554. Judging from the most authentic of his portraits—the one in red and black chalk, in the Basle Museum, which represents him in youthful years — he was a man of well-formed and regular features, expressive of a clear mind, a cheerful temper, and a quiet decision of character.[2]

Although, owing to the circumstance of his leaving his native town of Augsburg early, and his also residing but ten years in Basle, Holbein created, properly speaking, no school, yet some painters obviously formed their style from his. I may quote CHRISTOPHER AMBERGER, born at Nuremberg 1490, died 1563, who lived in Augsburg, and who occupies an important position as a portrait-painter. However inferior to Holbein in energy of conception and refinement of drawing, yet he occasionally surpasses him in transparency and warmth of colouring. Specimens of this class are the following: the portrait of the well-known geographer Sebastian Münster, in the Berlin Museum, No. 583; and of the Emperor Charles V., in the gallery at Siena. As an historical painter he is less successful: at the same time an altarpiece, dated 1554, representing the Virgin and Child surrounded with Saints, placed on the wall of the choir-sacristy in Augsburg cathedral, is skilfully composed and drawn, and the heads of refined and elevated character. The religious sentiment of this picture, though true to nature, is feeble in expression; the colouring is transparent. This painter, considered as an historical artist, embodies the transition from the early

---

[1] See further in 'Treasures,' &c., vol. i. pp. 203 and 236. Also, 'Galleries and Cabinets,' &c., p. 37, &c.
[2] A line-engraving from it is at the opening of Hegner's book.

German style to that of the more modern school, a movement which is more clearly seen in another altarpiece of the same subject, dated 1560, in the church of St. Anna at Augsburg.[1]

Another painter, of the name of HANS ASPER, shows the influence of Holbein in Switzerland. The portraits of Zuinglius and his wife in the library at Zurich are specimens of his art. I have not seen them, however.

Another Swiss painter from Berne, by name NICOLAS MANUEL, surnamed DEUTSCH, born 1484, died 1531, assumes, on the other hand, a far more independent position.[2] Although allied to Holbein in the realistic tendency of his art, yet he differs essentially from him in the mode of its expression. He also treated the subject of the Dance of Death with considerable humour, in 46 large fresco pictures on the churchyard wall of the Dominican convent at Berne. His conception, however, partakes in no way of the fearfully bitter sarcasm of the Holbein series, but has rather a light and goodtempered character. Thus Death is stroking the Abbot under his fat chin, is marching along with the soldier, and is enticing the child with the merry whistle of his pipe. All, therefore, except a fool, who resists, take his summons quietly. Unfortunately this work only exists in copies.[3] As Manuel, besides being painter, was poet, soldier, statesman, and reformer, it is not surprising that his art should, in point of development, by no means approach that of Holbein. Nor had he that great painter's feeling for beauty. His pictures are very unequal in merit. The richness and frequent beauty of his landscape backgrounds show the influence of Titian, with whom he spent some time in Venice, about the year 1511. He may be thoroughly studied in the Museum at Basle in the following works:—The Decollation of John the Baptist, No. 70. Here the expression of aversion in the figure of Salome, as she receives the bloody head from the half-averted executioner, is delicately conceived. The

[1] 'Künstler und Kunstwerke in Deutschland,' vol. ii. p. 62 and 67.
[2] Grüneisen's 'Nicolaus Manuel,' Stuttgart, 1837, p. 156 to 194.
[3] Lithographs of this work were published by R. Haag and Co. at Berne.

colouring is also fine, and the finish careful. The same merit of execution is observable in the David and Bathsheba, dated 1517, No. 68, which is painted in one colour with white lights. A Lucretia, of the same date and style of treatment, No. 69, shows rude and uncouth forms. Two pictures, in tempera on canvas, are also here, Nos. 66 and 67. The first consists of two scenes from the story of Pyramus and Thisbe, having the effect of a parody, the figures being attired in the stately costume of Upper Germany. The second, which is more carefully rendered, represents the Virgin and Child, with St. Anna and Saints, on clouds, and adored by a number of the faithful. Both these works are remarkable for their rich landscape. A large picture, in oil on canvas, representing a peasant wedding, in the possession of the Manuel family at Berne, shows how agreeably he could occasionally treat the busier compositions from common life, while a portrait of himself, in the Civic Library of the same town, proves him to have been a capital portrait-painter. In his art, also, we may see the deep interest which he took in the Reformation in his native land. A drawing of the Resurrection of Christ is in the possession of Dr. Grüneisen at Stuttgart. Here, however, the guardians of the sepulchre are not Roman soldiers, but Roman Catholic priests and monks, who are sitting round about with their concubines, and, scared by the appearance of the Saviour, are running away with all speed.

That branch of the Suabian school, also, which flourished in Ulm, produced in this period a very remarkable painter, MARTIN SCHAFFNER by name, who laboured from 1499 to 1535.[1] His tendency was realistic also, and in his earlier time he does not advance beyond a common portrait-like character of figures. Of this class is his Adoration of the three Kings, in the Chapel of St. Maurice at Nuremberg, No. 52. At the same time he exhibited, pretty early in his career, a power of expressing the cheerful innocence of young girls. As a specimen I may cite five youthful female saints, with one elderly saint, in

[1] Grüneisen and Manch, 'Ulm's Kunstleben,' p. 53, &c.

the Berlin Museum, No. 1234 a. Later in life, and owing probably to the study of Borgognone's works, he cultivated a feeling for beauty and for the higher expression of spiritual emotion. The finest specimens of this class are four pictures from the diocese of Wetterhausen, in the Munich Gallery, Nos. 17, 18, 25, 36. These are the Annunciation, the Presentation in the Temple (of the year 1524), the Descent of the Holy Ghost, and the Death of the Virgin. From these works we should be led to believe that Schaffner was a gentle and amiable man, full of deep feeling, and endowed with a strong sense of what was delicate and noble in form, more especially as regards the drawing of the heads. His colour only is defective, particularly in the flesh; it has a peculiarly clear greyish tone, without, however, being cold. The last of the pictures just referred to is remarkably good: the sinking form of the Virgin, who kneels in prayer with the Apostles (a peculiar and touching mode of conceiving the subject), and the different degrees of sympathy in the countenances of the latter, are very happily expressed. Another series from the Passion of Christ, in the same gallery, is treated more in the style of *genre*. Over the principal altar of the cathedral of Ulm is another important work by Schaffner, of the year 1521. The centre consists of a carving in wood, representing the Holy Family; the wings are painted by Schaffner; on the inside are family groups of the kindred of the Virgin, and on the outside different saints. The forms are somewhat round, and remind us of Italian art; the heads are soft in expression; the cast of the drapery is still occasionally angular, but grand in form, and in long masses. In all these pictures a delicate cool tone prevails more or less in the flesh. The general effect also pertains to the cool scale of colour. Martin Schaffner was also an excellent portrait-painter, as seen in his portrait of a Count Öettingen, dated 1508, now in the Munich Gallery, No. 156, a picture of refined feeling, though somewhat flat in modelling; also in his portraits in the Besser chapel and in the sacristy of the Ulm cathedral, both far more animated in character and powerful in colour.

Finally, a peculiar position in the Suabian school is taken by the painter HANS BALDUNG, called GRIEN, born 1470 at Gmund, died 1552 at Strasburg. No other master shows, in style of conception, drawing, and treatment, so decided an influence from Albert Durer, which makes it probable that he must have spent some time in the atélier of that master at Nuremberg. In point of feeling for beauty, harmony of colour, and general keeping, he is, however, inferior to the other Suabian masters. The character of his heads, which are roundish and unattractive in form, and too pronounced in single parts, is too often repeated. His chef-d'œuvre is a large altarpiece, signed 1516, in the Freiburg cathedral.[1] The centre picture represents the Coronation of the Virgin by the Almighty and Christ, with angels floating around and playing on musical instruments. The light clouds which sustain them are, on close observation, seen to consist entirely of cherubims' heads. The inner sides of the wings contain the twelve Apostles in adoration, robust individual heads. The outer sides of the wings and two stationary side pictures are occupied by the Visitation, the Nativity, the Flight into Egypt, and by the Annunciation: the last-named apparently by a different hand. In the Visitation the sweet expression of the Virgin and the mild and gentle countenance of Elizabeth are of great charm. In the Nativity the light proceeds from the Child; the group is further lighted by clear moonlight. Here, also, the expression of the Virgin and of the five angels is of great tenderness. But the most remarkable of the number, both as regards beauty and originality of composition and successful execution, is the Flight into Egypt. An angel has swung himself down from a date-palm, up which four other angels are climbing, on to the mule, and is extending fruit to the Child, who is clinging to the Virgin. On the back of the centre picture is a well-executed Crucifixion, after the composition by Albert Durer. The wings of the back contain SS. Martin,

[1] See Life of this master, and account of this work, by Schreiber, 'Das Münster zu Freiburg,' second edition, and 'Das Münster zu Strasburg,' second edition, p. 75.

George, John the Baptist, and Jerome, grand and characteristic figures. The portraits of the founders, on the predella, in adoration of the Virgin, under the Crucifixion, are very animated. Occasionally the painter degenerates into revolting exaggerations, as in the figures of those stoning St. Stephen. The head of the saint himself is elevated in character and vigorous in colouring. The picture, signed 1522, is in the Berlin Museum, No. 623. In the same gallery, No. 603, is a Crucifixion, dated 1512, and an admirable cartoon of the same subject is preserved in the collection of engravings. The fantastic element was also strongly developed in this painter, of which the large wings of an altarpiece at Colmar, and especially the Temptation of St. Anthony, give a striking example. The saint is conversing with Paul the Hermit. The landscape in this picture is very beautiful. Two women, also, with skeletons, in the Basle Museum, belong to this class of his works. They are very disagreeable subjects, but admirably executed. The best portrait by his hand known to me is one, dated 1515, of a light-haired youth, in the Gallery of Vienna. That of a Markgraf of Baden, dated 1517, in the Munich Gallery, Cabinets, No. 148, is drier. In his drawings, Hans Baldung approaches the precision of execution of Albert Durer, though far inferior to him in correctness. He executed two engravings with much skill, and a considerable number of designs, chiefly of a religious character, for wood-engravings.[1]

THE SCHOOLS OF THE LOWER RHINE AND OF WESTPHALIA.

The Netherlands exercised by their vicinity so preponderating an influence over these countries, that the painters they produced exhibit by no means so distinct an originality as those of the schools we have been considering. The influence of Quentin Massys especially, on the part of Belgium, is recognisable. With a tendency

---

[1] Bartsch mentions fifty-nine wood-engravings, 'Peintre Graveur,' vol. vii. p. 305.

decidedly realistic, they do not, in many instances, rise in their heads above a commonplace character, showing but little feeling for beauty, though often an intense and moving expression. In colouring they nearly approach the masters of the Netherlands, and also in the masterly rendering of detail, namely, in the often highly-finished character of the landscape backgrounds. As regards treatment, they may be distinguished by a certain dryness and by greater hardness of outlines. Here again Cologne forms the centre of pictorial activity, and a particular predilection is shown for scenes from the Passion, namely, such as the Descent from the Cross, which excite sorrowful emotions. After these, the Adoration of the three Kings, whose bones rest in the Cathedral of Cologne, is the subject most in vogue.

Foremost among this school is a Cologne master who flourished in the first third of the 16th century. His colouring and treatment of landscape backgrounds show the study of Quentin Massys' works. Later in life he visited Italy, without however his German feeling for art being affected in the most essential points by any impressions received there. In his pictures, which show in his later time a more judicious composition, an elevated and fervent religious feeling is observable. The heads of his women evince much feeling for beauty and spiritual purity; his male heads, on the other hand, though invariably truthful, are generally ugly in character; and his old men, in his earlier works, have an over softness of form more suitable to the other sex. The nude he frequently treats with a certain meagreness, though otherwise he is a tolerably good draughtsman. In his earlier works a great transparency and warmth of colouring appear, and his flesh is of a blooming reddish tone. In those later pictures, in which some influence from Italian art is traceable, this fine local colour is sacrificed to an attempt at greater modelling, but at the same time his heads are altogether of nobler form and purer taste. In the Netherlandish minutiæ of his landscape he remains always the same, except that his later pictures are in this respect somewhat heavier in tone. His earliest known work, dated 1515, is the Death of the Virgin, in the Museum at Cologne. The composition is certainly scattered, and the incidents wanting in repose; but the head of the Virgin is tender, the female saints on the wings of lovely character, and the portraits of the donors truthful. A large and originally far more important representation of the same subject was formerly also in a church at Cologne, but now forms part of the Boisserée collection in the Munich Gallery, where it still bears the arbitrary name of Schoreel. It agrees entirely in the wings with the above-mentioned picture, but differs greatly from it in the centre-piece. Like other pictures collected by the Boisserées it has been strongly overpainted with glazing colours, which give it a crude and gaudy look. The brick-red tones bestowed on the flesh parts are particularly disagreeable. An important picture in the Gallery at Naples, by the same master, corresponds entirely with that at Munich. The subject is a Crucifixion, with the Virgin, St. John, the Magdalen, and three angels who are catching the blood. On the wings are the donor with three sons presented by St. Jerome, and his wife with two daughters presented by St. Margaret, and the armorial bearings of the family.

One of the finest works however of this earlier time is in the collection of Mr. Blundell Weld, of Ince, near Liverpool, representing the Virgin contemplating the sleeping Child with intense love, and three singing angels.[1] A work of considerable size of the same time is a free copy, the property of Lord Heytesbury,[2] from the well-known Descent from the Cross by Rogier van der Weyden the younger, of which, as we have already said, three examples exist: two in the Madrid Gallery, and one in the Berlin Museum. The fact that one of these copies was formerly at Louvain proves that the Cologne master was for a time in the Netherlands. The difference in the composition lies only in the figure upon the ladder, and some of the heads are only altered in the expression. Instead

[1] 'Treasures of Art,' vol. iii. p. 250.
[2] 'Galleries and Cabinets,' &c., p. 386.

of the gold ground the copier has introduced a rich landscape. To the same period finally belongs an Adoration of the Kings in the Dresden Gallery, No. 1688. The transition from his earlier to his later style appears in a Pietà, with Joseph of Arimathea and St. Veronica, dated 1524, on the inner sides of the wings in the Städel Institute at Frankfort. It was formerly in the Lys church at Cologne. The early transparency of his colour is here seen combined with a higher character in some of the heads. The following are the chefs-d'œuvre of his later time:—An Adoration of the Kings, of very considerable size, in the Dresden Gallery, No. 1687. The character of the heads is very much the same as in his early days, but the colouring is greyer. It was probably painted for a church near Genoa, where it was formerly preserved.[1] A somewhat large altarpiece in the Louvre, No. 601, with a Pietà in the centre, St. Francis receiving the Stigmata in the lunette, and in the predella the Last Supper. The many motives from the Cena by Leonardo da Vinci prove the painter to have been in Milan. The arrangement of the centre composition is here more conformable to style, the types less truthful, but of greater elevation of character, the modelling more careful, but the colouring less warm and transparent.[2] Next in order, finally, is an Adoration of the Kings in the Gallery at Naples, there erroneously called Luca d' Ollanda, with two of the Kings upon the wings. The heads of the Virgin and of the kneeling King are here very beautiful; the chiaroscuro in which the procession is kept is particularly successful.

Another painter deserving mention is one who flourished in Cologne in the first decennium of the 16th century, and to whom the name of Lucas van Leyden was formerly erroneously given, and in later times, though also on insufficient grounds, that of CHRISTOPH. There is something antiquated in his meagre forms and in the awkward motives, in which at the same time an attempt at grace is observable.

[1] 'Remarks on the Exhibition, &c., of the Dresden Gallery,' Berlin, 1858, by Dr. Waagen, p. 42.
[2] 'Kunstwerke und Künstler in Paris,' p. 553, &c.

In his heads also the same insignificant and by no means attractive features are repeated, and generally with an affected smile. His hands especially are characterised by bony and scarcely tapering fingers. The flesh-tones incline to a cool pearl-grey colour; the draperies, in heavy and sharp breaks, consist generally of sumptuous stuffs executed with great minutia. The modelling, however, of every part is marvellous. Upon the whole the influence of Quentin Massys may also be traced in this painter. His earliest picture, known to have been executed about 1501, and formerly in the Chartreuse at Cologne, is now in the possession of Herr Haan at Cologne. It represents St. Thomas placing his finger in the side of the Saviour, who is assisting him in the act. At the sides are four saints, with angels playing on musical instruments on the grass. On the wings, outside and inside, are saints. Somewhat later in time, and from the same church and in the same hands, is the Crucifixion, with the disciples and St. Jerome. On the interior of the wings are saints, with the Annunciation, and SS. Peter and Paul on the exterior. Next in order are a series of single saints, five of whom in the Munich Gallery, Cabinets, Nos. 38-40, form an altar. The most remarkable figures are SS. James the younger, Bartholomew, and John the Evangelist. Two more are in the City Gallery at Mayence; and two, SS. Peter and Dorothea, No. 36, in the collection of the Prince Consort in Kensington Palace.[1] In all these the finish of the execution is marvellous. But his most remarkable work, as regards size and import, is a Descent from the Cross in the Louvre, No. 280, there called Quentin Massys. In composition, expression of the emotions, and warmer colour of the flesh, this is his most favourable specimen. The brown glazing shadows on the gold ground give it the look of a shrine.

In affinity with the first of these two anonymous masters may be mentioned JOHANN VON MELEM of Cologne, though several pictures of saints and donors in the Munich Gallery,

---

[1] 'Galleries and Cabinets,' &c., p. 228.

Cabinets, Nos. 74, 75, 77, 78, 80, 81, show him to be inferior in drawing, execution, and colouring.[1]

Among the Westphalian painters, all unknown by name to us, of this time, one especially is distinguished. His style of art approximates also in every respect to that of the Netherlands, though it bears a sterner and more antiquated form than that of the first-mentioned Cologne painter. His tendency is decidedly realistic, and his practice in every respect of great truthfulness; but unfortunately he is greatly deficient in feeling for beauty, his female heads being little attractive, and those of his children strikingly and also monotonously ugly. There is but little firmness in his drawing, and his outlines are sharp. On the other hand, there is something naïve both in his composition and feeling, his colouring is of extraordinary power, and his execution of great detail and solidity. His landscape backgrounds, for instance, which are enlivened with various attractive episodes, are among the best of the class which this period produced. The best specimen I know of him (a Nativity, dated 1512) is wrongfully termed an Albert Durer, in the Gallery at Naples (No. 342 of the Catalogue of 1842). The Child is lying on the ground beneath the ruins of a building, which, according to mediæval conception, betokened an antique temple, adored by the Virgin and Joseph, while a number of angels are singing the "Gloria in excelsis," accompanied by various musical instruments; at the sides are the donors, two men and two women, with their patron saints. In the rich hilly landscape of the background is seen a town upon a lake. The execution is wonderfully minute. A smaller but equally remarkable altarpiece is in the Berlin Museum, No. 607. In the centre of a rich and attractive landscape is the Virgin, with the Child in the act of benediction, and six angels. The insides of the wings represent the donor with St. Augustine, and the donor's wife with St. Barbara; the outsides, St. Anna with the Virgin and Child on her lap, and St. Elizabeth of Thü-

---

[1] I purposely reserve the mention of Haus von Calcar for a later occasion.

ringen with a beggar. A third winged altarpiece, dated 1515, is in the Antwerp Museum, Nos. 121-123. In the centre is the Virgin holding the Child, who is taking cherries from a basket held to him by an angel, while another angel is playing on a musical instrument. In the sky are the Almighty and the Dove. The Murder of the Innocents and the Flight into Egypt are both in the rich landscape. On the wings are the donor with St. Sebastian, and the donor's wife with the Magdalen.

In one painter only from the Lower Rhine, ANTON VON WORMS by name,[1] is the influence of Albert Durer perceptible. He flourished in Cologne from 1525 to 1531, principally as a designer for woodcuts, and also as a painter. His pictures, which are very rare, give evidence of a master who combined good drawing with a certain sense of beauty. One, signed with his monogram, is in the possession of Herr Merlo of Cologne. His good drawing appears also in the woodcuts taken from his designs. M. Sotzmann's investigations prove that of the eleven designs attributed to him by Bartsch,[2] one (No. 11) is by a feebler master; that his Passion is not copied from Albert Durer, but that only a few motives from that master have been adopted; these researches also add to the list various woodcuts of which he was the author, and especially one containing a large map of Cologne.

Among the pictures in the Museum at Cologne, and also in the churches of that city, may be seen many respectable though not important productions of this period. We may include the finely-coloured glass-painting in the north aisle of the cathedral of the year 1509.

[1] See Sotzmann on Anton von Worms, Cologne, 1819; and again in the 'Kunstblatt,' 1838, Nos. 55 and 56.
[2] 'Peintre Graveur,' vol. vii. p. 488.

BOOK IV.

THE TEUTONIC STYLE.

THIRD EPOCH, 1530—1600.

DETERIORATION OF THE TEUTONIC STYLE OF ART, AS REGARDS HISTORICAL PAINTING, ARISING FROM THE IMITATION OF THE ITALIANS. FURTHER DEVELOPMENT OF OTHER CLASSES OF PAINTING—GENRE, LANDSCAPES, ETC.

CHAPTER I.

PAINTING IN THE NETHERLANDS.

In consequence of the reputation of the great Italian masters Leonardo da Vinci, Michael Angelo, and Raphael, which spread throughout the Netherlands as well as Germany, many painters from these countries repaired to Italy. Here we find that precisely those qualities most opposed to their own feeling for art made the deepest impression on their minds; more especially such as showed excellences beyond the sphere of individual nature, viz., grandeur of beauty, and simplification of forms, masterly drawing of the nude, unrestrained freedom, boldness, and grace of movement—in short, all that is comprised in art under the term of the ideal. The attempt, however, to appropriate all these qualities could lead to no successful result. Being based on no inherent want on the part of their own original feeling for art, it became only the outward imitation of something foreign to themselves and already fully developed by others. They never succeeded therefore in mastering the complete understanding of form, or in adopting the true feeling for beauty of lines or grace of movement, and, in aiming at them, they degenerated into untruthfulness and artificiality of expression—into exaggeration of drawing and violence and tastelessness of attitude,—while the effort to model was generally at the expense of their own fine colouring. The pictures of this class, even of religious subjects, have accordingly but little to attract the eye; the more so as the withdrawal of genuine inspiration leaves the heads generally cold. But when they selected scenes from ancient mythology, and allegories decked out with an ostentation of learning, the result is positively disagreeable. Numerous, however, as were the painters in the Netherlands who followed this mistaken course, there were plenty whose sound feeling resisted the error, and impelled them to a different vocation. In lieu of religious subjects, the inspiration for which, as we have said, had ceased to flow, they began to take pleasure in scenes from common life, and struck into that path which had been opened by Lucas van Leyden. In this way religious themes subsided into mere accessories, and served only as a pretext for pictures which embodied their favourite studies. Others, who delighted especially in landscape, followed the steps of Patinier and Civetta; with this difference, that the landscape became their principal subject, and the gradually diminishing size of their figures reduced them at length to mere accessories of the foreground. But although all these masters, by the finish of their detail, by their animation, *naïveté*, and humour—and the landscape-painters especially, by their frequent poetic inventions—are incomparably more attractive than the imitators of Italian art, yet their propensity to the fantastic, their absence of simplicity in arrangement, their gaudy and crude colouring, and want of general keeping, must always assign to them a subordinate place in the feeling of lovers of art. The most satisfactory productions of this period will therefore be found in the department of portrait-painting, which, by its nature, throw the artist upon the exercise of his own original feeling for art. As this epoch is far more important as a link in the chain of history than for any pleasure arising from its own works, it will be sufficient to quote only the more important painters and a few of their principal pictures.

The first painter who deserted his native style of art, in which, as we have stated above, he had already greatly

L

excelled, was JAN VAN MABUSE. His works after 1512 are, with small exception, characterised by all the mistakes we have enumerated. Their redeeming quality is the masterly treatment. Among those of a religious class some of a small size are the most remarkable. The Ecce Homo in the Antwerp Museum, No. 57, so frequently copied by cotemporary painters, is a specimen of masterly modelling and vigorous colour; also two Madonnas with the Child, with rich architectural accessories, in the collection of Mr. Baring.[1] Mabuse is least successful in his nude figures; for instance, in his Adam and Eve at Hampton Court,[2] an original repetition of which is in the Berlin Museum, No. 642. But his most unpleasing efforts are such figures taken from mythology, viz., Neptune and Amphitrite, also in the Berlin Museum, No. 648, and Danaë and the Golden Shower, in the Munich Gallery, Cabinets, No. 41. On the other hand, his most attractive works of this time are portraits of a *genre*-like conception, such as a young girl weighing gold pieces, in the Museum at Berlin, No. 656 A.

Next in succession, of this class, is BERNHARD VAN ORLEY, born at Brussels 1471, died there 1541. Although almost cotemporary with Mabuse, yet we know of no pictures by him so worthily allied to the old school in moral and technical qualities as those executed by Mabuse before his visit to Italy. But, on the other hand, in the works imitative of the Italian style Bernhard van Orley is never so cold in feeling or so tasteless in form as Mabuse, who could never entirely shake off his Netherlandish feeling, and who, moreover, during a long residence in Rome, especially devoted himself to the imitation of Raphael. The works of the Brussels painter are composed with much discrimination; the earlier specimens often with earnest feeling, the later exhibiting well-drawn forms and good keeping; while the latest, it is true, lapse into the exaggerated and mannered forms of the later followers of Raphael. At the same time his execution is invariably careful, and

---

[1] 'Galleries and Cabinets,' &c., p. 98.
[2] 'Treasures,' &c., vol. ii. p. 368.

his colouring invariably cool in general effect, the flesh-tones inclining to a cold reddish colour. Bernhard van Orley was court-painter to Margaret of Austria, Governess of the Low Countries, and retained the same post under her successor, Mary of Hungary. The work by him bearing most signs of Netherlandish thought and practice is the Pietà, with portraits of the donors on the wings, in the Museum at Brussels. The heads are elevated in form and feeling—the portraits of great truthfulness. In close affinity with this is the altarpiece in the church of the town of Lierre, beyond the railway between Antwerp and Mechlin; the centre containing the Marriage of Joseph and the Virgin, the wings the Annunciation and the Presentation.[1] His most considerable work is a shrine with double wings in the church of our Lady at Lubeck. The outsides of the first pair of wings contain the Annunciation, which is not very satisfactory in conception; the inner sides, and again the outer ones of the second wings, the four Latin Fathers, of good draperies; and, finally, the inner sides of the last-mentioned, the Sibyl showing the Vision of the Virgin and Child to the Emperor Augustus, and St. John the Evangelist with the Vision of the Apocalypse; the centre represents the Trinity with adoring Saints, a free version from Albert Durer's picture.[2] This work is of great merit in many respects. Another picture, signed with his name, and in two compartments, is in the Gallery at Vienna. One division contains the Emperor Antiochus Epiphanes erecting an idol in the temple of Jerusalem; the other the Day of Pentecost, with St. Peter addressing the people. The heads are not pleasing, but the execution careful. His large Last Judgment in the chapel "des Orphelins" at Antwerp, with the Seven Works of Mercy on the predella, is most indicative of his adopted Italian manner. Though worthy of note for the able drawing of many of the figures, for the powerful tone of the flesh, and the vivacity of many portrait-like heads, yet the exaggeration of many of the actions—for instance, that of the Christ

---

[1] See further my article 'Kunstblatt,' 1847, p. 219, &c.
[2] See my article in 'Kunstblatt,' 1846, p. 115.

—the overladen character and the gaudiness of the colouring, give a very unpleasing effect, considered as a whole. One of his most attractive pictures is a Virgin and Child and Joseph, which is finely felt, and taken from a composition by Leonardo da Vinci in the Liverpool Institution.[1] On the other hand, in the worked hanging representing Abraham and Melchisedeck, and Rebecca at the Fountain,[2] at Hampton Court—probably taken from his cartoons, and decidedly of his latest time—he appears as a mannered imitator of Raphael.

JAN SCHOREEL, born 1495, died 1562;[3] scholar of Mabuse. This painter appears to have been the first to introduce the Italian style into his native country—Holland. On occasion of a pilgrimage to Palestine he happened to stop in Rome exactly as his countryman, Adrian VI., was raised to the papal dignity, 1521. He painted his likeness, and was appointed overseer of the objects of art in the Vatican. After the short reign of that pope Schoreel returned to Holland, and died at Utrecht, where he occupied the position of canon. In the one only historically authenticated picture by him, in the Town-hall at Utrecht, representing the Virgin seated, with the Child, in a landscape, with donors, he appears as an able draughtsman, and as an imitator of Raphael and Michael Angelo. On the other hand, the donors, and a set of portraits of pilgrims to Palestine, in the same place—among which is his own—show him to us as a painter of vigorous conception, warm tone of colour, and capital execution, in the style of the Netherlandish school.[4] The same may be said of the portraits of a man and his wife, dated 1539, in the Gallery at Vienna.[5] From a picture which was in the possession of the Methuen family at Corsham House in 1836, representing loving couples beguiling the time with music and the pleasures of the table, it is evident that he occasionally treated secular subjects

---

[1] 'Treasures,' &c., vol. iii. p. 236.
[2] Ibid., vol. ii. p. 367.
[3] Van Mander, fol. 154 a, and Joh. Secundi, Operæ Epist., lib. vii. 2.
[4] See article by Passavant, 'Kunstblatt,' 1841, No. 13.
[5] There erroneously called his own portrait.

with success. The treatment is truthful and lively, and the execution in a warm brownish tone of great mastery.[1]

MICHAEL VAN COXCYEN, commonly written Coxis, born at Mechlin 1499, died there 1592. He was at first scholar to his father, and afterwards to Bernhard van Orley.[2] He spent a number of years in Italy, where he adopted the outer form of Raphael's works, but remained unimbued with their spirit, so that the name of the Flemish Raphael which was given to him must be taken with much reserve. The numerous pictures which were the result of his long life are of very unequal merit. His frescoes in the church dell' Anima at Rome are unimportant and very mannered. In his compositions—which are frequently but too closely copied from Raphael—he shows in various portions much taste, and a sense of beauty in the heads; at the same time he is generally empty in expression, artificial in attitude, and exaggerated in the indication of muscles. Specimens of this class are in the Antwerp Museum, especially his Martyrdom of St. Sebastian, No. 88, and his Triumph of Christ, No. 93. A copy of the great picture, the Adoration of the Lamb, by the Van Eycks, which he executed for Philip II. of Spain, is full of merit as regards the life-sized figures, but is greatly inferior in those of a small scale.

LANCELOT BLONDEEL of Bruges flourished there about 1520 to 1574.[3] This master took delight in rich architectural backgrounds, conspicuous in which are whimsical Renaissance forms, generally executed in brown varnish on a gold ground, and therefore of very brilliant effect. His figures, which are chiefly conceived in the Italian taste, are often well set in action and of careful finish, but mannered, and of cold flesh-tones. The earliest picture known by him, signed 1523, in the church of St. Jacques at Bruges, represents SS. Cosmo and Damian; another, in the cathedral of the same town, dated 1545, the Virgin and Child, with SS.

---

[1] All other pictures, in Munich, Cologne, &c., attributed to this painter are not by him.

[2] Respecting the spelling of his name, and notices of his life, see 'Catalogue of Antwerp Museum,' von 1857, p. 82, &c.

[3] F. de Houdt's 'Deuxième Notice sur la Cheminée dans la Grande Salle du Franc de Brugge.' Gand, 1846, p. 42, &c.

Luke and Eligius. In the Museum at Berlin is also a Virgin and Child, No. 641, and a large Last Judgment, No. 656, an unsuccessful mixture of Netherlandish and Italian styles. The design for the mantelpiece in the large Council-hall at Bruges,[1] adorned with the statues of Charles V. and other princes, was by him as well.

JAN CORNELIS VERMEYEN, born 1500, died at Brussels 1559. How he gained instruction in art is not known; the fact, however, that Charles V. summoned him to Spain in 1534 for the purpose of his accompanying him the following year in his expedition to Tunis, where he drew the Siege of Tunis, with other events of the campaign—this fact is a proof that he must previously have distinguished himself as a painter. With the help of these drawings thus taken on the spot he executed ten large coloured cartoons, from which tapestries were worked by order of the Emperor, and probably in the Netherlands. These cartoons are preserved in a rolled-up state in the *Garderobe* of the Gallery at Vienna, and are said to have suffered much in parts. They are reported to be of great vivacity.[2] An evil star seems also to have presided over other works of this master, who was well known in his time, and who, firstly for his fine handsome person, and secondly for the length of his beard, was called El Mayo and Juan de Barbalonga in Spain. His pictures in the cathedral at Brussels were ruined by the Iconoclasts; and various landscapes, reported of great beauty, in the Palace of the Prado in Madrid, perished in the destruction of that building by fire in 1608. He is said to have been also a skilful portrait-painter.

MARTIN VAN VEEN, named from his birthplace MARTIN HEMSKERK, born 1498, died 1574. He was a scholar of Schoreel, from whom he received the Italian style of art, which he afterwards carried out in a most repelling form in Rome by the study of Michael Angelo and of the antique. His numerous pictures became very popular in Holland, but

---

[1] See the above-mentioned notices, and one of an earlier date by M. de Hondt.
[2] See article in 'Kunstblatt,' 1821, No. 51. My efforts to see at all events one of these cartoons were unsuccessful.

have now mostly disappeared. Momus criticising the Works of the Gods, dated 1561, in the Berlin Museum, is very characteristic of his art. The same may be said of the Silenus on an Ass with two Bacchante, in the Vienna Gallery.[1] As regards his treatment of Church-subjects, some pictures in the Hôtel de Ville at Delft and Haarlem are characteristic specimens. In the first is an altar with wings, signed and dated 1557, in the centre of which is the Elevation of the Brazen Serpent, in chiaroscuro. Also a second winged altarpiece, dated 1559, with the Ecce Homo in the centre. In a picture at Haarlem he has represented himself under the form of St. Luke painting the Virgin. If this picture be considered hard and mannered, a Martyrdom of two Saints, of the year 1575, is positively frightful.

LAMBERT SUSTERMANN, called LAMBERT LOMBARD, born at Liege 1506, died there 1560. He was a scholar of Mabuse, and adopted the Italian style from him, which afterwards, on occasion of accompanying Cardinal Pole to Italy, he further cultivated under Andrea del Sarto. On his return to Liege he opened a school which was numerously attended, and which was the means of further diffusing this style in the Netherlands. He also professed architecture, engraving, numismatics, archæology, and poetry. He is not deficient in feeling for beauty, either in heads or in action, though often very mannered in the last named. In the rendering of the muscular formation he is, compared with other painters of the time, somewhat subdued. His colouring is generally characterised by coolness, and by a *sfumato* which he probably adopted from Andrea del Sarto. In execution he is careful. His pictures are now very rare. The most remarkable—the Passage of the Red Sea, which is not successful; a Vision, which is more satisfactory; and the Scourges of the Almighty, Pestilence and Shipwreck, which are the most attractive of all—were in the collection of the King of Holland.[2] A Virgin with the sleeping Child, pale in colour,

---

[1] The numerous pictures in the Munich Gallery attributed to him are the work of Bartholomew de Bruyn.

[2] These pictures were withdrawn from the sale, and are now among the remaining pictures at the Hague.

but of refined feeling and tender completion, is in the Berlin Museum, No. 653.

FRANS DE VRIENDT, called FRANS FLORIS, born at Antwerp about 1520, died there 1570. He learnt his art from Lambert Lombard, and also visited Italy. As early as 1540 he was admitted into the guild of painters at Antwerp, and there opened a school which is said to have been frequented by one hundred and twenty scholars. In him the imitation of the Italian style attains its highest development. He was an artist of great talent, powers of invention, and facility of painting. He was deficient, however, in the sentiment of his heads, in grace of motive, and in understanding of drawing, so that his forms often exhibit marked exaggerations. On this account it is that his historical pictures are very unattractive. In his portraits only he is pleasing, as in them he was true to his Netherlandish nature. One of his earlier pictures, Vulcan exposing, to the sight of the Gods, Venus and Mars, round whom he has cast a net, dated 1547, and warmly coloured, in the Berlin Museum, No. 698, is a specimen both of his early attained mastery of hand, and of the tastelessness of his composition and insignificance of his heads. The Fall of the Angels, dated 1554, in the Antwerp Museum, No. 161, which is considered his chef-d'œuvre, is composed with great boldness, and shows a masterly power of painting, but it is tasteless in the animal heads of the demons, hard in outline, and crude in colour. An Adoration of the Shepherds, in the same gallery, No. 162, shows him to better advantage; the heads are animated and more true to nature than usual, and the chiaroscuro is well sustained: but the Virgin and Child are cold in the flesh-tones. Another picture there—St. Luke painting the Virgin, No. 163—is most attractive for the truthfulness and character of the heads. The saint is represented under the likeness of the painter Rykaert Aertsz; the colour-grinder under his own. The way in which the bull is here rendered shows again the tastelessness of the master.

MARTIN DE VOS, born at Antwerp 1531, died there 1603. He was the best of the numerous scholars of Frans Floris.

Afterwards he went to Italy, and had the benefit of Tintoretto's instruction at Venice. He then returned to Antwerp, and established a school. This painter was endowed with considerable powers of invention; and a number of his compositions are well known by means of engravings. Many of these are very attractive in character. Martin de Vos is less cold in feeling and less exaggerated in his muscular indications than Frans Floris; he is also generally careful in finish, and melting in touch; at the same time his motives are often mannered, his outlines hard, and his colouring crude. The Museum of Antwerp contains a whole series of his works; among them the altarpiece, dated 1574, the centre picture of which, the Incredulity of St. Thomas, No. 186, is remarkable for very finished execution. The Temptation of St. Anthony, No. 212, completed in 1594, showed a peculiar combination of the humorous and fantastic. Finally, a picture by him in the Berlin Museum, No. 709, dated 1589, with Christ appearing to the Disciples on the Sea of Tiberias on the one side, and the Prophet Jonah cast into the sea on the other, seems to herald, by the dramatic nature of the incidents, and the brilliant sunrise effect, the coming of such a master as Rubens.

Next in order among the scholars of Frans Floris may be mentioned some members of the family of painters by name of FRANCKEN; viz. three brothers, FRANS FRANCKEN THE ELDER, born 1544, died 1616; AMBROSIUS FRANCKEN THE ELDER, born 1545, died 1618; and JEROME FRANCKEN THE ELDER,— all of whom continued the style of the master. A number of works by the second brother are in the Antwerp Museum. Among these a picture on panel representing St. Sebastian healing Zoe the wife of Nicostrates, who was deaf and dumb, is remarkable for the vivacity of the five portraits. The three other painters Francken, who, having the same Christian names as the above-mentioned, are called the younger, painted pictures generally on a small scale. These partially betray the influence of Rubens, but, with few exceptions, are little satisfactory. We shall speak further of Frans Francken the younger, who was the most important of the three.

JOHANNES STRAET, commonly called STRADANUS, born at Bruges 1535, belongs also to this category. But as he repaired early in life to Florence, and died there at the advanced age of eighty-two, in 1618, he exercised no influence on the art of his native country. He imitated the manner of Michael Angelo, with the same unfortunate results as did Vasari, to whom he acted as an assistant. He painted, however, the sports of hunting and fishing, which brought his Netherlandish nature into play. The number of his pictures in oil and fresco were very large. Tapestries were also executed from his cartoons.[1]

But the most unattractive form in which the imitation of the Italian style displayed itself is seen in the works of BARTHOLOMEW SPRANGER, born in Antwerp 1546, died 1625. He was one of the favourite painters of the Emperor Rodolph II., at whose court at Prague he long resided. Parmigianino was the mistaken object of his imitation. His works show the most studied and forced attitudes, combined with an utter absence of feeling, and a cold tone of colour which is red in the flesh and greenish in the shadows. His chief merit in his better productions consists in an excellent modelling, and in an admirably fused treatment. Of the numerous pictures by him in the gallery at Vienna I quote one—Minerva treading Ignorance under foot—which is in every respect a characteristic work by him. Even this master when he took portrait in hand betrayed that feeling for the realistic in art which was his native Netherlandish inheritance. A proof of this is seen in his own portrait in the same gallery, which, though somewhat over-forcible in action, is truthfully felt, and painted in a warm colour.

HEINRICH GOLTZIUS, born 1558, died 1617, is a worthy companion to Spranger. He is less known by his rare pictures than by his numerous engravings, in which he shows no common versatility of power in the skilful imitation of very various masters, including Lucas van Leyden and Albert Durer; and also a wonderful mastery over his graver.[2] The great object of his imitation, however, is

---

[1] Van Mander, folio 184 a.
[2] Bartsch's Catalogue of his Works, vol. iii.

Michael Angelo, whom he seeks to rival by the most distorted attitudes, and the most violent play of spasmodically developed muscles. He treated both sacred and profane history, mythology and allegory, in the artificial taste of the day. He painted also portraiture and landscape. I will only mention here, of his historical compositions, the six called his masterpieces (Bartsch, No. 15-20), of which the Circumcision in the style of Albert Durer, and the Adoration of the Kings in that of Lucas van Leyden, are the most successful. He also appears to most advantage in his portraits, and namely in his own, which is the size of life (Bartsch, No. 172) and a real masterpiece. He also executed a few plates in chiaroscuro.

And here I may bring forward the name of CAREL VAN MANDER, born 1548, died 1608, who, though a devoted follower of this false style in art, deserves high praise as a writer upon art. Of all his numerous works, however, I know of none which I can mention with any certainty.

PIETER DE WITTE, born in Bruges,[1] was taken, when very young, by his parents to Florence. Here he became a skilful painter both in oil and fresco, and was variously employed by Vasari in his enormous fresco works in Rome and Florence. He thus acquired much knowledge, both in the arts of architecture and sculpture, and a particular aptitude in the decoration of buildings, all which accomplishments were called into action again in the service of the Duke of Bavaria at Munich on occasion of the building of the palace where the court resided. Although, of course, fettered by the perverted taste of his time, some of his pictures belong to the least unsatisfactory productions of the period. Those portions of the old palace at Munich which are still existing give evidence of his multifarious artistic powers. In Italy his name was translated into PIETRO CANDIDO, in consequence of which the Germans called him PETER CANDIT.

Various historical painters, in the ensuing generation, formed the transition to a better condition of art. Some of them, though still imitating the Italians, avoided the

[1] Van Mander, fol. 205 a.

repulsive exaggerations of their predecessors; others applied with some success to that truthfulness of nature and study of colour which was the real tendency of their native school.

At the head of these historical painters stands OTHON VAN VEEN, called OTTO VÆNIUS, born at Leyden 1558, died at Brussels 1629. Although the influence of the mannered painter, Federigo Zucchero, under whom he studied at Rome at the early age of seventeen, is seen in the frequently affected motives and gaudy colouring of his works, yet a certain moderation and taste in composition, and a sense of beauty in the heads, however deficient in warmth of feeling, are observable in his works. This coldness is increased by the far-fetched allegorical allusions to which a classical education of no common order tempted him. The number of his pictures is very considerable. Among those in the Antwerp Museum, the Calling of St. Matthew, No. 244; St. Paul before Felix, No. 248; and a portrait of Johann Miracus, Bishop of Antwerp, No. 247, are the most remarkable. This latter, compared with his historical works, displays the customary truthfulness of character and vigorous colouring. The six pictures at Munich—the Triumph of the Catholic Church, Cabinets Nos. 234-240,—though in themselves artificial, cold, and crude, are interesting as the models of similar compositions by Rubens.

HEINRICH VAN BALEN, born at Antwerp 1560, died there 1632. He is cold in feeling, generally mannered in motives, and glassy in colouring. In his nude figures, however, he shows a pleasing character, and the melting style of his execution is very finished. His ecclesiastical subjects—for instance the Ascension, in the church of St. Jacques at Antwerp—are the least satisfactory. His subjects taken from mythology, to which Jan Breughel frequently supplied the landscape backgrounds, are often more pleasing.

CORNELIS CORNELISSER, commonly called CORNELIS VAN HAARLEM, born at Haarlem 1562, died 1638. He first distinguished himself by a large portrait picture executed for the Guild of Marksmen in his native city; and though he afterwards treated Biblical subjects, and also scenes from common life, chiefly composed of nude figures, yet, upon the whole, he remained true to the realistic tendency. His pictures of the class just mentioned are very unequal in merit; the heads are often vulgar, and the motives tasteless. The best of them show a careful modelling and a warm and clear colouring. One of his chefs-d'œuvre is Bathsheba bathing with her attendants, dated 1617, in the Berlin Gallery, No. 734, in which, with characteristic conception, David is seen, scarcely visible, in a dark corner. But his talent was little adapted to the expression of strong emotions; the Murder of the Innocents, therefore, in the gallery of the Hague, is a very disagreeable picture. As regards the department of Mythology, his Venus, Cupid, and Ceres, in the Dresden Gallery, however little the heads are in keeping with the subject, is remarkable for force and transparency of colour, and for careful finish.

ABRAHAM BLOEMART, born at Gorcum 1564, died at Utrecht 1647. He constitutes in many respects the link of transition to the succeeding epoch; for however his frequently mannered motives, empty heads, over-soft execution, and occasionally gaudy colouring, betray the tasteless period in which he was born, yet his later pictures especially have a well-balanced general keeping, a purer taste, and a broad touch, which render them more satisfactory. His once numerous works have now principally disappeared. An Adoration of the Shepherds, dated 1604, in the Berlin Gallery, No. 745, conceived as a night-piece, is skilfully composed, and of powerful though somewhat gaudy effect. Joseph's Second Dream, with the Virgin and Child in the background, also at Berlin, No. 722, is mannered in the figure of the angel, but Joseph is a truthful and vigorous figure, and the keeping is well balanced. On the other hand, the Feast of the Gods, in the Hague Gallery, may be classed, by its crudeness and glassiness, with those works by him which partake of the character of the previous period. His raising of Lazarus, in the Munich Gallery, No. 193, is careful, and of better keeping and composition.

PIETER LASTMANN, born 1562, visited Rome in 1604,

where he evidently received an influence from Adam Elzheimer. On his return he attained such renown as to be summoned in 1619 and 1620 to paint pictures for a church in Copenhagen. He was a good draughtsman; his heads exhibit much sentiment, and his flesh colouring is warm and vigorous. In his landscape backgrounds, which generally are conspicuous parts of his pictures, the influence of Paul Bril is perceptible. Two works by him, St. Philip baptising the Eunuch, and a Holy Family, are in the Berlin Museum, Nos. 677 and 747.

ADRIAN VAN DER VENNE, born at Delft 1589, died at the Hague 1662, occupies a peculiar place among these painters. It was not till after he had received a classic and scientific education at Leyden that he devoted himself, under the instructions of Jerome van Diest, to the pursuit of painting. These circumstances not only influenced him in the preference of allegorical subjects in art, but contributed to divide his life between the occupations of an author and a painter. A moral element distinguishable in his pictures is his zeal for the Reformation, which just then rewarded the successful struggles of the Dutch, and his respect for the reigning princes of the House of Orange. In the mode in which he conceives such subjects he shows, however, a strong sympathy with the realistic tendency of his countrymen. His portraits, many of which he introduced into his allegorical and historical pieces, such as battles, &c., are not only well-drawn, of warm and clear colouring, and very careful finish, but the other figures in his pictures have also a portraitlike look. His realistic feeling is strongly seen in various *genre* pictures and landscapes. For Prince Maurice of Orange, the King of Denmark, and other patrons, he executed numerous pictures in chiaroscuro. The largest work I know by him—in the Amsterdam Museum, No. 337—represents Prince Maurice of Orange and his brothers, with other persons of distinction, on horseback, near the Hague—figures, about three-fourths the size of life. This work has, it is true, all the good qualities I have particularised above in point of keeping and execution, but also, like most of his other pictures, has something old-fashioned in character. He usually painted subjects with small figures, of which No. 337 in the Amsterdam Museum, called "la Pêche aux Ames," is a specimen.[1] The landscape here is painted by Jan Breughel, with Roman Catholics and Protestants on opposite sides of a stream. Several boats are also on the stream, the one containing Roman Catholic priests and monks, the other Protestant clergymen. Both are employed casting nets for figures swimming in the stream. Among the Roman Catholics are the portraits of Albert and Isabella; among the Protestants those of the Princes Maurice and Frederic Henry of Orange, and of the Elector Frederic of the Palatinate. Separate representations and inscriptions satirise the Papacy, and uphold the Evangelical Church. This rich picture is interesting both for its execution and subject. But a still more remarkable example of his art is No. 543 in the Louvre, which represents a festival in commemoration of the truce concluded between the Archduke Albert and the United Provinces of Holland in 1609, and is inscribed " A. V. Venne Fecit 1616." The landscape is also by Jan Breughel. The mixture of portrait figures—such as those of Albert and Isabella, with mythological and allegorical features—is very remarkable. The heads are very individual, and executed with great precision in a clear, golden tone. His inventions are as various as they are rich, as proved by the drawings he executed as illustrations for an edition of the works of Cats, the popular Dutch poet.

To various painters the decided and strongly realistic style with which Quentin Massys had occasionally painted scenes from common life, as for instance his Misers, became the model for their treatment, not only of similar subjects, but also for those of a biblical class. But none of them come up to his standard, degenerating generally into exaggeration and repelling vulgarity.

Foremost among them is JAN MASSYS, son of the master,

[1] This picture was formerly attributed to H. van Balen. The merit of having vindicated the real author belongs to M. Burger, in his ' Musées de la Hollande,' vol. i. p. 61, &c.

who lived from about 1500 to 1570. To his earlier time may be probably referred the repetitions of the Moneychangers and other pictures by his father, Van Mander expressly saying that he was engaged on such tasks. Remarkable specimens of this class are the Misers at Windsor Castle, the picture in the Berlin Museum, No. 671, and that at Munich, No. 80. Next in order is the St. Jerome, dated 1537, in the gallery at Vienna. All these works are of warm, powerful colouring, and careful though somewhat coarse treatment. His later pictures, on the other hand, exhibit in all respects—expression, colouring, and treatment—great feebleness; for instance, his Visitation, dated 1558, No. 156, and his Healing of Tobias, dated 1564, No. 157, of the Antwerp Museum.

JAN VAN HEMESSEN, born about 1500, died before 1566; if not the scholar, is the imitator of Quentin Massys. He displays usually a terrible vulgarity of forms and expression, is always hard in the outlines, and of a heavy brown colouring. He often copied Quentin Massys' works. I am acquainted with three copies by him of the Call of St. Matthew which I saw in England, one in the Antwerp Gallery, No. 94, and two in the Gallery at Vienna. One of his most pleasing pictures is a small Holy Family, dated 1541, in the Munich Gallery, Cabinets, No. 100—one of his most disagreeable, a St. Jerome in the Gallery at Vienna; but in the portrait of Jan van Mabuse, also at Vienna, he shows himself as a capital painter in this department.

Another painter, closely allied to the foregoing, and of a merit which is little known, is one of the name of HYUS, by whom a bagpipe-player, and an old woman, dated 1571, exist in the Berlin Museum, No. 693.

PIETER AERTSZEN, called LANGE-PEER, born 1507, died 1573, was scholar of Allard Claessen. He was a painter of extraordinary talent, and executed numerous large altarpieces in Louvain, Amsterdam, Delft, &c., all of which were destroyed by the Iconoclasts in 1566. Judging from the smaller, still existing pictures by him of Biblical subjects, they must have been conceived in a realistic and *genre*-like style. He was evidently a painter of keen observation, and as animated in composition as he was clever in practice. To these qualities is superadded, in his best works, forcible and clear colouring. A fine little picture by him is the Crucifixion in the Antwerp Museum, No. 159; also Christ bearing his Cross, in the Berlin Museum, No. 726, is a characteristic specimen. This latter subject is treated quite according to the customs of the painter's time. The two thieves are accompanied by a Dominican and a Franciscan, and the Bearing of the Cross forms only an episode in the middle distance. Occasionally he painted mere market scenes, a remarkable specimen of which is in the Gallery at Vienna.

JOACHIM BUECKLAER, the scholar of the foregoing, who flourished from about 1550 to 1570, walked quite in his master's steps. A Christ before Pilate, conceived in the same style as Pieter Aertszen's Bearing of the Cross, is in the Munich Gallery, No. 78. His market and kitchen scenes were also very popular.

PIETER BREUGHEL THE ELDER, also called PEASANT BREUGHEL, born about 1520, became member of the Painters' Guild in 1551, visited Rome about 1553, and died in Antwerp 1569. Although he also, on rare occasions, treated Biblical subjects in the same style as the preceding painters, yet he was the first who applied himself to the study of various forms of peasant life, and made it the chief subject of his art. His mode of viewing these scenes is always clever but coarse, and even sometimes vulgar. Occasionally he painted ghost and incantation scenes in the manner of Jerome Bosch. His treatment is in a warm tone, generally broad and sometimes slight. He also made skilful drawings, when travelling, from any landscapes which attracted him, and executed an etching of very picturesque character from one of these sketches. Woodcuts from his designs are occasionally met with. The Gallery at Vienna contains remarkable pictures by this master. Of his historical works, a Crucifixion, of the year 1563, a rich composition, is particularly worthy of note; the heads of the Virgin, &c., are of elevated expression. The Building of the Tower of Babel, of the same year, shows him in his fantastic landscape element. His humorous side is seen in his pictures of Winter, Spring, and Autumn (the latter a landscape of much poetry), and in a Fight between Carnival and Lent, dated 1559, which abounds with droll, and also with some coarse incidents. A Peasant Wedding, finally, is truthfully composed, and full of clever invention.

His eldest son, PIETER BREUGHEL THE YOUNGER, was also called, from the nature of his subjects, HELL BREUGHEL. In invention, colouring, and technical merit, he is far inferior to his father. His composition is generally lame, his heads spiritless, his flesh of a heavy leathery brown tone, and his touch very mechanical. Examples may be seen in his Christ bearing the Cross, in the Antwerp Museum, No. 255, and in a picture in the Berlin Museum, No. 721. The pictures called by his name at Dresden and Munich are by his younger brother Jan Breughel.

This JAN BREUGHEL, called VELVET BREUGHEL, born at Antwerp 1568, died there 1625, was a far more gifted painter, and of a versatility of talent which is rarely found. Though more especially a landscape-painter, in which aspect we shall presently regard him, he takes also as subject-painter an important place among his cotemporaries. His peasant subjects, though never rising above a coarse reality, are of lively character. The same may be said of his Scriptural pictures, on a very small scale—namely, his Scenes in Hell—and of his demoniacal subjects, laid sometimes in the ancient Tartarus, and which are conceived with strong effects of light. A clear and vigorous colouring, and a careful finish, are peculiar to these as well as to all his works. On the other hand, he is often wanting in general keeping. The Galleries of Dresden, Munich, and Berlin contain numerous pictures by him, and various specimens of those subjects.

DAVID VINCKEBOONS, commonly written VINCKEBOOMS, born at Mechlin 1578, died at Amsterdam 1629. This master is allied in many respects to the foregoing, though he moved in a far narrower circle. He also was a landscape as well as *genre* painter. He is fond of representing low life in the country, under those rude aspects which occur at fairs and festivals. His figures are of repelling ugliness and vulgarity, and his flesh-tones of a hard discordant red. Pictures of this kind are in the above-mentioned Galleries.

LUCAS VAN VALKENBURG, born at Mechlin, died 1625, painted scenes from peasant and soldier life in a somewhat grey but harmonious tone. His figures are of moderate drawing, but have a certain elegance. His execution is very finished. The best pictures I know by him are in the Vienna Gallery, where may also be seen specimens of his brothers FREDERICK and MARTIN VAN VALKENBURG, painters of the same class of subjects, but of weaker character.

SEBASTIAN VRANCX, born about 1573, is one of the earliest painters who especially devoted himself to battle-scenes, combats of horsemen, the plunder of villages, &c. His motives are truthful and touching, his brown-reddish colouring somewhat heavy, his execution tolerably broad, but careful. An excellent picture of this class is in the Vienna Gallery.

FRANS FRANCKEN THE YOUNGER, born at Antwerp 1581, died 1642. He was one of the best *genre*-painters appertaining to the last generation of this period. His works combine felicitous invention, much feeling for grace of action, able drawing, fine keeping, and a spirited touch. Only in his colour is he somewhat heavy. He painted the foreground figures in the architectural pictures of Pieter Neefs, of Van Bassen, and Josse de Momper, with great success. One of his most remarkable works is the Witch's Sabbath, dated 1607, in the Gallery at Vienna—perhaps the most complete representation that imagination has presented to us of this frightful world of fiction. In his later historical pictures, of which the Antwerp Museum possesses examples, he is less fortunate.

Upon the whole, the most satisfaction by far, at this period, as regards Netherlandish art, is, as I have before stated, derived from the portrait-painters.

The earliest of these is JOAS VAN CLEVE of Antwerp. Of the date of his birth and death nothing positive is known; he flourished from about 1530 to 1550. According to Vasari he visited Spain, and painted portraits for the Court of

France. At all events it is certain that he laboured for a time in England, where the great success of Sir Anthonis Moro is said to have disordered his brain. The few pictures however that can still be assigned to him thoroughly justify the high reputation he enjoyed in his time. His style of art may be classed between that of Holbein and Antonis Moro. His well-drawn forms are decided, without being hard; and the warm and transparent colouring recalls the great masters of the Venetian school. Two of his best works are the portraits of himself and wife in Windsor Castle. Not less successful is his own portrait in Lord Spencer's collection at Althorp. His pictures are frequently mistaken for those of Holbein, of which I have given some instances in my 'Treasures of Art.'

Next in order after Joas van Clevo comes SIR ANTONIS MORO, born 1518, died 1588.[1] He attended the school of Jan Schoreel in his youth, and afterwards visited Italy. On his return the recommendation of Cardinal Granvella procured him admission to the service of Charles V., with whom his art found such favour that the Emperor sent him to Lisbon to take the portrait of his son Philip's betrothed bride. Afterwards he repaired, and doubtless for a long period, to England, in order to paint Philip's second wife, Catholic Queen Mary. Subsequently he again spent some time at the Spanish Court at Madrid, and finally returned to the Netherlands, where he was much employed by the Duke of Alva. In all countries he earned praise, honours, and money. In his now rare historical pictures he exhibits one of the most repulsive forms of the Netherland-Italian style. In portraiture, on the other hand, his truthful feeling, good drawing, masterly and careful painting, and transparent and admirable colour, rendered him one of the best masters of his time. The portraits of his middle period are distinguished by their warmer and more vigorous colouring from the paler and less carefully finished works of his later time. Among his best pictures in England are those of Catholic Queen Mary and the Earl of Essex, in the collection of Lord Yarborough in London, and of Sir Henry

[1] His birth is sometimes assigned to 1512, and his death to 1575.

Sidney and his lady, dated 1553, in the collection of Colonel Egremont Wyndham at Petworth. No gallery is however so instructive, as regards this painter, as that of Vienna. Of his earlier time I will only cite his finely-felt and warmly-coloured picture, in a reddish tone, of Cardinal Granvella, dated 1549; his less warmly toned, but delilately conceived portrait of a young man with a scar, dated 1564; and the pictures of a young married couple, of cooler local tones and whitish lights, of 1575. The Dresden Gallery possesses also, under the erroneous name of Holbein, two female portraits of his best time, Nos. 1698 and 1701.

FRANS POURBUS THE ELDER, born 1540, died 1580. Though proceeding from the pernicious school of Frans Floris, this painter occupies a worthy place as portrait-painter. If inferior to the foregoing in refinement of drawing, he surpasses them all in golden and clear colouring. As an example of this class I may mention the portrait of a man, dated 1568, with his right hand on his side, his left on the hilt of his sword, in the Gallery at Vienna.

WILLEM KEY, born 1520, died 1568. This artist must have been a remarkable portrait-painter, the Duke of Alva having selected him to paint his portrait; but I cannot at this time assign with certainty any picture to him.

NICOLAS NEUCHATEL, called LUCIDEL, born 1550, died 1600. This admirable Belgian portrait-painter, who afterwards settled in Nuremberg, has left us the masterly portrait of the Mathematician instructing his Son, now in the Munich Gallery, No. 124. The relationship between the two figures gives the truthfully conceived heads a double interest. The local tones of the flesh are of a cool reddish, the shadows grey.

GUALDORP GORTZIUS, called GELDORP, born at Louvain, 1553, is seen to far greater advantage in his portraits than in his now chiefly vanished historical pictures, which are praised by Van Mander.[1] He was a scholar of Frans Franck the elder and of Frans Pourbus the elder, and settled later in Cologne, where several of his pictures are preserved. The

[1] Folio 195 b.

earlier are of lively conception, and carefully painted in a vigorous colour. In his later works he is cold in tone, and superficial in treatment.

Among the respectable portrait-painters of this time must also be reckoned CORNELIS KETEL, born at Gouda 1548. He painted Queen Elizabeth in 1578; later, various personages of her Court; and subsequently the Company of Marksmen at Amsterdam, and also some other company. My efforts to discover either of these pictures, or any in England by him, have not been successful.

On the other hand, a number of pictures exist by the hand of MARK GERARD of Bruges, one of the most favourite portrait-painters of the English Court in the reign of Elizabeth, who died in 1635. Not that he is by any means one of the best artists of this epoch, being somewhat tame in conception, and weak in drawing and colouring. The chief interest of his portraits therefore consists in the importance of his sitters, so that I may limit my notice to three very characteristic portraits—Queen Elizabeth, Lord Burleigh, and Lord Essex—in the collection of the Marquis of Exeter at Burleigh House.[1]

FRANS POURBUS THE YOUNGER, born 1570, died 1622, scholar of his father of the same name. Like him he was favourably distinguished as a portrait-painter, though inferior to him in warmth of colouring and solidity of impasto. He flourished for some time at the Court of Henry IV. of France, and took various portraits of that monarch, and also of his Queen, Mary of Medicis. The most important of his portraits in the Louvre is of that Queen, No. 396. The two smaller pictures also of the King, Nos. 394 and 395, deserve to be noticed.

PAUL VAN SOMER, born at Antwerp 1576, died 1624. He laboured for many years in England, where consequently his best works still remain. His conception is truthful and lively, his colouring warm and clear, and his execution finished. His portrait of Lord Bacon at Panshanger is excellent; also those of the well-known Earl of Arundel

---

[1] 'Treasures of Art,' &c., vol. iii. p. 407, &c.

and his Countess at Arundel Castle, seat of the Duke of Norfolk.

Most of the remaining portrait-painters of the latest generation of this epoch were Dutchmen.

MICHAEL JANSE MIEREVELT, born at Delft 1567, died 1651. With a simple and truthful feeling for his subject, he combines clear and often warm colouring. The number of his works is very considerable. A series of his works are in the Hôtel de Ville at Delft. In an archery piece of 1611, the largest picture by him known to me, with numerous figures, he does not appear to advantage. Although the heads are animated, the colouring is somewhat heavy, and the treatment rather mechanical. The portraits of William I. and II., and Maurice of Saxony, in the Burgomaster's room, are better. On the other hand, in respect of excellence of conception, clear colouring, and careful execution, the bust portrait of Hugo Grotius, in the same place, is admirable. Especially soft, for this master, are three children over the chimneypiece. Fine examples of his art are in the Dresden and Munich Galleries. Among his best scholars are his son PETER MIEREVELT, and PAUL MOREELSEE. An excellent picture by the latter is in the Berlin Museum.

In close affinity with the last is JOHANN WILHELM DELFT, by whom is another archery subject, signed and dated 1592, in the Hôtel de Ville at Delft. This picture contains many figures, and exhibits truthfulness of feeling and good painting, though it is somewhat hard in outline, and heavy in its brown colouring.

JACOB DELFT: by this painter is a remarkable female portrait in the Städel Institute at Frankfort.

DANIEL MYTENS, born at the Hague. Like Van Somer he spent his active years in England. In 1625 he was engaged by Charles I. at a salary of 20*l*., and it appears that he remained in that King's service till towards 1630. About that time he probably left England. This master is characterised by great simplicity of manner and a general effect of lightness of colour. In his flesh-tones he is often inclined to the silvery. His tenderly fused execution is careful. Two pictures of Charles I. and Henrietta Maria in their youthful days, with the dwarf Sir Geoffrey Hudson, various dogs and a grey horse, all life size, constitute his chefs-d'œuvre. The one is at the seat of Lord Galway, Serlby, Nottinghamshire; the other in the collection of the Countess of Dunmore, Dunmore Park, near Falkirk. Mytens occasionally painted small pictures of great delicacy. Two very pretty examples of this class, the portraits of Charles I. and Henrietta Maria, with architectural background by the elder Steenwyck, are in the Dresden Gallery, Nos. 965 and 966, under the erroneous title of Gonsales Coques. Another, with Charles and his Queen, and one of their children, in one picture, is in the Royal Gallery, Buckingham Palace.

CORNELIUS JANSEN, supposed to have been born in London of Flemish parents.[1] At all events he was long in England, where he painted for Charles I., and left it in 1648. He continued to paint portraits in Holland with great success till his death in 1665. He was an artist of refined feeling for nature, tasteful in composition, warm and tender in colouring, and of melting execution. Among the many pictures by him scattered through England, I will mention only that of Frederick, Elector of the Palatinate, in the Gallery of Hampton Court; of Lady Dorothy Neville, at Burleigh House; of John Taylor, master of the revels at the court of Charles I., and his own portrait, at Longford Castle. He also occasionally executed portraits on a small scale. An example is seen in that of Charles I. with persons of his Court in the Green Park, in the Royal Collection, Buckingham Palace.

In this time also the painters of animals grew into a distinct class, though some Biblical title, such as Adam and Eve in Paradise, was given to pictures whose chief interest lay in animal life. The best painter of this order was ROELANDT SAVERY, born at Courtray 1576, died 1639. His scenes, in which a very brown tone generally prevails, are often overfilled with animals, each singly of much truth of nature. One of his best pieces, Paradise, is in the Berlin

---

[1] Sandrart, vol. i. p. 319.

Museum, No. 710. Various pictures with wild rocky scenery, in which savage animals dwell, have something fantastic.

Next to him in this class is JAN BREUGHEL, already described as a *genre*-painter. His animal pieces often show the influence of Rubens, and surpass those of Roelandt Savery in transparency and truth of colouring. Good specimens of this kind are in the Dresden and Berlin Galleries, in the Louvre, and also at Madrid. His chief picture is also a Paradise in the Hague Gallery, in which the figures of Adam and Eve are finely painted by the hand of Rubens.

Jan Breughel was followed by FERDINAND VAN KESSEL, a painter of greater hardness and dryness.

Landscape painting, also, according to Van Mander's account, was carefully treated at this period; but, of the painters whom he celebrates as belonging to this class, FRANS MINNEBROER, JAN DE HOLLANDER, JACQUES GRIMMER, MICHAEL DE GAST, and HENDRIK VAN CLEEF, no picture ever reached my eyes. A few, however, by LUCAS GASSEL, who flourished before and after the middle of the 16th century, have been preserved. He continued the fantastic manner of Patinier, with strangely-formed rocks and a number of well-executed details. In colouring he is somewhat monotonous and cool. A landscape, with Judah and Thamar, in the Vienna Gallery, bears his monogram and the date 1548. I have seen other pictures, dated respectively 1538 and 1561, in private collections, though, in their liability to change hands, I do not quote them.

A remarkable advance in the art of landscape painting was made by the brothers MATTHEW BRIL, born at Antwerp 1550, died at Rome 1580, and PAUL BRIL, born 1556, died 1626. The early death of the elder gave no scope for any extended activity: he was, however, the instructor of his brother, who joined him in Rome and soon displayed the highest abilities of the two. Paul Bril painted both in oil and fresco, and left behind him a large number of works.[1]

[1] See regarding this master the notice by Ed. Fetis in the 'Bulletins de l'Académie Royale de Belgique' of 1855, p. 594-616.

He viewed nature with a fresh eye—selecting her natural and poetic rather than her arbitrary and fantastic features. He was the first to introduce a certain unity of light in his pictures, attaining thereby a far finer general effect than those who had preceded him. His deficiencies lie in the over force, and also in the monotonous green, of his foregrounds, and in the exaggerated blueness of his distances. Nevertheless, this painter exercised a considerable and beneficial influence over Rubens, Annibale Carracci, and Claude Lorraine, and must ever occupy an important position in the development of this branch of art. Only in his earlier works, and then rarely, does he betray the fantastic element, as, for instance, in his Building of the Tower of Babel, in the Berlin Museum, No. 731. His later qualities, and especially his treatment of the general lighting of a scene, are observable in a morning landscape, also at Berlin, No. 744. Fine examples of his best time are in the Louvre, especially Nos. 67, 71, and 73.

LUCAS VAN VALKENBURG.—We here again encounter this already mentioned painter and his brothers, under the character of landscape painters. They attached themselves more particularly to the earlier style, which was distinguished by its great minuteness of detail. The pictures by Lucas have frequently something naïve, and a peculiar poetic charm. The Vienna Gallery possesses the best landscapes by the three brothers.

JOSSE DE MOMPER, born probably at Antwerp 1559, died in 1634 or 1635.[1] Although younger than Paul Bril, he retains much more of the fantastic modes of conception which distinguished the earlier landscape painters. He generally introduces us to lofty hills and bold forms in striking sunlight, and is often untruthful in colour and of slight and mannered treatment. His pictures are numerous, for instance in the Dresden and Vienna Galleries. In his later works only he occasionally attained considerable power and keeping, as seen in a landscape in the Berlin Museum, No. 772. He was also a skilful etcher.

[1] I have taken these dates from the Catalogue of the Antwerp Museum of 1858, p. 175, &c.

The figures in his foregrounds were executed by various painters; by Peter Breughel the younger, several members of the numerous Francken family, David Teniers the elder, and Henrik van Balen.

And here again we come upon JAN BREUGHEL, who was a landscape painter of no mean merit. He treated the flat scenes of his native land, intersected with canals and rows of trees, with truthfulness and considerable detail, though he is wanting in the general keeping of the picture. His smaller pictures of this class are often attractive. Henrik van Balen, Rothenhammer, and even occasionally Rubens, painted ideal figures in his landscapes.

WILLEM VAN NIEULANDT, ANTON MYRON, and PETER GYSSENS, followed the same style as Jan Breughel, and their works are often mistaken for his.

Finally, we must not omit to notice two painters already mentioned, ROELANDT SAVERY and DAVID VINCKEBOONS, in their character as landscape painters. The first is inferior to Jan Breughel in truthfulness, but excels him in poetic feeling, especially in the representation of fine woods. An excellent example of his merits in this department is in the Berlin Museum, No. 749. Vinckeboons is somewhat heavy and gloomy in tone, but otherwise, compared with Jan Breughel, has much about the same qualities as Roelandt Savery.

Of the same period and tendency may be reckoned the already-mentioned PETER LASTMANN, ALEXANDER KIERINGS, and HANS PILEN. The pictures of the first named are distinguished by foreground figures, taken from scriptural subjects, and executed with much art.

Marine painting appears to have been first cultivated in Holland, where it subsequently attained its highest form of development. HEINRICH CORNELIUS VROOM, born at Haarlem in 1566, is the earliest known master of this class. He visited Spain and Italy, entering into an intimacy with Paul Bril, by which his art was greatly benefited. Afterwards he visited England, where he executed a drawing of the defeat of the Spanish Armada, for the Earl of Nottingham, High Admiral of England. Of his once highly-prized pictures only few are preserved. A picture of considerable size by him, in a side apartment of the Hôtel de la Ville at Haarlem, represents large vessels and a town in the background. The execution is careful and the sky clear, but the green water and the weak perspective show his department of art in a very primitive stage. A picture in the Antwerp Museum, No. 306, is, on the other hand, too broad and decorative in treatment.

ADAM WILLAERTS, born at Antwerp 1577, lived and died at Utrecht, probably in 1640. He painted pre-eminently coast and harbour scenes, and enlivened them with numerous figures. With all attention to detail, he combines also a successful effort at general keeping, and a broad and soft touch. He never quite succeeded in mastering the movement of the waves. A good specimen of him is in the Berlin Museum, No. 711. He sometimes diverged from his usual subjects and painted markets and festive scenes. A picture of this class, of vigorous colour and somewhat decorative treatment, is in the Antwerp Museum, No. 287.

BONAVENTURA PETERS, born at Antwerp 1614, died there 1653. He was a marine painter who especially represented the sea in its most tempestuous forms, with vessels running ashore or struck by lightning. His pictures have generally a very poetic character, though often untrue and mannered in the forms of the hills, the clouds, and in the movement of the waves. On the other hand, they have the merit of a great power and clearness of colour, and of a masterly handling. They are rare in public galleries, with the exception of Vienna, which possesses five,.and all of them signed. One of them, a vessel being wrecked in a raging storm, is poetic and very transparent, but the waves are too parallel in their action. The companion to it, with an ancient monument on the shore, though otherwise of great merit, is defective in the forms of the clouds. Two others, companions, dated 1645, one a Venetian fort stormed by Turks, with a mine in the act of exploding, and the other a fortified harbour, show a more refined feeling for form with the same transparency.

JAN PETERS, born at Antwerp 1625, died 1677, a younger

brother of the foregoing, painted similar subjects with success. A picture bearing his name in the Munich Gallery, No. 243, with a violent storm, and vessels being dashed against a rocky coast, is beautifully composed and lighted. But the over-brown colour of the rocks, and the coming up of the brown ground through the water, somewhat disturb the keeping.

The branch of architectural painting was comparatively early of development. JAN FREDEMANN DE VRIES was born at Leeuwarden in 1527. This artist went through a scientific study of the works of Vitruvius and Serlio, and devoted himself, with no common result, to this class of art. Like the landscape-painters before noticed, his works take their title from the figures in the foreground, though the rich architecture which occupies the surrounding space, and in which the laws both of lineal and aërial perspective are effectively observed, forms the real subject. The tone in which these architectural forms are treated is generally delicate, clear, and cool. The best works I know by him are a series of pictures in the fine summer council chamber in the Hôtel de Ville at Dantzic, in which, however, the figures are in the mannered taste of his time.

Architectural painting was further developed by HENDRIK VAN STEENWYCK, born 1550, died 1604, who was scholar of the preceding master. He painted chiefly interiors of Gothic churches, on a small scale, generally enlivened with figures by some of the numerous Francken family. He was the first to represent the effect of the light of torches and tapers on architectural forms. The fine perspective, both lineal and aërial, observed in his pictures, gives them a lasting value, though the execution of his architectural detail is somewhat hard and metallic. Admirable specimens of his art are in the Vienna Gallery.

PIETER NEEFS, born at Antwerp 1570, died 1651, was the best of Steenwyck's scholars. He painted quite in the same style, but excelled his master in power and warmth of tone, and also in the truthfulness of his torchlight effects. An excellent picture of this class is in the Louvre, No. 346. Other fine specimens by him are also there, and in the gallery at Vienna. Many of his works are enlivened by figures by Frans Francken the younger, by Jan Breughel, and by David Teniers the elder.

HENDRIK VAN STEENWYCK THE YOUNGER, son of the other Steenwyck, was a fellow-scholar with Pieter Neefs, but painted in a cooler tone, and was inferior to him in all respects. His works are also seen in the Vienna Gallery, and a larger one in the Berlin Museum. PIETER NEEFS THE YOUNGER, the son and pupil of the elder of this name, was also of inferior merit. Pictures by him are in the Vienna Gallery.

BARTHOLOMEW VAN BASSEN flourished from about 1610 to 1630. He formed his style independently of the preceding knot of artists; painted chiefly interiors of Renaissance churches, and also saloons of the same architectural character. His figures are usually the work of Frans Francken the younger. Though his pictures display careful detail and exact perspective, yet they are wanting in aim, and are often crude in effect and hard in forms. A specimen both of his church and of his saloon interiors is in the Berlin Museum.

The first examples of flower and fruit painting as a separate branch occur towards the end of this period, and here again we meet with the versatile hand of JAN BREUGHEL. His flower-pieces are comparatively rare; the single flowers are executed with feeling and great truthfulness of form and colour, but the general effect is without keeping. A chef-d'œuvre of this class is a large flower-piece in the Munich Gallery, Cabinets, No. 226. Also a large wreath of flowers in the Louvre, No. 429, with a Virgin and Child, by Rubens, painted in the centre.

Although miniature painting in this epoch, when so many monuments of art of greater size were in existence, no longer maintains that important position which we have accorded to her at an earlier period, yet two Belgian artists, who devoted themselves to this branch of painting in the second half of the 16th century, were so remarkable, and also so celebrated in their time, that I cannot pass them over in silence.

HANS BOL, born at Mechlin 1535, died in Amsterdam 1593. In his earlier time he devoted himself to the execution of larger pictures in size colours, but afterwards applied himself exclusively to miniature painting, in which he produced a large number of works. In his subjects taken from history the mannered taste of the school of Frans Floris prevails; but in his more numerous landscapes, with small figures from life, he combines picturesqueness of composition and good drawing with a very finished and clever execution. His general tone, however, is frequently too cold, and he is deficient in keeping. The merit of his portraits, animals, fruits, and flowers is their truth. Like the earlier miniature painters his practice was in body colours. True also to the old fashion, he decorated manuscripts with his miniatures, but more frequently painted small landscapes, on single sheets. As an example of the first kind, I mention a small prayerbook in the Imperial Library at Paris, Supplement Latin (No. 708), executed in 1582. Of the second class will be found some beautiful little pictures in the cabinet of miniatures at Munich, and in the cabinet of engravings at Berlin. Hans Bol also etched a small number of plates, with much success, from his own designs.

JOORIS HOEFNAGEL, born in Antwerp 1545, died in Vienna 1600. He received the instruction of Hans Bol; but, owing to a very careful education, he became an artist of much more extended powers. He travelled in France, Spain, Italy, and Germany. In the latter country he was first in the service of the Duke of Bavaria at Munich, afterwards in that of the Emperor Rodolph II. at Prague, but resided at Vienna. Owing to an uncommon facility of drawing, and to an untiring industry, the number of drawings, of every possible subject, made on these journeys, and also the amount of his miniatures, is astonishingly large. They comprise sacred and secular history, scenery, animals, plants, flowers, fruits, precious stones, pearls, &c. He also especially decorated manuscripts in the old manner and with the old technical materials. The most famous among them is a Roman missal, now in the

Imperial Library at Vienna (No. 1784), which he executed for the Archduke Ferdinand of the Tyrol, and on which he laboured from 1582 to 1590, a period of eight years. He here appears as a very clever eclectic painter, versed both in all the spiritual allusions of the early time, and also in the technical materials and forms of ornamentation,—a knowledge which he applied with great skill. Occasionally he shows signs of an allegorical, but often artificial mysticism peculiar to himself, and degenerates sometimes into an overladen and tasteless manner. He availed himself often of the emblematic representations from the Biblia Pauperum; and in his historical subjects made use of the motives of Raphael and other painters; in his ornaments also he adopted alternately, and with masterly handling, the earlier manner of the Netherlandish, German, and Italian miniature painters; and finally studied the miniatures of Giulio Clovio. Next to this missal I may mention two works executed for Rodolph II., one of which represents, in four books, the walking, the creeping, the flying, and the swimming animals; the other books contain various subjects. Hoefnagel also often painted single pieces; for instance, the Glorification of the Spanish Monarchy, dated 1573, in the Library at Brussels. The numerous emblematic representations are in the artificial and tasteless spirit of the times; but the execution is of indescribable pains and finish.

CHAPTER II.

PAINTING IN GERMANY.

THE aspect of painting in Germany and Switzerland at this period is less satisfactory than in the Netherlands. We especially miss a chief centre of activity, such as Antwerp afforded. The early schools of Nuremberg, Augsburg, Ulm, and Cologne had died out, and in their stead, both in these and other places, only isolated painters occur. Historical painting, it is true, took the same course as in the Netherlands, but its few scattered masters appeared later on the scene. That rich development of subject and landscape painting also, for which the Netherlands had been distinguished, found no equivalent here. Portrait painting, on the other hand, was successfully pursued, though not so as to rival the best masters of the Flemish and Dutch school.

HANS STEPHANUS, known in the history of art by the name of HANS VON CALCAR, from the town of that name on the Lower Rhine, where he was probably born 1510.[1] He was the first to turn, and with great success, to the Italian school, residing in Venice from 1536 to 1537, in the school of Titian, whose manner he so entirely adopted that it becomes occasionally difficult to distinguish their respective works. He there executed the admirable drawings for the woodcuts which illustrate the well-known work by Vesalius on anatomy, and afterwards went to Naples, where Vasari became acquainted with him in 1545, and where, according to Van Mander, he died in 1546. I know no historical picture by him; but his very rare existing portraits thoroughly justify the favourable witness of Vasari. They show also a really great affinity to Titian, being less energetic, but very delicate in feeling for nature, in which they approach close to Giovanni Battista Morone, excellent in drawing, and very carefully coloured in a clear, warm, and somewhat reddish tone. A very fine portrait of a man, formerly attributed alternately to Paris Bordone and to Tintoretto, is in the Louvre; another, with a letter in his hand, at Vienna; a third in the Museum at Berlin, No. 190.

Many of the German painters, in their earlier efforts, adhered, even in this department, to the style of the former period, and only sought to adopt the qualities of Italian art at a later time. Conspicuous among this class is BARTHOLOMEW DE BRUYN, who flourished in Cologne from

[1] The statement of his having been born in 1500 is destitute of all foundation.

1520 to 1560. His earlier works approximate closely to those of his master, the painter of the Death of the Virgin. His principal work of this time are the wings of the large shrine upon the high altar of the church of Xanten, executed in 1534. The inner sides contain events from the legends of SS. Victor, Sylvester, and Helena; the outer ones the figures of three saints, with the Virgin and Child, SS. Gereon and Constantine, and four half circles. The heads and figures are of elevated character, the forms fullish, the execution very able, and the tone of uncommon warmth and vigour. His portraits of the same period, such as the burgomaster Jan van Ryht, painted 1525, in the Berlin Museum, No. 588, and of one Browiller, painted 1535, in the Cologne Museum, so closely resemble Holbein as generally to be designated by his name. His Descent from the Cross, with wings, in the Munich Gallery, Nos. 112, 113, and 114, is also a good work of the same epoch. Although he deteriorated afterwards, both in thoroughness of execution and in truth of tone, yet he retains the same Holbein-like style of treatment. This we see in a Virgin and Child adored by a Duke of Cleves, in the Berlin Museum, No. 639. After this time he attempted to adopt the characteristics of Italian art, after the fashion of Martin van Hemskerk, the results of which were heads devoid of interest, tasteless motives, cold and insipid colouring, and slight execution. Even his portraits of this time are poorly coloured and slightly painted. A number of his works of this class are to be seen in the Munich and Cologne Galleries, where, excepting Nos. 76 and 80, they all bear the name of M. van Heemskerck.

In Westphalia we find a family of painters, by the name of TOM RING at Munster. LUDGER, THE ELDER, may be seen in his principal work, dated 1538, in the collection of the Westphalian Art Union, which represents Christ and the Virgin interceding with the Almighty, who, surrounded with angels, is about to destroy the sinful world. The painter here decidedly adheres to the early German school, showing dignified and stern feeling, and thorough execution. His son HERRMANN TOM RING, on the other hand, judged by his chief work, the Resurrection of Lazarus, of the year 1546, in the Munster cathedral, evinces in many respects the influence of Italy. The architecture, with well-executed white busts, is of Italian taste. But his portrait-like heads are not important, and his actions are mannered. The portrait of the donor is animated, but Martha and Mary have the aspect of nuns. The colouring is gaudy, the chiaroscuro well observed, and the finish, especially of the accessories, good. In his later pictures he appears as a feeble painter in the manner of Frans Floris.

The son of Herrmann, LUDGER TOM RING THE YOUNGER, like many a Netherlander, devoted himself to the imitation of the details of real life. Thus his pictures of sacred subjects are so in little more than name. Of this class is a Marriage at Cana, dated 1562, in the Berlin Museum, No. 708—literally a large kitchen piece with numerous skilfully executed details, but totally devoid of keeping. The subject itself is seen in a corner of the background.

At Nuremberg, at about the same period, lived a master of the name of VIRGILIUS SOLIS, painter, engraver, and designer upon wood, born 1514, died 1562. His pictures are now become very rare. From his numerous engravings, however, treating as they do the most various subjects, and from the woodcuts taken from his designs,[1] it appears that in his earlier time he attached himself, though but in a mechanical fashion, to the school of Albert Durer, devoting himself subsequently to the imitation of Italian art, in which he displays great readiness of hand, but little feeling.

MICHAEL OSTENDORFER flourished in Regensburg about 1550. He formed himself after Albrecht Altdorfer, though inferior to him in feeling and skill. Like Lucas Cranach he sought to embody the doctrines of Luther in his art. An altarpiece of this class is in the collection of the Historical Museum at Regensburg.[2]

---

[1] Bartsch, vol. ix. p. 242, &c., quotes 558 engravings by his hand, and various long series of woodcuts from his designs.
[2] 'Kunstwerke und Künstler in Deutschland,' vol. ii. p. 125, &c.

At about the same period we find in Munich a painter by name HANS MÜLICH, generally but erroneously called Mielich, born 1515, died 1572. His portraits are now rare; one of a woman, in the collection of the King of Prussia, shows that he followed the early German style. The treatment is truthful, and the colouring clear. The same qualities appear in his portraits of Duke Albrecht V. of Bavaria and his Duchess Anna, and of other individuals—among the rest of himself, executed in miniature for the above-named princess, in the illuminated MSS. of the music of the Seven Penitential Psalms, by Orlando di Lasso, and in the motetts by Ciprian de Rore.[1] On the other hand, the historical subjects introduced into these works by him show him as a feeble imitator of Italian artists.

In this time also occurs the name of HANS SEBALD LAUTENSACK, who laboured in Vienna, and who decidedly descended from the painter family of the same name at Nuremberg. No picture, however, by him is known to me. As regards his engravings[2] he appears most to advantage in his landscapes and views of towns, following in his fantastic feeling and mechanical treatment the style of Altdorfer. His portraits, which are weak in drawing and hardly treated, show also his adherence to the early German school.

A somewhat later generation than those we have just considered gave themselves still more determinately to the imitation of Italian art, of which their productions show us the most perverted examples. In the whole field of ideal art, whether mythology, allegory, or Holy Scripture, they are alike mannered and devoid of taste, and especially so where nude figures constitute the chief subject. Their treatment of realistic scenes from their own cotemporary history and from common life, as well as their portraits and landscape, are somewhat more endurable, though far less truthful and careful in character, than

---

[1] See the same in the Munich Court Library among the rarest treasures called there "Cimelien," Nos. 51 and 52.

[2] Bartsch, vol. ix. p. 207, &c., mentions fifty-nine engravings and two woodcuts by him.

the works of the Netherlandish masters of the same time. The following are the most notable names.

TOBIAS STIMMER, born at Schaffhausen 1534. According to the fashion then prevalent in Germany, he decorated with frescoes the façades of many houses in his native city, and in Strasburg and Frankfort. No example of these has, however, been preserved. His oil pictures are also very rare. The portraits of a Herr von Schwyz, bannerman of Zurich, and of his wife, in the collection of Mr. Carl Waagen of Munich, show skill and truthfulness. His whole style may be gathered from several hundred woodcuts executed from his designs.[1] He died at Strasburg in the prime of life.

JOST AMMAN, born at Zurich 1539, removed to Nuremberg in 1560, and died there 1591. I know no example surviving of his pictures in oil and on glass. But various engravings, and a large number of woodcuts from his designs, give evidence of his great diligence.[2]

CHRISTOPH MAURER, born at Zurich 1558, died 1614. He was the scholar of Tobias Stimmer, and closely followed his style. He also is only known by a small number of plates and woodcuts, the first etched by himself, the second from his designs, which have now become very rare.[3]

HANS BOCK, known by his diffuse frescoes, inside and outside the Hôtel de Ville at Basle, some of which still survive. He is very mannered in style, but of great energy, as for example his picture of the Calumny of Apelles in the same Hôtel de Ville.

The following masters enjoyed much favour at this period at the courts of the Duke of Bavaria at Munich, and of the Emperor Rodolph II. at Prague.

HANS VAN ACHEN, born at Cologne 1552, died at Prague 1615; studied at Cologne in the school of the painter Jerrigh. On his return from Italy he was successively employed at both the above-mentioned courts. His best pictures are those in which we trace the study of Tintoretto, viz. his Bathsheba bathing, in the Vienna Gallery;

---

[1] Bartsch, vol. ix. p. 330.   [2] Ibid. p. 351.   [3] Ibid. p. 385.

his least attractive are those in which he took his friend Bartholomew Spranger for his model, namely, his Bacchus with Venus, his Jupiter and Antiope, in the same gallery. Specimens of his ecclesiastical pictures are in the church of the Jesuits and in the church of Our Lady at Munich.

JOSEPH HEINZ, born probably at Berne. According to Van Mander he was a scholar of Hans van Achen, and one of the favourite painters of Rodolph II. He died in Prague 1609. His pictures are occasionally distinguished by a cold sumptuousness; as for example his Venus and Adonis in the Vienna Gallery; also by a feeling for elegance of form, as in his Diana and Actæon in the same gallery. His colouring is gaudy and untruthful, but his touch melting and masterly. His most unattractive works are those taken from Scripture, as seen in the Crucifixion at Vienna. He appears to most advantage in his portraits, namely, in that of the Emperor Rodolph II., also at Vienna.

CHRISTOPHER SCHWARTZ, born at Ingolstadt, in Bavaria, died 1594. He formed himself in Venice, more especially after the works of Tintoretto, and afterwards became court painter at Munich. His forms are pleasing and his actions graceful, though often mannered. His heads are insipid, and his colouring either gaudy and crude or too faint. He also decorated the exteriors of houses with frescoes. The most notable of his pictures are a Virgin and Child in glory, in the Munich Gallery, No. 105. Also a family portrait, No. 115, in which Tintoretto is his obvious model.

JOHANN ROTHENHAMMER, born at Munich 1564, died at Augsburg 1623. He was scholar of Hans Donnauer, and visited Italy, where he also studied Tintoretto especially. He painted a number of large pictures, but is chiefly known by those on a smaller scale, in which he collaborated alternately with Jan Breughel and Paul Bril; he executing the department of mythology or allegory, they that of landscape. In his earlier pictures—such as his Death of Adonis, in the Louvre, No. 424—he approaches Tintoretto in force, warmth, and clearness. His forms also partake of the same elegant character; unfortunately he adopted the Venetian master's arbitrary and confused arrangement of lines. His later pictures—for example, his Virgin in Glory, in the Munich Gallery, No. 111—have a disagreeable effect from the brick-red tones of the flesh and the greenish shadows. In his numerous small pictures he is known by the tenderly fused character of his execution. Plenty of this class are found in all galleries.

By far the most attractive painter whom Germany displays at this unsatisfactory period of the art is ADAM ELZHEIMER, born at Frankfort on the Maine 1574,[1] died at Rome 1620. He early showed his artistic talents, and was placed under the Frankfort master, Philip Uffenbach, after which he travelled through Germany to Rome, where he married an Italian. He had a profound and refined feeling for nature, further developed by ceaseless study, and admirable technical qualities, which told to great advantage in his uniformly small pictures. His historical works, scriptural or mythological, are of decidedly realistic character, well arranged and drawn, occasionally approaching Rembrandt in warmth of tone, and executed throughout in a fine body of colour, and with the utmost attention to detail. Effects of torch and candle light were also his favourite study. Although well paid for his pictures, the time he devoted to them was so considerable, that, having a numerous family, he was thrown into prison for debt, and died in bitter poverty. His most admirable works are his landscapes, which have a miniature-like character, as if we looked on nature through a diminishing glass. In the small space which they occupy, he gives a wide expanse of diversified scenery, illuminated by broken gleams of light—woods in deep shadow, water with its clear bright surface, and the graceful alternations of mountain and valley; the eye, which at a little distance enjoys the harmony of this little world, loses nothing when it approaches to view more closely the minutest details of execution, or the spirited indication of the different objects. There is no want of pleasing figures

---

[1] Sandrart, vol. i. p. 294, and Schnaase's 'Niederländische Briefe,' p. 26.

subordinate to the landscape. Here we have a Holy Family journeying through a still, moonlight landscape—there a thick forest, in which John the Baptist preaches to the assembled people—now a night-piece, with Æneas leading his followers from the burning city. Owing to his laborious mode of operation he left but a small number of pictures, which are now become exceedingly rare. Some of them have also lost their original charm by the darkening of the colours. His best examples known to me are the following. A Flight into Egypt, in Devonshire House. Tobit and the Angel, in the collection of the late Hon[ble.] Edmund Phipps, a picture engraved by the Chevalier Goudt; Cupid and Psyche, in the Fitzwilliam Museum at Cambridge; a Venus, in the Mesman Collection at Cambridge; St. Paul on the Island of Melita, at Corsham Court; the Delivery of Peter from Prison, at Broom Hall; the Flight into Egypt, and the Good Samaritan, in the Louvre, Nos. 159 and 160; Paul and Barnabas at Lystra, and Christ with the Disciples at Emmaus, in the Städel Institute at Frankfort; the Flight into Egypt, engraved by the Chevalier Goudt, in the Munich Gallery; a Repose in Egypt, and another Flight into Egypt, in the Vienna Gallery; and the Triumph of Psyche, in the Uffizi at Florence.[1]

[1] This picture is falsely called by the name of Paul Bril. On the other hand, the ten pictures there ascribed to Elzheimer are the work of Poelemberg.

www.ingramcontent.com/pod-product-compliance
Lightning Source LLC
Chambersburg PA
CBHW032356230426
43672CB00007B/718